18

P9-DGO-592

SQUADRON

SQUADRON

*Ending the
African Slave Trade*

JOHN BROICH

Overlook Duckworth
New York • London

This edition first published in the United States and the United Kingdom in 2017
by Overlook Duckworth, Peter Mayer Publishers, Inc.

NEW YORK
141 Wooster Street
New York, NY 10012
www.overlookpress.com

For bulk and special orders, please contact sales@overlookny.com,
or write us at the above address.

LONDON
30 Calvin Street
London E1 6NW
T: 020 7490 7300
E: info@duckworth-publishers.co.uk
www.ducknet.co.uk

For bulk and special sales please contact sales@duckworth-publishers.co.uk

Cataloging-in-Publication Data is available from the Library of Congress

A catalogue record for this book is available from the British Library

Text design and typesetting by Tetragon, London
Manufactured in the United States of America

ISBN: 978-1-4683-1398-7 (US)
ISBN: 978-0-7156-5231-2 (UK)

2 4 6 8 10 9 7 5 3 1

'The worst of men is the seller of men.'

MUHAMMAD

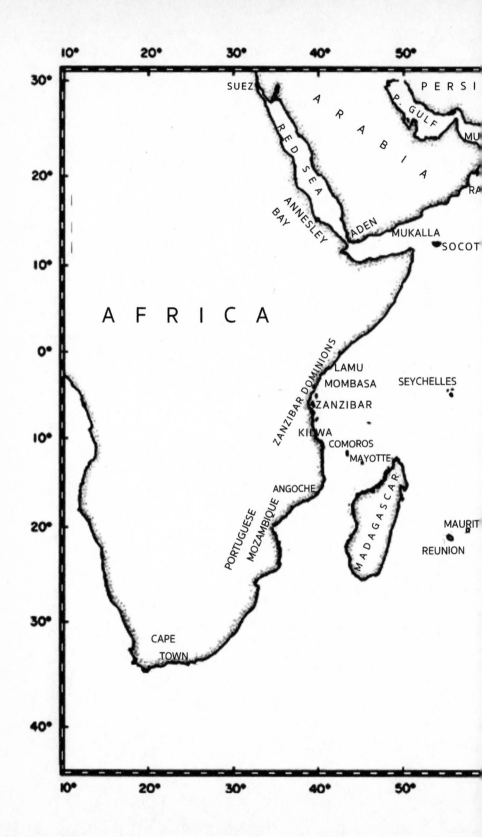

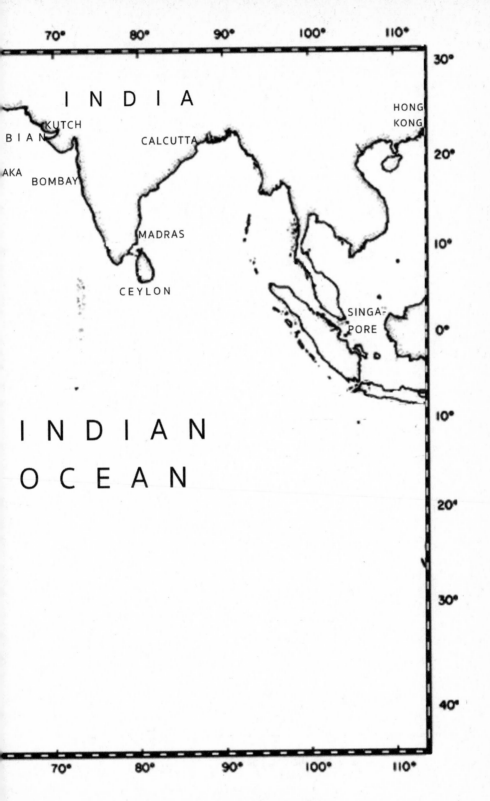

Map 1: The Indian Ocean

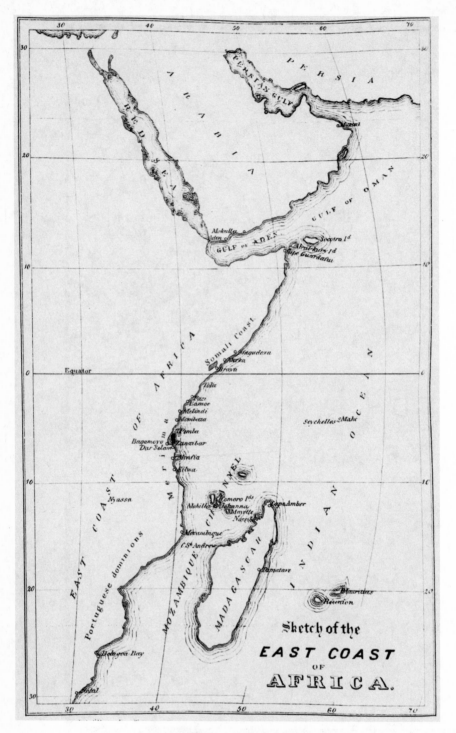

Map 2: The East Coast of Africa

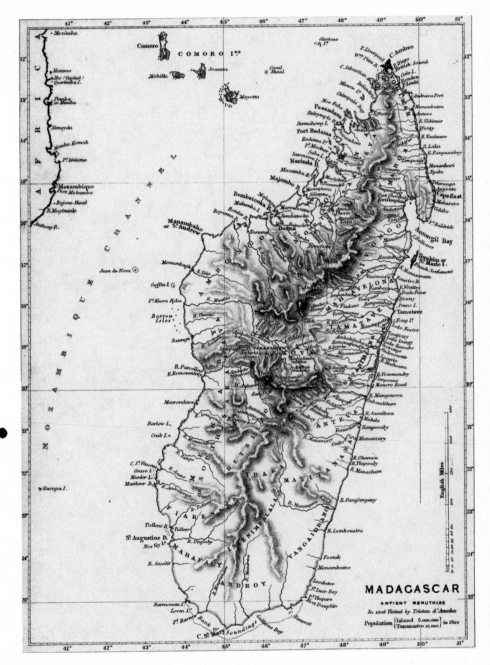

Map 3: Madagascar

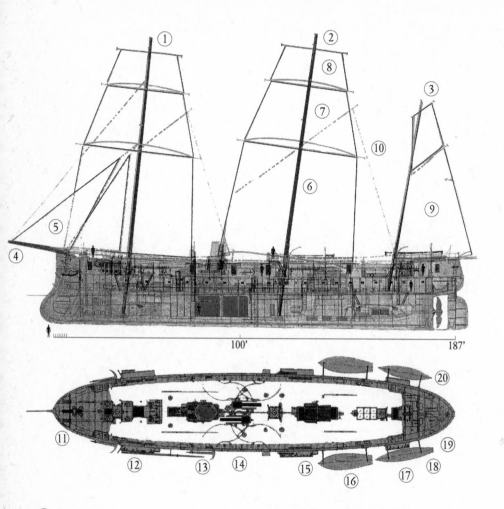

①	Foremast	⑪	7" rifled, muzzle-loaded gun under f'ocsle
②	Mainmast	⑫	Above, center: the forehatch
③	Mizzenmast	⑬	Funnel siutated over boilers
④	Bowsprit	⑭	Two 64-pounder guns on rails
⑤	Jib	⑮	Vents over engines
⑥	Mainsail	⑯	25' cutters shown hanging off davits
⑦	Main Topsail	⑰	Above, center: wheel, under poop deck
⑧	Main Topgallant	⑱	25' whale boat
⑨	Spanker	⑲	Commander's cabin under poop deck
⑩	Hashed outlines show lateen sails	⑳	Gig

Cut-away profile and aerial view of the Amazon-class sloop

CONTENTS

PART II · 'A DANGEROUS SEA'

PART III · 'SOLD TO SLAVERY, OF MY REDEMPTION THENCE'

LIST OF ILLUSTRATIONS

GLOSSARY OF HISTORICAL FIGURES

Philip Colomb	Commander, Royal Navy; captain of HMS *Dryad*
Leopold Heath	Captain, Royal Navy; commodore of the East Indies Station, Bombay
Edward Meara	Commander, Royal Navy; captain of HMS *Nymphe*
George Sulivan	Commander (later Captain), Royal Navy; captain of HMS *Daphne*

Minor figures

Henry Churchill	British consul, Zanzibar
Sir Henry Bartle Frere	Diplomat, head of the British mission to Zanzibar 1872
Dr John Kirk	Acting British consul, Zanzibar
David Livingstone	Missionary explorer in East Africa
Conolly Pakenham	British consul, Madagascar
Colonel Lewis Pelly	Former British consul at Zanzibar, diplomat in charge of Persian Gulf matters, based in Persia
Ranavalona II	Queen of Madagascar and eventual Anglican convert
Henry Rothery	Lawyer in the ecclesiastical and Admiralty court in London; legal advisor to the Treasury on slave trade matters
Majid bin Said	Sultan of Zanzibar 1856–1870
Barghash bin Said	Brother of Majid and Sultan of Zanzibar 1870–1888

GLOSSARY OF MID-NINETEENTH-CENTURY ROYAL NAVY RANKS

Flag, commissioned, and subordinate officers in order from highest to lowest rank:

Admiral, Vice Admiral, Rear Admiral

Commodore (a rank that a captain holds while leading a squadron or on a special task)

(Post-)Captain

Commander (called 'Captain' when leading a ship)

Lieutenant

Master

Chaplain

Surgeon

Paymaster

Sub-Lieutenant (formerly Mate)

Midshipman

Warrant officers. Order does not necessarily denote rank hierarchy because these and other non-commissioned officers often reported directly to the captain, lieutenant, or other officers.

Gunner

Boatswain/Bosun

Carpenter

Chief Engineer

Assistant Engineer

Petty officers. Order does not necessarily denote rank hierarchy.

Master-at-Arms

Captain of the Forecastle and captains of various sail positions

Captain's Coxswain

Quartermaster

Ship's Corporal

Sailmaker

Ropemaker

Caulker

Blacksmith

Leading Stoker

Cooper

Armourer

Head Krooman

Leading rates and seamen. Order does not necessarily denote rank hierarchy.

Leading Seaman

Shipwright

Able Seaman

Captain's Steward

Captain's Cook

Ward/Gun Room Steward

Ward/Gun Room Cook

Ordinary Seaman

Barber

Krooman

Boy 1st Class, Boy 2nd Class

THE ARABIAN SEA, MAY 1869

EIGHTY MEN, women and children were squeezed in a space forty feet long and not twenty-five wide. They were in the dark, under a bamboo deck, in airless heat – bent, crouched, huddled. Limbs welded stiff, they could not have stood even had the deck above their heads miraculously disappeared. The meagre hull moved north along the coast. Above it was dawn. But dark, always, under the deck.

In that dark was Kiada, born near the shores of the great lake Nyasa. Over a year before, war came to her village and her brother was killed. She and another brother were seized by men who made them walk uncountable miles far across hills and forests until they came to the edge of a sea, even greater than Nyasa whose shores stretched beyond seeing. She was held in a town on the edge of the sea for a year. There she was made to pound rice, removing the chaff. For some reason she was then placed on a ship to cross the water and it soon sailed the short distance to the island of Zanzibar about fifty miles from the East African coast, the island itself only sixty miles long. Then men displayed her in the slave market there. She had been purchased and packed in this dhow many days ago. She was now twelve years old.

Aminha was sixteen years old and a year before had been at home with her parents. She was abducted, forced to the coast, then transported to Zanzibar where she was made a labourer, carrying loads around the island. But even amid fear and captivity she found some consolation – a husband, another one of her master's slaves. She loved him, but not long ago she had become desperately sick, beyond the help of her husband. Her master was alarmed, not that she was suffering but because he seemed about to lose his investment. He decided to cut his losses, selling her out of his estate and away from her husband forever.

The boy Bakaat was born at the coastal town of Kilwa to enslaved parents. He had been kidnapped from his father one year ago when he was eleven years old and sold into slavery at Zanzibar.

Mabluk, the same age, was from the country around Lake Nyasa. He had been held on Zanzibar for two years. Before that, he had been given to slavers by his own brother. The two were starving, eating grass in desperation, and when an opportunity came, his brother sent him with a slaver hoping that Mabluk, at least, would get food. The boy was held by an Indian trader in Zanzibar before being sold and stowed in this ship.

Masumamhe was terribly hungry. Fifteen years old, she had been seized in a raid on her village three years ago. Men marched her overland to a port and then shipped her across the short passage to Zanzibar, where she was made to collect coconuts. Then, in the middle of the day, while she was carrying her load, unknown men had seized her, taken her to a house and hidden her away. There were around ten others captive there and they were kept like this for many weeks. Finally the men took her out at night and packed her away in this shallow hold.

Masuk was abducted when there was war in the lands around his village. He had been just a child then. He was sixteen now, a long-time servant of a merchant in Zanzibar. Then, for some reason – he never learned why – he was taken to the slave market and sold. That had been some months ago. Then one day he learned that he was to be carried from the island on a ship to some unknown port. But when the time approached he was told that the ship had been seized and burned by foreigners. Nevertheless, after a time he was crowded into this small ship.

In the dark there were eighty men, women and children bound for a destiny unknown other than that it was a future as property – brute labour, farm work, war-making, house servant, sexual property.

The small ship moved north along the coast. Then came a noise like thunder, but not thunder – as loud as thunder, but sudden, then gone. Something was happening.[1]

If a country has the military power to stop an obvious evil, should it take direct action? If a foreign military murders its country's minority children with nerve gas, tortures them to death? If nationalist revolutionaries create rape and torture camps, commit ethnic cleansing? If a powerful country that discovers such evils has the physical might to stop them, must it stop them in order to be 'good'? Does it have, in other words, an ethical imperative? Otherwise, should it be condemned by history for having sat on its hands?

Or should the powerful country refrain from military force? Act through diplomatic channels or through market forces to employ the carrot or stick? For perhaps acting with deadly force is itself an evil, compounds destruction and pain, leads to unforeseeable consequences and imperial extension. And what begins as humanitarian intervention might degenerate into quagmire. But such diplomatic or economic approaches are often slower, indirect, or incomplete. Meanwhile, evil acts fast and ruthlessly. So it is arguable that those favouring this approach leave children to torment and death while waiting for juntas to buckle under pressure or for revolutionaries to become capitalists.

This is the story of four men for whom these were not mere ruminations, but questions that they had to answer on a daily basis, four Royal Navy officers who, in their ships, had the power to level towns. In their cannon, rifles, marines and sailors they had the power to kill, sink, burn and terrorise. Theirs was a military power unrivalled in history, let alone in their own time. And these men were faced with absolute evil – the slave trade. They looked upon slave ships full of children, their bodies cadaverous; they saw ships full of women being smuggled to a life of sexual slavery; and they saw men being carried with their sons to slave markets at which they would be separated forever – fathers whose essential purpose and meaning, their ability even to attempt to protect their children, was stripped from them.

This is the story of four men who, faced with evil, capable of murdering the murderers at a command, struggled to walk the line between direct justice and civilised restraint, having to choose between the most basic eternal law and the law of modern governments. On one side was a bloody instinct righteously to destroy the perpetrators; on the other side were their orders, which discouraged violence if possible and required adjudication. Those dispassionate edicts emanated from a government and culture wedded to the idea that the good influences of the international marketplace, of free trade, would stop such evils – eventually, given enough time. But how long did Kiada, Aminha, Bakaat and the others have?

In the late 1860s, when this story begins, the British public had reason to be proud of their country's efforts against the slave trade. Abolitionists were a powerful political force from the late 1700s. Subjects of the British empire were banned from participating in the trade in the first years of the 1800s, and in the early 1830s parliament declared an end to the institution of slavery itself throughout the empire (in some places it was phased out over six years). To enforce their fight against slavery, the British entered into treaties with the kingdoms of Africa's west coast. They won the right to police those waters for slave traders to the Americas. For many decades the parents of Britain sent their sons to that feverish coast to struggle and die in what most trusted was a righteous effort.

By the late 1860s the British had reason to be proud, but also to believe the matter closed. By the mid-1850s the squadron hunting slavers off West Africa was reporting fewer and fewer of them. A series of South American countries abolished slavery in the same decade, and then the United States nearly tore themselves apart over the issue in the early 1860s, with the North and Emancipation winning.

But the matter was not closed with the wind-down of the Atlantic trade or the end of the American Civil War, for there was a far less publicised trade in the Indian Ocean. There were still slave ships bearing hundreds of captives packed on pestilent slave decks, vast territories decimated by slave raiders and the wars they sparked. Slavers, many from the Arabian Sea coasts and Persian Gulf, carried African abductees to clove, coconut, millet and sugar plantations throughout the Indian Ocean, to the white-walled towns of the Persian Gulf to act as house slaves, or to Madagascar to be made soldiers or sexual property.

The Royal Navy knew about the trade, and in fits and starts roused itself to police it in the mid-1800s. But the imperial sub-capital of Bombay, charged with policing the Persian Gulf, Arabian Sea and western Indian Ocean, took little notice. Very few ships were ever appointed to fight the trade, and the news-reading public in Britain heard little about it. There was a brief spark of interest when David Livingstone published some affecting depictions of the murder and starvation caused by slavers on the East African mainland in 1866, but it seemed not to take hold. The abolitionists, the British and Foreign Anti-Slavery Society, knew of the Indian Ocean trade and tried to focus attention on it, but they struggled to sustain interest.

That changed when an officer took over the Royal Navy squadron at Bombay and re-energised and re-focused its anti-slaver efforts. This, however, called down the wrath of his superiors and civilian overseers on himself and his squadron. In the end, something happened to call the attention of the British public to the issue and forced the British empire to either admit to a complicity in the trade or take decisive action against it.[2]

Leopold Heath, George Sulivan, Edward Meara and Philip Colomb are names lost to time outside a small handful of scholarly mentions. But in a gruelling year-and-a-half campaign at sea they hastened the end of the slave trade along Africa and Arabia's coasts as no one had before. Theirs is a dramatic story of success and despair, cat-and-mouse intrigues and desperate races. But besides the action at sea, it is a story as much about these very characters themselves, allowing us to watch four men's different reactions to the human catastrophe with which they come face to face. They were not just any bystanders: they were individuals who had at their command the potential power to annihilate the perpetrators. When presented with this opportunity – and they were – would they remain dispassionate? Stick to Admiralty instructions that strictly limited their actions? Or cross the line into the renegadism of which some ultimately accuse them?

They represented an empire which sometimes practised blatant expansionism and avarice – typified by the Opium Wars which the Royal Navy fought and whose brutish settlements it enforced. They represented an empire that sometimes embodied wilful inequality and racial superiority, as displayed in appalling responses to the Irish potato famine and other famines in India. Yet they represented, too, an empire that spent vast treasure and sacrificed generations of sons policing the slave trade from West Africa from 1807 to 1860, prompted by figures like William Wilberforce and a religious movement that pushed for justice.

In their individual personalities the four officers embodied these divergent things: in Sulivan an evangelical sense of equality and justice like that of Wilberforce; in Colomb a faith in white racial superiority and a belief in the overriding importance of the role of market forces in ending the trade; in Heath a frustration with limits imposed on Royal Navy power and independence; in Meara a rather black-and-white view of right and wrong and the conviction that he was the right judge thereof. Of course, as complicated humans, the four were never as consistent as these thumbnail sketches suggest; their attitudes were challenged and inconsistent.

In their personal and professional backgrounds, as veterans of Crimean and Chinese actions and Arctic adventures, the commodore and captains personified much about the make-up of the Royal Navy of Victoria's heyday. Two had brutal experience of what was involved in the dogged effort to rid the west coast of Africa of the slave trade, a hallmark of service among those who enlisted in the early and mid-1800s.

That effort to check the trade in the enslaved was perhaps the most expensive humanitarian campaign the world has known. It lasted over half a century, consuming hundreds of thousands of pounds a year – about 0.3–1.3% of Great Britain's annual national expenditure in direct costs alone. And the African blockade cost the lives of about one in ten to twenty of a rough average of 2,000 sailors on the patrol each year. Yet it diverted around 150,000 people bound for slavery in the New World from the Middle Passage.

The effort grew out of a sense of British complicity in the trade before 1808, along with evangelical humanitarianism in Britain, but it also aimed at other countries' trades. It hunted American slavers – a US law barred its ships and sailors from the trade in 1808 – and Portuguese, Swedish, French and Spanish slavers as each country banned the trade over the next couple of decades. Even after the traffic in kidnap victims to the US and other American countries was outlawed, adventurers continued to run the blockade, tempted by prices that skyrocketed after the bans. And just because the trade was outlawed did not mean that countries like the US had the will or military power to enforce the bans. Even in Britain the will to police the illegal trade was difficult for abolitionists to sustain in the face of high costs in treasure, sweat and blood.[3]

One group of slaver fighters deserves special mention here as a community of men almost entirely lost to history except among a small group of scholars. Their service exemplified something profound. West African sailors served in the British suppression squadron from its earliest years in a crucial role. Called 'Kroomen' after the Kru coast east of what is today southeast Liberia, these African men – many descended from the enslaved and some of them former slaves – had a reputation for sobriety, courage and experience – often they were far more experienced and far more sober than the British sailors and even officers with whom they sailed. And, many captains believed, Kroomen's constitutions protected them from the malarial miasmas that plagued this part of the world. Their strength was renowned, as was their skill at using a canoe, which they seemed to be able to pilot in any kind of sea. They usually brought their own distinctive canoes on board with them, using them for bearing messages, running quickly ashore, or saving men who had fallen overboard. Some were tattooed with a broad blue-black arrow from hairline to nose, and many wore tattoos of former ships, a kind of history on the skin that grew over the years. Veteran Kroomen knew the landscape, could withstand the promised physical and mental trials, and understood the challenge; every ship on the Bombay station carried them. The Kroomen had a saying, 'An Englishman goes to the Devil, a Krooman goes with him.'

When a Royal Navy ship arrived in Sierra Leone to take its place in the anti-slavery squadron its captain typically made his way to Kru Town to take on a complement, usually offering pay equal to that of an ordinary seaman. He would seek out an experienced 'Head Krooman' responsible for bringing on half a dozen or more Kroomen. The Head Krooman would vouch for the others, instruct them, and intercede between them and their officers. This avoided problems: the Kroomen were often extremely practised sailors, sharing a well-earned sense of professional pride; but a novice seaman or even officer might treat a Krooman with ignorance and abuse. Having the Head Krooman responsible for correcting his own division helped avoid such instances. The alternative, and it happened, was for an ignorant teenage midshipman or bosun to curse or strike a Krooman vastly his superior in merit – and then for all of the Kroomen to disappear at the next port.

When a young Leopold Heath led a bloody raid under the guns of Lagos, a Krooman was shot down not far from him on the beach. And when a young midshipman, Edward Meara, boarded a boat and pulled

up a wide African river to attack slavers, Kroomen boarded too. As this
story will show, the service of the Kroomen in Commodore Heath's East
African campaign was critical. The Royal Navy's fight against slavers was
not simply a story of white men trying to save black men. African men like
King Kosoko and his minions were slavers; African men like the Kroomen
hunted them.[4]

PART I

'Set a squadron
in the field'

CHAPTER 1

'ON THE BROW O' THE SEA'

Meara, Heath, Sulivan and Colomb before their convergence

THIS STORY BEGINS when the men who eventually changed everything on the east coast of Africa were learning their trade as slaver-fighters on the west coast amid anguish and devastation.

Edward Meara's childhood was as genteel as his years at sea were violent. He was born into wealth on a leaf-green estate but as a third son was unlikely to inherit. For boys in such a position this left two typical career paths: church or military. The Royal Navy was largely officered by well-born men, for there was a centuries-old belief that they possessed a special aptitude for command and that sailors preferred to sail under high-born officers.

Two things from Edward Meara's past combined to shape his actions in the fight against slavery on the east coast when he joined the squadron to captain the *Nymphe*. One was a kind of impatience and high-handedness that might have been bred of privilege; perhaps a sense, too, that his station and welfare were secured by fortune and not by the good opinion of the Admiralty. The other was a history of dealing directly and violently with slavers earlier in his career. Both seemed to contribute to brute action. In the coming months, it would become clear that he also simply had an uncomplicated view of the just way to respond to the slave trade.

His story starts in County Waterford, Ireland, in the 1830s. On the banks of the wide Suir River below Waterford, not two miles from the sea, stood the genteel Georgian estate, May Park. Its master, George Meara, was the factotum of the young nobleman, Lord Waterford. For his patron, Meara did the rough work of politics and business above which Lord Waterford was supposed to stand. When tenants needed evicting, enticements needed paying, even documents destroying, loyal George Meara did the job. When he was not playing the flinty right-hand man, George Meara played the squire. He hunted foxes and mused over the right quality of salt to make the best Waterford butter, while his gardener grew famous strawberries. He married a Viscount's daughter and ascended in the rank of gentlemen.

Children began quickly to appear in the nursery of the fine house with its splendid views. First twin boys, followed by a girl. Then, in 1831, another boy baptised Edward Spencer Meara. Then, a year later, another girl. The baby girl's delivery was the last great effort of her mother, who died shortly after giving birth.

The first-born of the twin boys would be heir to May Park, running the farms, the garden, the tree nursery and the staff. The path for the other boys was the same as for many other gentlemen's second and third sons. The elder, William, would have a commission in the army, and Edward, after some schooling in England, would enter the brig *Heroine* as a midshipman at the age of eighteen. While his older brother George was being groomed, attending balls, moving in great circles, Edward was serving in the West African anti-slavery squadron and making war.[1]

January 1850, HMS *Heroine*, south of Sierra Leone, West Africa

In January 1850, Midshipman Edward Spencer Meara was on the *Heroine* lying off the coast of West Africa. The brig carried six guns, spanned ninety-five feet, and carried seventy souls. She was captained by Commander John Marsh, charged with hunting slave ships: American, Brazilian, Cuban and Portuguese. She lay at single anchor off the mouth of the steaming

Gallinas River, a place dotted with islands, the sorts of places slavers hid their pens. They had filled slave stockades there not long ago, but in recent years the British had convinced more and more rulers on this coast to forswear dealing in slaves, including the countries bordering the Gallinas and Solyman Rivers, slow waterways that snaked deep into the African hinterland. For the rulers that expelled the foreign slave traders this meant less war-making, and the British promised to replace lost income through greater trade with Britain.

Piecemeal, in fits and starts, the traffic here was slowing. But now there was trouble, rumours of war. A people in the region, the Zaro, refused to free their slaves and give up the trade, and word had it that they meant to make war on those who submitted to the British. In this they were encouraged and helped by American and European slave traders. The *Heroine* was watching the shore intensely.

The long sentry duty was wearing. Supplies had recently run short and the New Year passed with the spirit room empty. A midshipman had answered the captain shortly; a young ship's boy had died in the night. But in this still, soupy water they could not bury him in the normal way, by gently sliding him from a plank or table into the sea. The morning after his death they laid him in the dinghy, rowed a considerable distance from the ship, and only then consigned his mortal remains, wrapped in sailcloth, to the deep. Far from home, far now even from his shipmates, he sunk alone.

Then one hazy afternoon a boat pulled away from the shore, in it a man who had been stationed on shore as lookout. He came up the side with a letter for Captain Marsh. He brought certain news of war: the Zaro had indeed descended on the lands that had quit the slave-trade.

The next morning the drum beat to muster, then Edward Meara boarded the *Heroine*'s sailed pinnace, a small gun fitted onto it and manned by the coxswain and a few of his crew. Finally, Captain Marsh boarded behind them. As the little flotilla prepared to depart the *Heroine*'s side, the first lieutenant appeared, quietly steaming to be missing the action – perhaps the best chance for promotion he would ever know.

The *Heroine* fired a gun to alert the lookout on shore that they were coming, and the men pulled, and the pulling was hard. There was a steady north-east wind almost directly in their faces, and sandy shoals near the river's mouth hindered even the shallow-bottomed pinnace. Finally on shore, they found the lookout and interpreter. He in turn took Captain Marsh and his men to a war council with several princes of the coast and river lands, where they learned that the Zaro had seized the town of Juring, a place about six hours up the river by canoe. So John Marsh and the princes drew up plans for driving the Zaro out of these lands. Plans laid, Marsh had a signal sent to the *Heroine*: he wanted his marines. They and a small group of trusted sailors arrived on the beach by that evening and the collected men made camp for the night.

At sunrise, Edward Meara and the war party departed. Red-coated marines, blue-coated officers and able-seamen in a fleet of boats, several leaders of the countries lying on the Gallinas and Solyman in their own long war canoes. Around them, their men-at-arms in more canoes. Midshipman Meara was in the pinnace, and his men pulled more easily now against the slow, wide rivers. Shortly after the sun began its descent in the sky the company reached the town of Juring. All was quiet and unmoving as the sailors and marines got out of the boats. They explored, finding the stockade walls undefended. There was evidence that goods and supplies and people had been borne away. The Zaro, it seemed, had heard of the boats' approach well before they had arrived.

Commander Marsh called a council and the princes gathered around to plan their next move. Then there was a noise and a man appeared from the edge of the town, running towards them. Quickly it was apparent that he was no threat and he yielded himself. He was, he explained, a slave escaped from the Zaro. Those people, he said, had taken another town three miles upriver called Siman, and he had heard them discussing their next target, yet another town above that one.

The company acted quickly, re-boarding and pulling fast for Siman. They were not too late this time. The boats were greeted by musket-fire coming from a stockade fort close by the river. Not only musket fire: the enemy had a small gun of their own. The captain's coxswain and gig's crew began working the pinnace's gun while Midshipman Meara and Lieutenant Corneck coordinated the pinnace's crew. Meanwhile the marines returned the stockade's fire and the defenders started falling. One. Several. Five. But none of the Royal Navy sailors or allied West Africans had been struck down. In time, smoke poured from the stockade. Then smoke and licking flame appeared in the town behind it.

The Zaro men inside began to abandon the burning fort, many moving for cover in the scrub along the river. Still the pinnace's small gun fired on. Now the men loaded it with grapeshot and spattered the river's edge with iron balls. Again it was loaded with the cluster of iron grapes; again came the shower of metal and dust. Now the sailors loaded it with a tin case packed with smaller musket balls; again the blast. Round after round after round. On top of that, hundreds upon hundreds of musket and pistol shots. Lead and iron sowed – death and dying reaped – along the river bank.

Finally, enemy fire was silenced, the Zaro fighters obliterated. John Marsh and his men did not bother to count the enemy dead on that riverside. Their purpose was achieved. The captain, fearing miasma, wanted to get his men away from the dead and from the river, and so ordered his boats to return.

On the way back down to the coast the fleet stopped at a village of one of the African allies for a ceremonial meal of victory and thanksgiving, but they did not stay long. The Royal Navy men re-boarded, descended to the coast, and made camp on the beach above the waves. And Midshipman Meara – who would receive a commendation from his commodore for his role in the attack – was back on the *Heroine* the next afternoon.[2]

HMS *Niger*, November 1851, off Lagos, slave coast of West Africa

Less than a year after Edward Meara's first immersion in the sweat and blood of the slave trade fight on the west coast of Africa, the Royal Navy struck at that coast's most powerful slaver king. But the action was a debacle, improvised on the run, with marines and sailors storming a beach and fortified town in the face of iron and lead. Leading the charge up the beach was Commander Leopold Heath. The confused nightmare that he lived that day may have instilled in him his powerful inclination towards careful planning and tactics. The cost of extemporisation that day was paid in men's lives.

The son of a wealthy judge, the thirty-four-year-old Heath was broad-shouldered and large-fisted, but the impression of brawn was moderated by the roundness of his face. He looked precisely like the keeper of a pub in a suspect part of a town, with shoulders and hands that could shift barrels with ease, or pummel the unruly. His face might be genial so long as the clientele behaved; otherwise it might become coldly fierce with only a slight shift. Heath had risen quickly, and his first command was a plum commission for a new commander. She would have been suitable for

Leopold Heath, photographed at the end of his career,
after having been made Rear Admiral, 1871

a post-captain's command, with fourteen guns throwing 32-pound shot, a great twelve-foot screw that could drive her at ten knots, a crew of 160, and only a few years old when Commander Leopold Heath had led her from Portsmouth.

Leopold Heath and HMS *Niger* were summoned to Lagos from their patrolling grounds to the west on the slave coast. On arriving off Lagos, Heath saw several men-of-war huddled, the brigs *Harlequin* and *Waterwitch*, and the iron paddle gunboat *Bloodhound*. The fast-looking brig *Philomel* was there too, and a signal soon ordered Heath to appear on her.

There he met the other commanders and the coast's consul, John Beecroft, about sixty years old, grey-whiskered, with long experience in West Africa. There was something hard and uncompromising in his face. A council began, and Beecroft reported that the government in London had lost patience with Lagos and its slaver-king, Kosoko. London had had its diplomatic approaches rebuffed, and the British community and liberated Africans in the region had been threatened. London viewed Kosoko as one of the last great hindrances to the end of the slave trade on the west coast, and had ordered John Beecroft to try to make a treaty with Lagos for the suppression of the trade. The consul should strongly hint that Britain would otherwise support Kosoko's dynastic rival and see him deposed.

So Beecroft asked the collected officers to put him ashore under a white flag – but supported by a large flotilla of boats for his protection. A show of force, but not an attack. Beecroft said that he knew the character of such African chiefs. All they needed was a show of British power to come to terms quickly. The senior officer of the gathered ships deferred to the Crown's representative, and preparations began to cross to Lagos at sunrise.

Back on his ship, Heath gave orders for *Niger*'s contribution to the flotilla. Lagos was a dangerous place, many of its people experienced in war-making, an army of some thousands, well-armed with good muskets provided by Portuguese and Brazilian slave agents. The town overlooked a river and extensive lagoon and had a navy of war-canoes with which it

commanded the network of lagoons and rivers in the area. The town itself
was protected by scores of guns. Not many years past, its approaches had
been hung with severed heads.

Well before dawn, Heath issued orders to *Niger*'s senior officers. He
would go with six boats – two gigs, three cutters and a twelve-oared pinnace. He would bring eight of his officers, fifty-one sailors and sixteen
marines. In the dark, Heath climbed down into his gig with his boat's crew,
the master's assistant and a marine. His boats pulled off to join those of the
other collected ships. The black iron *Bloodhound* would tow the flotilla as
close to shore as she could. Twenty-two boats, including a Krooman canoe,
gathered; over three hundred men. Consul Beecroft was indeed bringing
a show of force behind that white flag.

At six o'clock in the morning the group moved across the short distance
of sea for the entrance to Lagos. First was a small gig with the consul in it,
flying a very broad white flag. Then came the black iron paddler, flying
its own white flag. The boat fleet trailed behind her. As they entered the
river road for Lagos and came around a bend, shots cracked from the right
bank. The flotilla was still several miles from the town and Heath could not
be sure whether this was the beginning of an ambush or a group acting on
their own. The muskets were out of range for now, in any case.

The senior captain in the group ordered the two flags of truce to be kept
flying and carried on steadily, though fire from the bank increased. Now it
seemed less likely to be the result of men acting alone. *Bloodhound*, which
was towing the boats, plunged into mud, wallowing and coming to a stop.
Musket balls were falling around the boats. Then crashes sounded from
the direction of the town a mile away. Lagos had opened fire with cannon
on the white flag of truce.

The British hauled down the white flag. This was no longer a diplomatic
mission. Then, from a point where muskets were firing on the riverbank,
several war canoes pulled away from the shore. It seemed they would cross
to the other side of the river and trap the British flotilla in crossfire, so a
group of British boats moved away to head them off. There were small

cannon mounted on some of these, including some of Heath's, and they began hurling shrapnel at the enemy.

Bloodhound remained stuck in the river's ooze and could not bring its long gun or two carronades to bear. From a distance, beyond the surf, the *Niger*'s guns occasionally popped, but they could not reach those of Lagos. One choice was for the boats to retreat to sea, leaving the *Bloodhound* to defend itself until the tide lifted it or it could be towed off. Another was to push forward to the town and attack, perhaps silencing the guns there. After an hour of exchanging fire with the forces on the riverbank and sustaining fire from the town, the senior captain ordered a landing. Some of the boats would cover the debarkation while about 175 men landed under the town.

Heath and his men would lead the attack. His boat crews pulled into constant musket fire, and he estimated that five large guns from above in the town were also targeting them. Heath could see that the defenders were organised and well-positioned. They never intended to receive a diplomatic visit, they were prepared for an assault, probably reacting to the aggressive appearance of the flotilla. And the men defending the beach were not shrinking. Leopold Heath could see their resolve and the long stretch was stubbornly defended. They fired with skill, too. But still Heath's boat and the others drove on into the waiting onslaught.

Heath leapt as the gig touched sand, his feet among the first on the shore, his men leaping out behind him. The other boats touched and the marines and sailors poured out of them. The two young mates of the *Niger* hurried to his side to lead with him. The first houses of the town were not far from the river, and there were some low stone walls. He and his men were utterly exposed on the beach. There could be no slowing, no stopping. Heath ran and his men ran.

Somehow, Leopold Heath survived the desperate crossing to the first stone buildings, but still he and his boats' crews were exposed to fire. Somewhere a swivel gun, more than one, was pounding at them with small shot. Onward into the town they had to go to confront their attackers and perhaps silence the swivel guns and big guns. And so they plunged on.

It was a warren, a maze of alleys. As they struggled up an alley, they were shot at from intersecting streets. Henry Hall was shot at Heath's side and lay dying or dead; John Dyer fell dead. Now the boat crews of one of the other ships had landed and were also trying to advance into the town, but they were being barraged and the boats trying to cover the landing were being pelted. A man was shot in the back. A marine's arm was splintered by a cannon shot.

But Leopold Heath's men were taking the brunt of the fire. At sea, a captain was aware of his enemy. Survival was a matter of wind, manoeuvre, gunnery, the response of the crew. Not all of these forces were in his control, certainly, but the fight was not this blind plunge into desperation, like being thrown into a ring blindfolded, expected to defeat five opponents who could see you and threw their punches at their discretion. They were being constantly outmanoeuvred and outflanked. The amount of incoming fire only increased as Heath and the sailors and marines pushed up. The Lagos fighters contended every intersection. Now a marine fell, and sailors John McCarthy, Bill Hall and Tom Todhunter.

Finally, having advanced no more than three hundred yards into the town at bloody cost, never finding the cannon firing on the boats, Leopold Heath decided it was enough. He could not ask the men to fight further. There was no possible tactic for success. When they managed to dislodge one of the defenders from his place, he only circled around to take up a new position. Meanwhile, Heath's men were falling and dying: two dead and six or seven brought down. This was the cost of an improvised landing in unknown conditions.

He ordered the neighbouring houses and buildings put to the torch. The fire was punitive, but also offered some cover for their dangerous retreat. Turning and running would have meant more murder of his men, so Heath led them in a careful withdrawal. Covering for one another, they began to edge down to the beach and the waiting boats. An explosion sounded somewhere amid the flames, then another. There was not much wind so there was no spreading firestorm, but the fire seemed to be covering their backs. The survivors made it, bloodied, into the riddled boats.

As the surgeon tended to the many wounded officers, marines and sailors, *Niger* limped to a rendezvous with the squadron's commodore, Henry Bruce. Bruce was furious. Consul Beecroft had practically invited the fight. The senior captain on the spot should never have agreed to the plan since a blockade would have brought King Kosoko to his knees as surely as an assault, far better. While Heath and his landers had fought bravely, they never should have been placed in that position. A consul, waving a directive from the Foreign Office, did not supernaturally transform into an experienced naval officer with experience in executing a controlled, overwhelming landing. He should never have been followed into the fiasco.[3]

In these years, it was difficult for abolitionists to focus the will of Britain to keep up the fight against the trade on Africa's west coast as costs mounted, lives were claimed, and Britain's complicity seemed to fade into the past. But in the same period there was a trade on the east coast at which Britain directed almost no will at all. That is because this trade was simply too far away, it historically involved fewer British perpetrators, and the empire had no territorial presence on that coast. Yet in the 1850s and 1860s roughly 15,000 people were forced overseas by slavers from regions today called Malawi, Mozambique, Tanzania and Kenya. The kidnappers themselves were sometimes Portuguese, sometimes Arab, sometimes African, but often of mixed ethnicity. The dealers who collected the victims at the coast might be any of these. Purchasers on the coast could be French or Portuguese, sometimes operating under the cover of legal fictions that called them dealers in 'migrant labourers' instead of slavers. Other purchasers were Arab or mixed Arab-African middlemen who carried slaves to markets in Portuguese Mozambique, Madagascar or Zanzibar. From these markets, the abductees might be forced to labour on East African island plantations growing sugar or cloves for Indian, Arab, French and occasionally English masters. They might be forced to Madagascar or all the way to the Persian Gulf to be forced labour on date plantations, slave soldiers, domestic slaves, or sexual slaves. Often those who financed the slaving operations – providing silver or trade-stuff, ships and crews – were Indians or Omanis. On a wider scale, those who underwrote the trade were those who bought the ivory that some captives were forced to carry to the coasts on their way to slave pens and the spices or produce harvested on slave labour farms.

The will to police the east coast trade had to be encouraged over the heads of those who profited from the status quo. That was hard enough, but it also had to be policed without an east coast Royal Navy station as there were on the west coast. In those moments when attention was paid to the slave trade on the Indian Ocean side, Britain had to secure treaties with coastal rulers allowing the Royal Navy to inspect ships. These were hard to come by and very limited, and the work itself had to be directed either from Bombay or the Cape – both very distant – or from the island of Zanzibar, which was itself the largest slave market on the coast.[4]

HMS *Castor*'s pinnace, November 1849, Mozambique Channel

It is on the east coast of Africa, not far from the island of Zanzibar, that young George Sulivan enters the story in 1849. Heath and Meara were gentlemen's sons, and in the Victorian Royal Navy as in Lord Nelson's, most of the officer class were gleaned from such men. George Sulivan had no land or title, but his name itself meant something. In their native corner of Cornwall, the Sulivan name evoked respect. George's father had battled Frenchman, Spaniard and American in Britain's long war with Napoleon. His grandfather had too, amassing for himself and his sailors a hoard of prize money (which he promptly spent). His brother had been a lieutenant on the *Beagle* under Fitzroy and was a friend of the naturalist Darwin. Cousins proliferated throughout the service.

George Sulivan

Seventeen-year-old Midshipman George Sulivan, with scores of sailors of HMS *Castor*, prepared to attack a slaver fort. Sulivan boarded the *Castor*'s sailed pinnace and twenty other men packed in, preparing for a voyage of several days. Their target was near a river-mouth island called Angoche. It was in African territory claimed by the Portuguese, but the Portuguese could not control it. The fort was held by Arab and African traders, pirates and slavers. Spanish and US slave traders had been seen visiting it disguised as whalers in order to collect captives by the hundred for sale in Brazil. The Royal Navy was acting at the request of the Portuguese, so the slaver fort and any ships there were fair game.

Loaded, five boats sailed, and by nightfall had drawn within six hours of the fort. Time to stop for the night, and the boats anchored close together at a place called Monkey Island. The lieutenant leading the expedition ordered an extra-large ration of spirits portioned out and with it a dose of quinine for every man. The boats' crews each sang in turn, keeping it up long into the night.

At daylight the boat fleet continued for the island. After noon Sulivan saw the fort's walls in the far distance, a red flag flying above them. The palisades overlooked a very shallow tidal inlet — the reason that these shallow-draft boats were chosen for the attack. Trees closely hemmed the bay. The boats moved on. A couple of hours passed and a tide began lifting them in toward the fort, but very slowly. Now they were only several hundred yards away. At two hundred yards the fort opened fire. There was roundshot, but also grape, masses of small iron balls meant to tear apart the human body. A sailor fell, then another, his ribs hammered in by hard metal. The boats were having trouble approaching the fort. The tide was not lifting them quickly enough, and even these shallow craft were scraping the bottom. It was like a nightmare in which one is helpless to move in the face of danger.

The fort fired on. There were more guns than the British had expected, and more men. Some fired from a dhow anchored close under the fort's walls, while the Royal Navy boats struggled to manoeuvre. Only the crew of Sulivan's managed to bring their single small gun to bear; they loaded it with exploding canister shot and lobbed fire over the fort's walls. Finally, the fire from the fort beginning to slow, another boat managed to rush the dhow anchored under the fort. The sailors scaled it and attacked, and soon it was on fire. But as the men began their retreat they came under new musket fire from the nearby tree line. Two more sailors fell and had to be carried off the burning dhow.

Sulivan guessed that there were over 2,000 defenders of the place while the attackers were fewer than 100. There was little doubt that there were enslaved Africans penned nearby the fort, collected for the next American or Brazilian customer, but there was no hope for them. The small gun on Sulivan's boat was working some vengeance, but what would it mean to the Mozambicans in the slave pens? Now the tide was receding; the boats would ground if the flotilla did not abandon the attack and retreat from the inlet soon. And so they did, bleeding and tending their wounded.

Some months after the raid a letter arrived at the Cape for Midshipman Sulivan. It was from his mother; whose father, grandfather, husband and two sons were Royal Navy officers. *I think of you a great deal in that place,* she wrote. *I don't like your going up rivers after slavers. You know a little makes me anxious, although my trust for all things that concern my children is fixed on God.*[5]

HMS *Phoenix*, Cape Desolation, south-west Greenland, May 1854

Philip Colomb began his navy career as a fifteen-year-old in HMS *Sidon* serving in the Mediterranean. He was born in Scotland, his father a successful general and his mother the daughter of a baronet, twice Lord Mayor of Dublin. Colomb entered the navy already a midshipman like Heath, Meara and Sulivan. As a fifteen-year-old he had been thrust above veteran able-bodied seamen who had sailed the world over and fought Napoleon's navy before Colomb was born. But at the same time Colomb was on the receiving end of his lieutenant's thrashings, ordered to stand double watches on the precarious bitt in the ship's bow, or atop the paddles' box, or to have precious shore leave denied.

Five years later, twenty-three-year-old Philip Colomb found himself mate of HMS *Phoenix*. 'Mate' was a sort of in-between rank. He had passed out of the ranks of the midshipmen not two years before, but was not yet a lieutenant; no longer a 'young gentleman', not yet a commanding figure. Still, he had responsibility for a watch and sometimes commanded the quarterdeck.

The *Phoenix* was near the Arctic Circle on a mission to find explorer Captain Edward Belcher. Belcher, in turn, was on a mission to rescue the famous Sir John Franklin whose last quest to find the Northwest Passage, it was known, had met with disaster. Belcher had searched for almost two years with no luck. His time was up, and *Phoenix* was sent for him. The Admiralty decided that quite enough sailors had died on the ice.

The Admiralty sent an experienced arctic surveyor, Edward Augustus Inglefield, and his old workhorse of a ship, *Phoenix*: 174 feet, 10 guns, 135 souls, and quite modest speed under steam. Inglefield was a capable captain, lettered and conscientious about guiding his young officers in character. An eager photographer and painter, he relished observing these hard landscapes. He photographed the deeply cleft inlets and ice-scapes, getting indifferent Inuit to stand still long enough for successful exposures.

By inclination, Colomb was not one to share his captain's interest in the sublime. *Fantastic peaks,* he reflected, *and gracefully-shaped icebergs are few. The ordinary Arctic scene is dull and monotonous.* At this moment as he headed to take the watch the sea was shrouded in fog. *Phoenix* had a transport in company for picking up Belcher's crew in case they were wrecked or ice-bound, but the transport was out of sight in this fog. The *Phoenix* had to fire a gun on occasion to show her position and encourage the transport to stay close.

On *Phoenix*'s mission with Colomb was Lieutenant Edward Spencer Meara. Sometimes Colomb would relieve Meara from his watch in the wet, 40-degree subarctic air. It was not the last time Colomb would lend Meara a hand. In the subtropical waters off East Africa Colomb would one day try to extricate Meara from a tangle.[6]

Three of the captains in this story were veterans of the fight against slavers; the fourth, Philip Colomb, was not. But he had a reputation as a tactical thinker. It was a distinction Leopold Heath knew well; as commodore, Heath had an idea about how to utilise Colomb's tactician's brain in his anti-slavery campaign.

HMS *Defence*, English Channel, July 1863

Advance the clock nine years to 1863, and Lieutenant Philip Colomb could be found on the weather deck of the colossal ironclad *Defence* in the English Channel. The lieutenant had just fifteen minutes to teach two signalmen how to use a machine they had never seen before. The device before them was on trial on this July day. It looked something like an organ grinder's machine, a kind of hurdy-gurdy with a barrel organ cylinder and crank. A long arm extended upwards from this and at the top was a lantern with a shutter covering it.

It was a signalling machine, and Colomb quickly showed the two men how to input a number into it. The number corresponded to a phrase – the sorts of phrases flags had communicated between Royal Navy ships for centuries – *Enemy in sight. Cease firing. Require assistance.* Colomb showed the men how they might also input Morse code into the machine. Then he cranked the wheel. Whatever the rate of cranking, the machine lifted and lowered the shade atop the lantern with perfect regularity. Short-long, long-short-short-short, long-short-long-short. Flags had served the Royal Navy for centuries, but at night they had never much served at all.

The road to this day and this trial had been long. The Admiralty was a famously conservative place and the word 'innovation' constituted an invective. Colomb's machine was not welcomed, even called foolish, and he met many closed doors. He demonstrated it many times, but trials he thought were successes they called failures. Though just a lieutenant, Colomb wrote appeals to challenge these judgments, to ask for new trials. He wrote letters to those who opposed him, appealing to their reason. He came close to impertinence, but stayed just short of the line. But his was a forced, tenuous humility. He believed what was reasonable was right. Might, in the form of a rear admiral's pennant, did not make right – reason did.

He might have been betrayed by a face that tended to suggest smugness. His eyebrows arched naturally, imperiously. He had the long nose common in his family and it could give the impression that he was looking down it. If his face did not suggest smugness, it suggested that he knew something amusing, maybe about you.

He was well-bred, but Lieutenant Colomb suffered from being the third son in a family that had a better name than estate. To develop his machine and keep promoting it, he had to sign away significant rights to any future earnings that it might make from selling it to the navy. He had little money. A year before, Colomb had won an important supporter. He was a captain who had seen the Russians put flashing signal lights to good – or ill – use at the Crimea. This man had made a name for himself as a capable organiser when he took responsibility for landings near Sebastopol. He was Captain Leopold Heath. Perhaps Heath's endorsement had helped Colomb get this latest trial.

Colomb quickly finished his tutorial to the signalmen, then the trial began. The rear admiral of the Channel fleet stood by. A distant ship received and responded to the signal with ease; it was a clear success. By the end of 1863 the Channel fleet had adopted the system, and Philip Colomb was promoted to commander.[7]

CHAPTER 2

'THE VALIANT OF THIS WARLIKE ISLE'

The commodore's resolution and the journey of the Daphne

WHY DID MEARA, Heath, Sulivan and Colomb launch their unprecedented attack on the East African slave trade from 1868? First and foremost, because Leopold Heath as the squadron's commodore determined to do it. Heath's Royal Navy superiors and political overseers gave him no special order to do this. Policing piracy and slavery in the Indian Ocean and Arabian Sea was one item in his station's portfolio of roles. But he smashed precedent in the focus and scale of power he committed to fighting the slave trade.

As Heath was resolving in his mind to launch his campaign in 1868, he was unwittingly sailing into a whirlwind of contending forces and philosophies swirling around the question of slavery, race, economic dogma and the role of government. The commodore formed his decision in the context of a culture that predominantly deemed slavery repugnant on many grounds; expressing support for the institution itself was no longer a publicly acceptable stance, as it had been when parliament had debated the question of eliminating it throughout the empire in the 1820s and early 1830s. An 1833 Act eliminated the status of slavery in the empire from 1834 (1835 on Mauritius and later in other East India Company territory). Of course, it had taken a ruinous war in the USA to settle the question of the validity of slavery there. Meanwhile, in many states and kingdoms across the globe, slavery remained after America's Civil War: in Brazil, China, Cuba, Madagascar, the Portuguese colonies, many parts of West and East Africa, Persia and Gulf principalities, Zanzibar and its East African footholds, and elsewhere.

But if the basic consensus against slavery in Britain was certain in 1868, what to do about slavery and the trade outside the empire was not at all. There were all kinds of opinions about the extent and limits of British action, about what actions exactly to take. The same abolitionist groups that won success in the empire worked to focus attention on the East African trade in the 1850s and 1860s, but they often failed. And working against their arguments for action were powerful currents in British politics pushing for fewer international commitments and less government spending – including on the Royal Navy.

Related to this were those who believed that free trade – a watchword of the age – would eventually end the slave trade on Africa's east coast. In their vision, British and Indian merchants would spread throughout African ports and, by trading for raw resources other than black ivory, slowly but surely re-orient African markets away from trading in the enslaved.

Among others, the influential Scottish missionary David Livingstone encouraged this solution. An agent of the London Missionary Society, directed to convert the natives around a small outpost in East Africa as a young man, Livingstone decided that he could better spread Christianity and abolish slavery by being an explorer. By exploring, he could encourage the trade that ultimately, he believed, would meet his goals. In the 1850s and 1860s he became a household name as a pioneer and adventurer. The British public lost contact with him in the late 1860s and he was feared dead. When reliable news reached Leopold Heath at Zanzibar that he was alive in 1869, and when Henry Stanley subsequently sought him out in 1871, it helped refocus attention on East Africa and the slave trade there. Newspapers printed new tales from Livingstone describing the warfare, famine and depopulation that went hand-in-hand with slave trading. But

Livingstone and his allies still looked to Christianity and commerce for an eventual solution.

Related to arguments against actively pushing for emancipation and in favour of the power of market forces were popular ideas about race. These held that 'the negroes' were lazy, naturally servile, and possessed no innate desire for freedom. If you gave them freedom, they would only use it to refuse to work. Forcing freedom on such people, the argument went, was hardly good for the African at all. In the Caribbean, after parliament abolished the institution, formerly enslaved people were forced to be unpaid 'apprentices' for a further four years on the theory that an imagined black race was innately apathetic and needed to be taught habits of work once the slave-driver disappeared.

This was a line of race thinking represented on Heath's squadron by Philip Colomb, but these opinions were not shared by all. Others, like George Sulivan, rejected such theories, thinking in terms common from Wilberforce to Harriet Beecher Stowe: that Africans were more like Europeans than not, and were as worthy of freedom as any European. Public ideas of race and slavery were mixed: Dickens could write about Africans being little superior to animals, yet write, 'still they must be free'. Anthony Trollope could write that 'God for his own purposes ... has created men of inferior and superior race' while nevertheless arguing in 1860 that 'if we can assist in driving slavery from the earth, in God's name let us still be doing'. On the other hand, some pointed to the recent American Civil War as the bloody price of 'human-equality fanaticism' and 'abolition mania'. Yet others criticised the tremendous national expense of suppressing other countries' slave-trading at the behest of naïve abolitionists.

With regard to the east coast slave trade, about which public and official Britain knew less than the west coast trade, some argued in the 1860s that expense should be spared because there, as opposed to the West Indies or Americas, 'slavery was of a domestic character'. One MP said, 'We have already done enough, and having carried out a great measure of justice at a cost of £20,000,000 ... I think we should abandon the Quixotic idea of constituting ourselves the knights-errant of the sea at a time when non-intervention was the order of the day.'

As Heath was resolving in his mind to launch his campaign, he was unwittingly sailing into a storm of contending political forces. There was a slavery suppression bureaucracy in London, including corners of the Foreign Office, Treasury and Admiralty. Further, there was the government of India, the consular and diplomatic framework throughout the Indian Ocean and Arabia, and Downing Street. All of these Heath threatened to disrupt with his sudden departure from the status quo.[1]

Annesley Bay, Red Sea, January 1868

To find Leopold Heath in the moments when he decided to launch his campaign against the slave trade, advance the calendar seventeen years from the time when a younger Heath retreated from the slave fortress of Lagos through smoke and blood, past years fighting the Russians in the Black Sea, patrolling the English Channel, and teaching gunnery, and go to Annesley Bay in Abyssinia (today's Eritrea and Ethiopia), north-east Africa, in 1868.

Commodore Heath had charge of a massive landing. He stood on the quarterdeck of his flagship, HMS *Octavia*, his broad blue pennant flying above on the mizzenmast. On board was Sir Robert Napier, a lieutenant general of long experience in Indian campaigning. Napier had a sweeping moustache and a permanent squint as if etched by the Indian sun. Heath was thickly built without being fat, and had penetrating eyes set in a straight line. Napier wore bright red, Heath dark blue. Standing on deck, Heath and the other officers could see white tents on a plain reflecting the intense sun, the advance force. There were some red coats moving about and an English flag flying. A wharf was under construction.

Annesley Bay opened onto the Red Sea at the north. Coral islands at the mouth tamped down waves blown by the perennial northern winds. The easy seas would aid Heath in his unloading. But the coral islands, narrow opening of the bay and shallow waters presented a challenge.

The British government had determined to remove the king of Abyssinia, and it was Heath's duty, being in charge of the Royal Navy's Indian Ocean fleet, to put the men on the ground who would remove that king. Heath was to move over ten thousand men, thousands of horses and mules, hundreds of guns, and uncounted tons of material from Bombay to the Red Sea. He had personal charge of over two hundred ships, including a hospital ship and a factory ship. He had eleven captains to direct, had responsibility for mail communications, and, most critically, was responsible for creating water for the entire operation through some of his ships' steam distillation systems. He carried material for building a railway. He even had twenty elephants to transport.

First, to deliver the general who would shepherd war. It was early evening and the *Octavia*'s crew, ordered to line the yards, scrambled up and stood high above the deck. The commodore's barge came to the side and Sir Robert descended in state. The barge pulling away, *Octavia*'s guns fired a salute of fifteen blasts multiplied by echoes; from shore, the smaller sound of the field guns firing a receiving salute echoed back. Napier was welcomed by an honour guard on the new wharf. This done, Heath could begin the work of delivering war to Africa with his usual efficiency.

When Heath was a far younger officer he had organised a landing under the enemy guns of Sevastopol during the Crimean campaign. He had spoken up in a meeting of vastly superior officers and convinced them to follow his proposals for landing thousands of men and guns under the eyes of the Russians. When the moment for the attempt arrived, Heath himself was ordered to take command of one half of the beachhead. He went ashore and from there carefully directed landings at his section. Thousands of men guided, massive guns transferred from the element of water to earth, steam tugs working quickly but successfully, and all in heavy waves. Meanwhile, the Russians who were encamped not far from the landing site withdrew. The success helped make Heath's career. It also represented everything that the disastrous Lagos attack was not: it embodied order, control and execution of a sound plan. And it was this visible order, Heath believed, that had kept the Russians from attempting anything.[2]

Commodore Leopold Heath was in his element again. Follow the most direct route between order and execution. Turn debris into constituent parts of a coherent whole. He understood his orders, knew to whom he was responsible, and had the ships and officers he needed to complete his work. And he succeeded: he commanded the birth of a port city in a salt marsh, orchestrated port operations on a daily basis, and directed the tasks of his station squadron.

After the force was landed, but still with many responsibilities as temporary governor of the newfound harbour, Heath turned his mind to the problem of the slave trade. Before he had departed Bombay he had already collected the records and opinions of past officers and officials on the subject of fighting the trade. Old treaties made with earlier rulers of Zanzibar and Madagascar gave the Royal Navy the authority to stop slaves from being carried across the Indian Ocean. That is, while the British could not force those rulers to halt the institution of slavery in their lands, they had made it illegal for slaves from the Zanzibar market to be borne abroad beyond Zanzibari territory and for captives to be brought from the African mainland to Madagascar. But the promise of extremely high returns on investment meant smugglers pierced the blockade north and south along the coast, sped by monsoon winds, and headed to Madagascar and sugar islands nearby.

His letters to his Admiralty superiors make it clear that Heath took for granted that fighting the slave trade was the 'undoubted duty of England'. He made clear his deep frustration with the failure of half-hearted routine that had resulted in failure on the east coast. Yet he had no more than a half-dozen ships on his small station to perform every duty demanded by London and Calcutta in the Red Sea, Persian Gulf, and western Indian Ocean from Bombay to the Cape. He could not possibly stop every fleeting dhow running the blockade in every direction. In previous years efforts had been haphazard and unsustained – a state of things unacceptable to the man.

He began thinking, planning. If his assignment in charge of the East Indies station were a typical length, he would have no more than a few years to correct a generation of official apathy and incoherence. He had on *Octavia* a young officer who was a slaver-hunter of some experience. William Maxwell had served on HMS *Lyra* in Zanzibar waters and Heath interviewed him. The two spoke as they explored the sage and dust hinterlands near Annesley Bay on horseback, sometimes hearing jackals' calls.

Heath began to envisage a kind of trap laid for the slavers running up the east coast for destinations in the Persian Gulf and elsewhere. Once the campaign in Abyssinia was over he would be able to test it. Finally, six months after landing, the army marched back victorious from the Abyssinian interior to another naval salute at Annesley Bay. Not long after, *Octavia* left the Red Sea for the Indian Ocean and the commodore's new undertaking.[3]

HMS *Daphne*, Plymouth, June 1867

At steamy Annesley Bay Leopold Heath had with him another navy officer with experience of hunting slavers on the east coast of Africa: George Sulivan. And Commander Sulivan captained a new ship that held special promise for executing the kinds of tactics that were revolving in Heath's mind. (Heath and others had pleaded with the Admiralty for better, faster ships for this squadron.) A year before this Sulivan had been in his ancestral country of Cornwall, where he one day found his heart's desire in the post.

It was June 1867 when, after a few months on land on half-pay, George Sulivan received a letter from the Admiralty, a light-blue paper coveted by every commander. It was a new commission. He was to get a brand new sloop ready for sea, and was *hereby required and directed to cause the utmost dispatch to be used.* He was ordered to take her to Bombay, the Royal Navy's East Indies station, but there was a world of work to be done first.

So to Plymouth and to the dockyard on its west side, Devonport, with its rows of workshops and sheds, pools and slips; the great sorted stacks of timber; the long ropery, forges, and over all of it coal smoke. There he first saw *Daphne*: black, much larger than his previous ship *Pantaloon*, longer and higher in the water, a bit under 190 feet long and 36 feet broad at mid-ship. She was bluff and brawny at the waterline like a larger man-of-war, and would force her way through the water rather than cutting it as had the sleeker *Pantaloon*. She had three raking masts, and when they were properly rigged they would be adorned with some square and some triangular sails. This was known as being 'barque-rigged'. She would thus wear some square sails for being pushed before the wind, and some triangular for being pulled forward by a wind cutting across her or even somewhat in her face. It was a kind of compromise rig. Beneath the water-line she concealed a massive engine and boilers to drive a fifteen-foot screw when the wind failed.

Sketch of *Dryad* drying her sails in the harbour of Zanzibar

Daphne was one of the new *Amazon* class, and she and her sisters were the largest commander's commands in the Royal Navy. The great line-of-battle ships were hard ironclads, but the new *Amazons* wore no armour, though they hid iron deck beams, upright stanchions, and other iron reinforcements. Nor did the *Amazons* show long rows of gun ports: four only for them. But they were powerful guns, persuasive, with carriages set on tracks to pivot.

The new class was created as an answer to the CSS *Alabama*. In 1862, the rebellious southern states of America had purchased a fast yet hard-hitting ship from a Liverpool shipbuilder. The *Alabama* proceeded to wreak havoc on United States shipping throughout the world. The Admiralty imagined what ships like the *Alabama* chasing down British trade might do in a future war, so they set out to match her. *Alabama* had eight guns, including two heavy long-range guns on pivoting carriages like the *Amazons*. And she was quick, up to thirteen knots under sail and steam, while the *Amazons* could make twelve.

The role of the *Amazons* was to match the pace and striking-power of an *Alabama*, but also to put an end to arguments before they got too heated and settle things from a distance. The *Amazons* could be sent into the harbour of this bloody pirate or that rebellious chief, then – pridefully, deliberately – level a fort, explode a magazine, or ruin city walls. The *Amazons* embodied a rather insistent style of diplomacy.

It was not the *Amazons'* style to brawl at close quarters, but they possessed one experimental weapon meant to be delivered as directly as possible: a ram. *Daphne*'s gently curved ram evoked the rams of ancient Greek triremes: metal-reinforced, sweeping forward at the waterline. The Greeks painted theirs like sea monsters; not so the Royal Navy. The thinking was that in a fleet action in which ironclads were hammering each other ineffectually, a fast ram-bowed ship might be sent in under full steam to charge the enemy. The 1862 US Civil War 'Battle of Hampton Roads' between the iron *Monitor* of the North and *Merrimac* of the South seemed to provide an illustration: the two had exchanged hammer blows to no avail for three hours. Many ironclads lay precariously low in the water, and ramming them, some thought, might bear them down. The low, heavy *Monitor* was indeed eventually fated to sink in heavy seas. Reinforcing the enthusiasm for rams, meanwhile, was the 1866 Battle of Lissa in which the Austrians successfully used the tactic against the Italians.

On a bright June day Sulivan went aboard *Daphne*, finding her mostly empty. No crew, no one to whom he could read his commission, per ancient tradition. About an hour later the master hurried on board. He would take most responsibility in navigating her and had good experience of piloting a gun vessel in Chinese waters. The next afternoon came Sulivan's first lieutenant, aged twenty-four, a man who had flitted quickly from ship to ship in his career. He had never run a ship like *Daphne* and it remained to be seen whether he could handle it.

It took weeks to assemble the ship's complement. Twelve men from the recently broken-up old *Cambridge*; seventeen from *Indus,* guard ship of Plymouth harbour; twenty-four men from the antique French prize, *Canopus.* A great many of these were receiving-ship men, raw recruits. A contingent of marines joined from the Plymouth division. They had just returned from Ireland where they had been hunting a phantom Fenian uprising – supposedly stoked up by American Civil War veterans – that never materalised.

Sulivan and his lieutenants not only had to make one crew of the men and boys, but transmute many a landsman into a sailor. Hammocks were issued, the crew was drilled at fire stations, new sails bent and stowed, and rifles, pistols and swords counted and locked away. They hoisted aboard their new boats, painted white. They fitted one of these boats with a six-pound gun, and carefully filled the *Daphne*'s magazines with shot, shell, and – in its fire-proof room – powder. They heaped ton after ton of coal in the many chutes that dotted the ship's weather deck. They fitted a new capstan for raising the anchor.

A speed trial of the new engine took place a month after Sulivan took her in hand. On the baptismal day *Daphne* demanded a blood sacrifice. In the rush of work to get the maximum speed out of the ship a bag of coals came crashing down on the head of stoker Dick Osborne. He never rose again. It was far from the last sacrifice *Daphne* would demand.[4]

HMS *Daphne*, West Africa, September 1867

After some adjustments to her machinery and rigging, *Daphne* parted in late summer from England for Africa. Thus, on a bright, warm September mid-morning, *Daphne* was sailing eastward just above the equator to Sierra Leone with topsails and topgallants high above on iron masts that approached 100 feet. The wind was light, and *Daphne* was reaching for all she could. She should raise the crouching-lion hill above Freetown in a few hours. George Sulivan ordered the men mustered as he wanted to read the Articles of War before anchoring in the harbour. The Articles were a warning and ward, and every port had its lures. He read:

> All persons in or belonging to His Majesty's ships or vessels of war, being guilty of profane oaths, cursings, execrations, drunkenness, uncleanness, or other scandalous actions, in derogation of God's honour, and corruption of good manners, shall incur such punishment as a court martial shall think fit to impose, and as the nature and degree of their offence shall deserve.

By noon they had sighted the hills and cape. The officer of the watch shortened sail, the leadsman cast his lead-weighted line to sound out the bottom, and a few hours later *Daphne* lay at single anchor in the deep water of Freetown harbour. Her captain meant to keep *Daphne* in port as briefly as possible, but there was much to do in that time. There were well over 100 tons of coal to be dumped in the pitch-black vaults down below, damp sails to be loosed to dry against mouldering, and all the other tasks and business after a long passage.

Most important, Sulivan would complete his complement: he needed Kroomen. Sulivan was in luck. An old and trusted shipmate from the *Pantaloon*, John Bull, was in the Kroo-Town section of Freetown. Bull had spent years doing hard service on Africa's east coast. Sulivan made Bull Head Krooman, responsible for bringing on seven more Kroomen. They came on board bringing their log canoe. Then *Daphne*'s Amazonian sister *Nymphe* glided into Freetown harbour shortly after *Daphne* to take on the usual contingent of Kroomen. After just three days, *Daphne* steamed out of the harbour against the wind and bucking the current. Next, to lonely Ascension Island, then Cape Town, and around the Cape for East Africa.

A day beyond the Cape the wind rose and rose. After long hours with Sulivan refusing to leave the watch, a sail tore away in a gust and he ordered braces adjusted to reinforce the straining yards. The waves were contrary and growing and *Daphne* started rolling on the heaving sea. Some hours before dawn an extraordinary sea threw itself high over the bulwarks and bashed the ship's boats. There was an explosion of masts, yards, blocks, stanchions and oars. Two steel boathooks went flying as if to murder. The long cutter was flung from its high place on its davits but saved from the sea by the scrambling men. Sulivan commanded the struggle to right the chaos. Finally, still before sunrise, he relinquished the watch and withdrew to his cabin.

More restless hours passed with the cross-seas constantly shoving *Daphne* until a titanic wave hurled itself onto her. It hammered the ship so forcefully that securely latched iron ports on the bulwarks blew open. The water tore nettings that enclosed railings from their places. The upper deck was a sea that gushed down hatchways to the decks below until it covered them. In his cabin under the poop deck Sulivan was unaware of the deluge – in fact none of the officers were fully aware of what had happened. After a couple of minutes Gardner, the first lieutenant, came up the companionway and managed to reach Sulivan's door. He told the captain of water sloshing around the deck below. Should he batten down?

Something was wrong. The sub-lieutenant, Richard Orton, was stationed up on the iron conning bridge that spanned the ship port to starboard above the bulwarks. From there, Orton should have raised the alarm when water started pouring in the ports and hatchways, but there had been silence. Just then the bosun's mate who had been on deck came hurrying aft. *Man overboard.* The force of the monstrous wave, the blind swing of a reeling titan, had hurled Orton from high on the bridge and the sea took him in.

Alarms and a rush of orders; the wheel yanked around; *Daphne*'s head straining to come about as close to the wind as possible. Someone sighted Orton already half a mile astern. It had taken too long to raise the alarm. Still, Orton swam, strong, at twenty-one-years old. The men flung life-buoys.

Daphne managed to slow, at least, the rate at which Orton was drawing away from her. Sulivan ordered the fires built in the cold boilers below, but it would be at least two hours before he could call for power from them. Orton, Sulivan measured, had a matter of minutes in such waves. Sulivan had saved several sailors from drowning in his time, but diving into such seas was self-murder. First one man, then another, asked – begged, even – to be allowed to lower a boat and pull for Orton. But Sulivan knew that lowering a boat in such wind and seas meant losing both a boat and that boat's crew. *If you men won't consider your death,* Sulivan thought, *then I must.* Sulivan knew that Orton was a capable swimmer, but there was no hope, regardless. *He must sink,* thought Sulivan.

Soon the youth was lost to sight. After an hour in the cold darkness, far longer than the boy had life, Sulivan gave the order to abandon the fight against wind and waves. Resume course. The order given, despair – a sorrow he could never after put into words – took him. He turned and left the deck.[5]

HMS *Daphne*, Mahé Island, Seychelles, August 1868

HMS *Daphne* arrived at the East Indies Station in Bombay just in time to join the massive flotilla for Annesley Bay. After some repairs, she took a factory ship, a floating workshop, in tow. She took her position in the amassed fleet and sailed west. For months she took her turn as guard ship and ran errands to and from Aden on the bottom of the Arabian peninsula up to Suez where the canal was being built, up and down the Red Sea. She carried messages, shipped pay, bore passengers. Whatever the flagship *Octavia* signalled, *Daphne* jumped to do.

After the troops marched back from the interior of Abyssinia, the commodore released *Daphne* from the Red Sea. Now she was gliding between the islands of the Seychelles, drawn on by a steady light wind under bright blue skies interspersed with cloud. It was midday, with a southerly wind, 75 degrees, and seas the same temperature. This was a reprieve from far hotter days at berth in Annesley Bay. There, unsteady, weakly winds faintly gasped as weed grew on *Daphne*'s belly.

The passage had not been easy. The day she set out from the Red Sea, seaman George Young fell from a main yard. Icarus's neck was probably saved when he glanced off the Kroomen's canoe hung in its place, so that he splashed into the sea instead of crunching onto the oak deck. They got Young out of the waves alive. Weeks later in the crossing, *Daphne* cracked the same main yard when she was surprised by a rogue blast of wind. Meanwhile, the sick-room list grew to twenty.

Soon Sulivan hoped to raise Mahé, the main island of the Seychelles chain. *A healthy island,* Sulivan thought, *which can't be said of any other part of most islands in this sea or the African coast.* At two o'clock the lookout raised the island and the officer of the watch gave orders. The *Daphne*'s crew trimmed sails, set the tall, trapezial gaff mainsail, and cast the lead and line as the sandy beach began to rise under her keel. With equatorial evening falling, the sloop approached her anchoring place off the marked approach to the port. There lay Commodore Heath's flagship, the long *Octavia*. Orders to fire a rocket and burn a blazing pyrotechnic light, furl sails, and drop anchor. Night fell fully with a few passing showers meandering across the Indian Ocean.

The morning's sun showed a variety of green on the island. Here and there a brown cliff broke through the cover. A peak of several thousand feet rose beyond the little port, green to the top. Sulivan paid his duty to the commodore on board the flagship and reported on the passage. He made a point of telling the commodore how young Midshipman Stuart and Head Krooman Bull had worked together to save George Young from drowning after he glanced off a canoe. And he had to ask the commodore for a new main topsail yard out of *Octavia*'s spares, though a great yard was a precious thing half an ocean away from the nearest dockyard store. The request was granted.

There was work to do, but Sulivan also wanted to give his men leave since they would not be in such a green, benign place for a long while. So one watch went ashore while the other took on water, coaled, and rattled down yards. Then they switched. Boats were repaired, the ship cleaned, the new yard hauled up and fitted. Four days of leave, and the sick-room began to empty.

After a week, before they were to part, *Octavia* signalled Sulivan to dinner. The commodore's orders were ready. Sulivan was to patrol the African coast, Madagascar, and the south-west Indian Ocean islands. First he was to call on the British consul in Madagascar to show the flag and learn what slave trading was going on there. Heath would sail directly to Zanzibar to speak to the sultan and visit the slave market.[6]

CHAPTER 3

'HIS BARK IS STOUTLY TIMBER'D'

*Commodore Heath declares
his intent and the* Amazons
prepare for their campaign

ZANZIBAR WAS THE CAPITAL of an East African coastal empire, the Zanzibari sultans originally from Oman on the Arabian peninsula far to the north. The Europeans were not the only ones who colonised and meddled in Africa in the modern period. Neither were European empires the only ones to grow fat feeding on the blood of African slavery. Zanzibar was the centre of an extensive slave trade, and the sultanate's main source of wealth was the tax it collected on imported human merchandise. Traders brought as many as 20,000 Africans to the island each year, both to replace the dead on Zanzibar's plantations and for re-export beyond the island.

Its harbour was a busy entrepôt, a place where cargoes were loaded, off-loaded, resold, reloaded and reshipped. Ivory flowed to Zanzibar from the mainland, and it was re-exported to Bombay or London or Marseille. Copal, hardened tree resin used in making varnish, was dug on the east coast, imported to Zanzibar, and re-exported to Europe and the US. An Omani pioneer introduced clove trees to Zanzibar and its neighbouring island, Pemba, in the early 1800s. By 1868, the two islands produced almost 4,000 tons of cloves per year. (Clove harvesting was intensive work, since gathering the stem with the bud from the end of the branch risked breaking the branch; stems then had to be separated from the bud before the bud was dried. This process was repeated several times over two annual seasons.) Cloves were sold to Bombay and London and throughout the world. This created a wealthy plantation class, and that in its turn created a hunger for another critical import, enslaved East Africans. Abductees came from the East African hinterland often carrying ivory tusks on their backs, and often in a state of semi-starvation after experiencing war in their homelands and a brutal forced march to the sea.

Zanzibar and Pemba's large clove operations had slave labour forces of 2,000 or more. To feed and clothe these thousands, cotton flowed inward from the US and India, rice and other food supplies from around the Indian Ocean from many nations and principalities. The cotton cloth sometimes served to purchase more war-slaves in the interior. It was a tidy circular trade.

Treaties made between the Zanzibari sultanate and the British Crown prohibited the sale of slaves to any Christian, banned the long-distance slave trade, required that traders be licensed by the sultan, and limited the slaving season to some degree. The trade could only be carried on within a roughly 500-mile stretch of coast and must not pass eastward to into the heart of the Indian Ocean. But based on many years of observation, Heath and others in the Royal Navy suspected many thousands of the enslaved were being taken to ports well beyond the treaty limits.

The treaties empowered the Royal Navy to enforce these limitations at sea, but the station charged with stopping the forbidden long-distance trade – Bombay's East Indies station – was overstretched. It had only a handful of ships to devote to the East African coast and Arabian Sea and a long list of duties. Occasionally an officer would arrive among the squadron who focused on slaver-hunting and won some successes. But the squadron had a reputation for being comprised of some of the most worn-out ships in the navy. Frequently it could devote no ships at all to the mission, with worn vessels in dry-dock or pressing duties calling ships elsewhere.

HMS *Pantaloon*, Zanzibar harbour, July 1866

A scene from George Sulivan's previous commission just prior to receiving the *Daphne* captures the compromised position of the British in Zanzibar – a position in which they could do nothing about the trafficking in humans occurring right before them.

HMS *Pantaloon* was in Zanzibar harbour and her captain was in his cabin, a space not ten feet at its widest and not five feet high. It held a small square table, a little stove, and small cabinets fitted into every possible place. There was a knock at the cabin door and the ship's interpreter, Jumah, entered, slipping off his sandals.

'My master,' he said, 'suppose you come on deck? I show you something.'

Sulivan followed up the ladder-way outside his cabin door and across the threshold of brightness onto the quarterdeck. There was activity all around the ship. *Pantaloon* was being tended to after hardworking weeks in the Indian Ocean and quarters were being whitewashed. And still the mizzen topsail needed repairing and booms and masts needed scraping and painting.

Ships and boats crowded the harbour of Zanzibar, the island capital of Sultan Majid bin Said, who ruled a coastal empire from the spot. French and German merchant ships often visited his port; American and English ships too, carrying away ivory from the mainland and cloves from Zanzibar's plantations. Outnumbering these were smaller ships, dhows, the work-horses of the East African coast. Familiar throughout the Arabian Sea and Indian Ocean, they were low in the water and narrow, but high in the stern, usually with one or two leaning masts and sweeping triangular sails. They embodied speed – not power or permanence, but haste.

Among all these was the 11-gun sloop HMS *Pantaloon*. Her three masts, slightly leaning or raked, stood well above the dhows in the harbour. She was far longer, too, at 150 feet, with a distinctive keel that stretched far diagonally aft over the water behind her. The dhows that moved in its shadow had crews of thirty at the very most, usually far less, while the *Pantaloon* had 130. But though it dwarfed the dhows, though its guns threw 32-pound iron shot, though a steam engine and boilers burned at its heart, the *Pantaloon* was impotent in this harbour.

The interpreter Jumah pointed out a particularly large dhow coasting into the harbour. Sulivan could easily see that it was crammed with Africans from the mainland, kidnapped, bound for Zanzibar's busy slave market. It was a sight with which he was familiar.

The *Pantaloon's* captain, Commander George Sulivan, was a slight man. It was as if his years sailing tropical waters had steamed away some of his mass and this gave him an ascetic air. But his face was broad, mouth wide, and eyes set at a distance. The open eyes looked fit for a pastor, incongruous for a veteran of around twenty years, witness to a long record of inhumanity and violence.

'What's the use, Jumah? We can't take her here.'

The large dhow passed under the *Pantaloon's* stern, showing a crowd of men, women and children on its bamboo deck. It was packed so tightly that only the raised poop deck was visible. The dhow's captain and chief hands looked up at Sulivan and Jumah. They called to them, laughing.

'What does he say, Jumah?'

'Why you not come and take us?' Jumah translated. 'Are you afraid?'

Jumah shouted back a challenge in Arabic. The dhow's captain replied.

'I got lots of slaves on board,' Jumah translated, 'tell the captain to come and see.'

More laughter, and the large slaver coasted to a rest. Just a pistol-shot away, marked Sulivan. In an hour it would be emptied. An agent, quite possibly one of the Indian traders who owned a significant share of the business on the island, would force the captives to the market to be groomed for resale in the near future. *If this were any other sea and one ship attacked another and kidnapped its people,* reflected Sulivan, *we would declare them pirates, seize them, and hang the kidnappers.* But here, now, Sulivan and *Pantaloon* were powerless.

Though the official stance of the British government was that slavery was an abomination, and while the institution was outlawed in the empire, this was not the British empire. The oak under Sulivan's feet was, but Zanzibar was not. The British had a treaty with the sultan of Zanzibar permitting the Royal Navy to arrest his subjects and seize their ships when involved in the distant overseas slave trade – the trade bound well beyond these waters. But the British only won the treaty by agreeing to overlook the trade between Zanzibar and the African coast to the west. There, middlemen took receipt of people kidnapped in the interior and then sold them to slave traders on the coast who bore them to a number of Indian Ocean markets, often the market in Zanzibar. From there, the Africans were sent to the clove plantations on and near this island, or set to other labour in town or on farms, or made sexual chattels. This activity was perfectly legal according to the letter of the treaty. The *Pantaloon* could not touch this slave ship.[1]

HMS *Octavia*, Zanzibar, August 1868

Now, in summer 1868, Heath's flagship *Octavia* sailed into Zanzibar harbour with booming salutes. Heath sent his humble appeal to the sultan of Zanzibar, Majid bin Said, and was soon approaching his seafront palace, Beit al-Sahel, a whitewashed two-storey building, forty yards wide, with a broad, shady portico. It was red-roofed, with green shutters over windows set very high. A platform of nine cannon stood before it. Amid the palace compound were a family mosque, tomb and large stables. Neighbouring the whole was the small crenellated fort which housed the sultan's men-at-arms. Not an army, really, but a household guard comprised of some slaves and some Baluchi mercenaries – men from a famously fierce land. But the sultan's power did not lie in the fort, it resided in the customs house next to it. There the sultan extracted taxes from every ship that arrived at this famous Indian Ocean crossroads. These included – most importantly — licensed slave ships. Close by the customs house were the British, French and American consulates.

Approaching the palace with Leopold Heath was the British consul to the kingdom, Henry Churchill, only forty years old but a veteran of diplomatic posts in Persia, Syria and Algiers, Churchill was a scholar, sometime archaeologist, onetime denizen of a Russian dungeon. He had dark eyes and hair and the Romantic look of the previous age.

Heath and Churchill entered the palace and were guided to the long and open reception hall, with dark wooden beams that spanned the ceiling. Beneath their feet was a chequered floor of black and white marble. Ornament in the hall went little further; it had the elegance of measure and discipline. Then there was the sultan, a man of thirty or thirty-five with a very slight build that conveyed austerity. He had a short, carefully kept beard and moustaches. His forehead was broad and smooth. He had a gentle bearing, but his eyes revealed intense energy.

The sultan greeted Heath with courtesy. Then the long hall emptied of retainers. Speaking through the multilingual Churchill, Heath told the sultan why he was there.

The commodore informed the sultan that he was turning his full attention to putting down the slave trade, devoting both his mind and his men-of-war to the problem. Heath was tactful, not threatening or blustering. And he told the sultan that he had no special assignment from Her Majesty's Government, nor did he bear a proposal from London for a new treaty. He was committing himself on his own account to better fight the outlaws who violated the existing treaty. Heath left unspoken his awareness that the sultan's power depended in part on slave soldiers, on slave-worked plantations, and on the taxes gleaned from slave imports. The sultan's merchant subjects were powerful, independent-minded, and made rich on the blood of slavery. Even if the sultan had wanted it, an end to slavery would gravely risk his own head. Heath could not hope to stop the trade completely if the British empire itself condoned it here.

So, he told the sultan, he wanted to find a way for his captains to distinguish quickly between an authorised trader and the smugglers who ran the blockade for distant ports. These men, Heath told the sultan, operate under cover of the legal trade, thus perpetuating the Indian Ocean slave trade. Unless changes were made, there would be no chance of putting it down. After listening to Heath's proposals with courtesy, Majid bin Said asked that the commodore kindly draft his concerns and proposals in writing. Heath and Churchill took their leave.

Leopold Heath did submit his concerns in writing, but he never heard back from the sultan's court. When he did not, Heath felt, as he wrote to his superiors, that 'the ground is clear for other arrangements' and 'more earnest efforts'.[2]

HMS *Dryad*, Portsmouth, August 1868

Heath could not have been surprised by the lack of response from a ruler whose riches and position depended on the continuation of the traffic in abductees. And now he was free to try his new strategy for choking the trade. Heath had sent Sulivan to gather information in Madagascar, patrol the East African coast, then begin a trial of Heath's new tactics. It only remained for the other two captains Heath would commit to this mission to arrive in the Indian Ocean.

Commander Philip Colomb was almost on his way. He stood on the docks in Portsmouth harbour flanked by friends, fellow officers in the service. They congratulated him on his appointment to the great new sloop *Dryad*, then patrolling in the Red Sea and Indian Ocean. But Colomb was preoccupied with how to survive the voyage to Alexandria, the overland passage across northern Egypt, and the trip via Pacific and Orient (P&O) Lines down the length of the Red Sea. Once he reached the British port of Aden at the bottom of the Arabian peninsula, and his new command, his days would be filled with problems to be solved, solutions to be tested. But until then he would be a mere passenger under the command of a civilian captain. Several weeks he would be stowed in the *Damascus*, subject to the banalities of imposed companions: effusive Frenchmen, inquisitive Americans and God knew what else. Confined and, worst of all to a man like Colomb, wasting time.

Colomb and his comrades set off back into the heart of Portsmouth to purchase the essentials for his trial. First they located a folding deck-chair, fabric-seated, far more comfortable than those provided by P&O. Next came a stop at the newsagents where Colomb was laden with an armful of newspapers. And, though the literary Colomb knew they were tawdry, he selected a stack of shilling novels to make the miles pass. For the Mediterranean was wide.

Colomb's friends saw him and his time-killing materials onto the *Damascus*. The three found the ship's bar, raised their glasses, and drank one another's health. 'To our next merry meeting,' one of them said. Between Royal Navy officers that might take place at any of the hundred ports in the empire or on any of the world's seas. Shortly, conversation scraped aground.

Somewhere below, stokers were at work making steam and finally the three officers were relieved by the bell for embarkation. Colomb handed his friends one last letter before they hurried away and the *Damascus*'s twin paddle wheels began their roll. A woman in the crowd of waving handkerchiefs cried for the departure of her husband, Colomb's steward. And Colomb imagined his own wife, far away at home with the children, crying too.

After a brief reprieve from boredom at Gibraltar, every Royal Navy sailor's home away from home, Colomb dozed as often as he could in his prized deck-chair, feet propped on a backgammon table. Between dozing and feeding, Colomb contemplated his fifty or so fellow passengers and made idle observations in his journal. Upper middle class, conservative, veering towards uncharitableness as the weeks passed. There was little space, few baths and limited games and books aboard. The passengers formed tribes and competed over them. The *Pax Britannica*, thanks in large part to men-of-war captained by the likes of Colomb, held firm sway in the Mediterranean. So, safe from the threats of Frenchmen, Turk, or pirate, the Hamilton clan could devote its attention to the threat that the O'Connor clan represented to the best breakfast table, chess set, or beef roast.

At one meal, Colomb and his forced messmates heard one tale of charity. One of the P&O officers related how, not long before, one of their steamers had come upon a heavily laden ship apparently in some need. It turned out to be a slave ship crammed with human beings. It was bearing them from some East African port to Madagascar perhaps, or some port in the Arabian Sea or Persian Gulf, or even Brazil. It seemed that the wind had failed them and the slavers' food and water had run out. The victims were starving, so the English passengers had supplied the ship with food and water.

Colomb reflected in his journal that this was a humane response, no doubt, and a mercy to the desperate slaves. But at the same time it was a kindness to the slavers. It meant the preservation of their investment. Saved chattel, saved profits, in his estimation. Colomb would return to hard reflections on the economics of the slave trade again and again in the coming months.

Philip Colomb had an academic bent, was thoughtful and speculative. When he ran into the problems or limitations of ships or systems or techniques, he tended not to accept them but to set his mind to alternatives. His was an impatient and inventive mind. He would be led by cool logic and not, he assured himself, by sentimentality or soft sympathy for the Africans.

He had heard more of this slave trade in the last few years. The missionary explorer Dr David Livingstone – now feared dead in unmapped Arica – had published widely read accounts of the trade, including the warfare that produced a supply of victims. Other famous explorers, Speke, Burton, Baker – household names – wrote similar reports of blood and slavery. Colomb believed that the public at home was awakening, at last, to knowledge. In his view, the Admiralty was taking a greater interest in suppressing the trade because in recent years jurisdiction over Indian

Ocean affairs had passed from the government in India to the government in London. The British Indian government had a more 'offhand' approach to the slave trade, at best. That is why Colomb was steaming east to meet the *Dryad*. But he was still a novice slaver-hunter.

'Capture plenty of dhows,' one of his friends had called as Colomb departed Portsmouth some weeks before. *But how is this capturing of dhows done*, he wondered, and *what kind of thing is a dhow?*[3]

HMS *Nymphe*, Bombay, November 1868

On the station Colomb would meet his old shipmate from the *Phoenix*'s arctic venture, Edward Meara, who was taking command of one of the other *Amazons* at about the same time. In the months to come Meara would prove in many ways Colomb's opposite. If Colomb was dispassionate, Meara was vengeful. Colomb was cautious, Meara bold. And in the months to come Colomb would have to help his more hot-headed comrade out of trouble.

Meara's prized commission to join Heath's squadron and captain the *Nymphe* had found him patrolling home waters as coastguard. Months later found him being rowed over Bombay harbour in 90-degree tropical air in a dark blue uniform as only a sickly wind sighed and vanished. Meara had sailed the West Indies, coasted Brazil, and served in the miasmatic waters off Sierra Leone in a naval career that had taken him to all the world's oceans, but he had spent the last three years based around his native Ireland. There he had inhabited fog, boarded limping ships in ice gales. Yes, Meara had known heat like this as a young man raiding up the rivers of West Africa, but not recently.

Still, he was finally experiencing the moment for which he had waited 5,000 miles. HMS *Nymphe*, sister ship of *Daphne* and *Dryad*, lay ahead. Her teak sides were painted black, as were her tubular iron masts. Two towered high in front of a shorter mizzenmast, and all leaned slightly as if swaying

Photo of former kidnapees on board *Daphne*, 1868

from speed. Unlike most ships, the *Nymphe*'s bow reached forward at the waterline as if she meant force her way through it. Amidships rose her funnel, incongruously straight and stumpy below her proud, tall masts. Her stern was covered with boats hanging on their davits.

Who were the ship's crew-members, and what was their life like aboard? Following Meara aboard the first time provides some insights. Coming to her side shortly before noon, Meara was piped aboard the *Nymphe*'s upper deck. Now, at exactly noon, it was time for the sacramental reading of Meara's commission. This done, Meara was now captain of the *Nymphe*. The bell rang and afternoon watch replaced the forenoon.

Visible from the quarterdeck, the space of command on the ship's top – or weather – deck, were more boats cradled amidships, as were the guns. Slightly forward were two large cannon on trucks, while slightly aft were two hulks – six-ton cannon that threw 64-pound shells of 7-inch diameter well over a mile. They straddled tracks so that they could be pivoted and aimed by a relatively small crew of sailors and Royal Marine artillery. The *Nymphe* and her sisters were meant to destroy from afar, to fire calmly, deliberately. The *Amazons* threw their insults from a distance, almost indifferently. Still, they shattered.

Soon the bosun called all hands to quarters for muster. The crew took their positions about ship. In this and other musters, Meara began to learn about his crew and vessel. A crew of 150 was a kaleidoscopic society. There were a dozen marines in red, more than a dozen cooks, stewards, and servants, the carpenter's crew, sailmaker's crew, armourer's crew, sixteen able and fourteen ordinary seamen, and more. There was James Barton, ship's boy from York. The helmsman came from Cork, one of the carpenters from Dublin. William Whitehead, able-bodied sailor, was from London, and William Mitchell, AB, like so many sailors, came from Devon. As with all ships on the station, Kroomen served on the *Nymphe*. There was Tom King, of long experience on this coast, Juma Matarka, and Ben Johnson: eight Kroomen in all. Young Nobie Rosekie, a refugee from slavers, had recently come on board from Socotra Island off the Horn of Africa and now hunted the slavers who once hunted him.

Down the steep companionway from the weather deck was the main deck, the middle deck on this ship. It was thirty-six feet at its widest and only the ship's boys could walk it without ducking under oak beams. It was huddled, but it was a huddled world. It was a delineated world of regions and districts. Along the sides were the cabins of the lieutenants, master, paymaster, surgeon, engineer, and captain's steward and wardroom steward. Cupboards in essence, each of these were barely long enough to hold a short bed and encompass outstretched arms. But in a crowded ship where privacy was otherwise non-existent, they were fortresses of isolation. The berth for the several midshipmen was hardly larger than these cabins for one, but these teenage boys still knew luxury that veteran able-bodied seamen, many superior sailormen, would never know. All of these small spaces opened onto the wardroom, a shared sphere, vast at sixteen by sixteen feet, where officers and surgeon dined elbow to elbow. Here they mended, played cards, and drank cocoa or coffee under a broad skylight waited on by servants.

The engineers were not citizens of the wardroom, so further forward, amidships, they had their place, less grand by far than the wardroom. The engineers had their own small mess cabin roughly ten by seven feet. Lockers, drawers, racks and shelves were tucked into every available corner for the special tools of their trade. But they had one luxury – a small stall in which they could shower. The engineers inhabited the dark realm of coal encompassing the lower deck. Warm water piped from the boiler room rinsed the coating of black dust from their bodies at the end of their watches. In this neighbourhood, too, the warrant officers – chief carpenter, gunner, bosun and master – had their small cabins tucked in among little pantries, rifle racks, shell lockers and small worktables.

Forward, before the mainmast, was the sailor's home. Their country took up about half of the main deck. They messed here on tables that could be stowed up amid the beams. And here the sailors slung their hammocks when it was their turn to sleep. Lining the hull were racks for their ditty bags and uniforms, effectively all they had in the world. Through the heart of this place rose the large funnel that emanated from the boiler room directly below. When the engine fires were stoked, the funnel warmed with intense fever and the deck underfoot became warm. When the fires were rolling, the lower deck warmed to around 100 degrees even in cool waters, and the *Nymphe* had not inhabited cool waters in a long time. Indian sun above the sailors, engine-fires below.

Close by, a little further forward, was the galley. Here the cook's crew and stewards worked in the heat of a large stove to feed 150 mouths. Here there were worktables, cupboards and coal boxes. The cooks could pump salt water into a basin for cleaning, as well as fresh cooking and drinking water from iron tanks below. Provisions came up through a nearby hatch.

Near here was the way to the infernal stoke hole. There squatted four large, dark boilers, fat devils bound to the screw shaft. Their iron skins were dark but their glowing red mouths showed their true essence as things of fire, and treacherous. They consumed as much coal as offered by their supplicant feeders, the stokers. Windsails fed air all the way down here

since the fires consumed air as much as coal. From far above, too, a telegraph line led from a place near the wheel and compass on the upper deck
so that the stokers could be told how much to feed the mouths. Close by
were the large coal rooms, taking up one-fifth of the entire deck. Over two
hundred tons of coal could fit in these – or the weight of thirty of *Nymphe*'s
monstrous guns. Here there were condensers in which seawater could be
made fresh for feeding the boilers. Then the engine room, where the steam
from the boilers exploded in three cylinders, thereby shoving a piston and
rod, turning a crankshaft, and finally spinning the shaft that led all the way
out of the stern and the fifteen-foot screw.

Down here on the dark orlop deck were store after store. Carpenters'
and engineers' stores, huge spools of cable, the bread room, the spirit room.
Separate, but not too far away from the brooding boilers, was the powder
magazine. There was a pump here for fighting fire. Fire here would have
meant cataclysm.

At some point after salutes, introductions, inspections, Commander – now
called 'Captain' – Meara found himself in his cabin. It was not his first
command. As a lieutenant, ten years ago, he had the little *Magnet* serving
in home waters. *Magnet* was no plum. She was a humble gunboat that
had been rushed out of the dockyard with scores of others to serve in the
'Russian' or Crimean War. Some of her timbers might even have been
green. Not so the *Nymphe*. Practically new, designed by the greatest naval
architect of the age, iron-braced, very large for a sloop, fast under steam.
And now Meara was in her stateroom. Relative to every other quarter in
the *Nymphe*, it was boundless. Twenty feet at its widest, easily accommo-
dating two wide lounges and, nestling in the stern, a curving cupboard.
And a substantial table at its centre at which the captain could spread charts,
examine accounts and host members of the wardroom for dinner. There
were three large portholes, two on each side and one looking straight
astern – gun ports, really, in the unlikely event that a gun, a stern chaser,

needed to be rolled into the cabin. Above all this, a skylight. Opening on to the commander's cabin was a bed cabin with its own desk and watercloset. A second small cabin opened on to the stateroom which could serve as a bed cabin for important passengers. Eventually, Meara slept.

When he rose the next day, he rose an administrator. The *Nymphe* needed to be overhauled. Tropical seas had worn her vitality. Weed grew from the hull and dragged at her, while rope and sails rotted. Meara and his lieutenants directed weeks of cleaning down to the last corners after which the ship was painted and painted again. The crew mounted masts and yards to paint them. Chains were brought out of their places and inspected, as was rope. The men replaced gear and sail and fitted new braces, caulkers moved over the ship clicking away, and Meara had the titanic guns shifted to new positions.

To get at the weed, the *Nymphe* had to be brought into a dock so her copper sheathing could be scraped. This meant the crew had to remove to reside in a hulk for some weeks. This was a massive renunciation of routine, but still the crew was frequently mustered and inspected. And kept busy: when the circumstance of a dock-stranded ship meant that the crew could not perform their usual duties, they were lent out to the dockyard for work.

When hands were idle, the devil made tools of them. George Hill of the sailmaker's crew was cited and marines Henry Feighly and James Hutchinson demoted for violating the Articles of War. A wardroom cook disappeared. Late one warm night a sailor spotted a body floating not far off. The officer of the watch sent some men in a boat to investigate, but the body sunk before the boat reached it. Meanwhile, the sick list grew.[4]

CHAPTER 4

'THE IMMINENT DEADLY BREACH'

Daphne *hunts and draws first blood*

WHILE THE CAPTAINS of the *Dryad* and *Nymphe* were still heading for the Indian Ocean, Sulivan began the work of gathering intelligence, patrolling, and preparing to test his commodore's new tactics. First, he pointed towards Madagascar.

HMS *Daphne*, Tamatave, Madagascar, September 1868

After busy days of working to windward south from his parting with Heath at the Seychelles, *Daphne* came to anchor off of Tamatave, a modest port on the eastern side of the great island. Salutes fired, salutes returned, and a boat lowered for Captain Sulivan to head for shore.

This was the station of Consul Conolly Pakenham, scion of an exalted and formidable English family, but for some reason sent here to spend his life on the opposite end of the planet in this small post. Pakenham's main duty was to strengthen the relationship between Britain and the new government of Madagascar. After generations of struggle over the island, one Madagascar caste and dynasty won sovereignty over most of the large island early in the nineteenth century. But in the 1830s that dynasty reacted to European – especially French – meddling and missionary activity by throwing them out of the country and forcing renunciations from Christian converts.

After decades of rebuffing European and American forays, the royal court began allowing more foreign interaction around 1863. But the king who had tried opening things up was targeted by traditionalist elements of the aristocracy and eventually strangled. Madagascar had a tradition of female monarchs in addition to male, so it was natural for the king's widow to take the throne. She ruled for the next five years and, despite the fate of her husband, continued opening Madagascar to the world, protected by a crafty prime minister.

Only months before Sulivan's arrival, Madagascar crowned a new queen upon the death of the old: Ranavalona II, another widow of the assassinated king. For the previous five years she had been tutored by the newly arrived British missionaries. At her coronation, a gold chain woven in her hair, a Bible was on display next to her seat as she declared the state religion to be Christian – better still for the British, Protestant. This was no small thing given that the French were competing with the British for influence on the island as they had many decades before. Her royal seat was on the island's central plateau. The court's control of the coasts, especially the African-facing west and south, was less established than elsewhere, though officially the island was united. Pro- and anti-Europe, pro-French and pro-British cliques competed in the royal court.

The Kingdom of Madagascar was a dominion of slaves. Generations of conquest by the central capital created uncounted thousands of war captives. There was a class of masters and a larger mass of the enslaved. Twenty-five or thirty years ago, foreign slave traders, especially French, crowded the ports. But in 1865, Ranavalona II's predecessor signed a treaty with the British declaring the trade to and from the island illegal. The institution itself, though, foully slinked on.

Slave ships still came and went in the shadows, but they were no longer visible in the ports. With little Royal Navy presence, slavers dodged and ran the paper blockade to out-of-the-way coasts. If he could catch them, Pakenham could legally demand that the Malagasy punish the slavers and recover the East African abductees. But catching the slave traders was difficult. The Africans came from the territories nominally controlled by the Portuguese, sometimes directly, sometimes through the French-influenced Comoro Islands. The French bought slaves on the African coast, declared them 'free' but liable for indentured servitude in exchange for the price of their purchase. They were supposed to stay in French territory, but they were taken here under the French flag with the designation of passengers or indentured workers, called *engagés*.

Pakenham briefed Sulivan. And when the commander parted from the consul he carried away a good impression of Pakenham. A British consul might be expected to enforce an anti-slavery treaty as a matter of duty, but Sulivan thought he could be trusted to act on principle, too. A credit to Britain, he thought, a man who would act with energy if only the Malagasy could be shown to be cheating the treaty. If only the Royal Navy could catch them at it. That was up to Sulivan and the rest of the East Indies squadron.

On the *Daphne*, the men worked on perennial repairs, parties went ashore to attend church in the village, others took cattle aboard. Some days later, as *Daphne*'s stokers summoned steam for her departure, a French man-of-war jealously looked in at the port. The implicit competition between French and British in these waters was also perennial.

Daphne then patrolled along the north-west end of the island, the most notorious for slaving. But over several days her searches produced nothing and, turning her head north before a southerly wind, she left Madagascar behind under plain sail.

Next, to the nearby Comoro Islands, a mix of petty sultanates and kingdoms. Some of these were under British influence, while some had been grabbed by the French. All abetted the slave trade. On a warm mid-September morning the wind faded to nearly nothing. The stokers renewed the fires in the heat below, and *Daphne* began steaming past one of Comoros, Johanna. It had a treaty with the British allowing trade to or from the island to be inspected. But still, falsehoods under the French flag – carrying supposed 'immigrant labourers' – perpetuated the slave traffic, as did Arab and Swahili outlaws.

Sulivan looked at the peak 6,000 feet above the little island, lushly emerald. And he knew it was a place of pure sweet water, fruit and sweet potatoes – a contrast to the society on the island which he found rotten and squalid, a miserable collection that passed for a town, with slave labour farms beyond it. More squalid still, the English consul of Johanna, William Sunley, had been caught using slave labour on his own sugar plantation on the west coast of the island. Retired from the Royal Navy, Sunley had set out to make his fortune as a sugar planter. He had been caught using 500 slaves. They were loaned to him from neighbouring plantations, but paying their masters for their use was supporting the trade. A visitor from the Cape made the discovery and reported Sunley to London. London, in turn, ordered him to stop using slave labour or resign his consulship. The man had the gall to refuse to quit either, and the London authorities forcibly stripped his consulship from him. Sulivan knew that Sunley was still on the island. A living slander against Britain, Sulivan thought – living, breathing hypocrisy.

After two more weeks of skimming between the Comoros and easy sailing up the mainland African coast, the *Daphne* slowly approached the mouth of the Kiswara River. North-east of this shore, not far, was the island of Zanzibar. These were familiar waters to Sulivan who had hunted slavers here in years past. This coast, he knew, fed Zanzibar's demand for forced labour.

Darkness was falling as *Daphne* swam cautiously on her approach to the river mouth. Sulivan raised steam to move with even more deliberation, as men on the sides dropped the lead and line often to feel out the bottom. In the dark *Daphne* dropped one anchor.

Before sunrise the next morning, Sulivan ordered the small dinghy lowered into the dark warm water. On this day he and the *Daphne*'s doctor would go exploring. Above, a mix of star and cloud, and a light, swinging wind. Sulivan took the oars while Surgeon Mortimer, a veteran of many ships and seas, descended in the dark. After two rifles had been passed down to the boat Sulivan started pulling towards the river's mouth and into living Africa. Miles passed, and dawn showed a world of green, a gently rolling land of grass and mounds of trees. Behind these were gradually rising hills. Eventually Sulivan chose a spot on the lightening riverbank to pull the dinghy up.

The two men walked and, as the sun emerged fully from the Indian Ocean it was gentle for a change. They aimed up a hill to look around the country. More miles, and they found the summit and their view: a broad valley with a small stream running through it, and woods on the valley's opposite end. It reminded Sulivan of the best views of England, though something was missing. Had this been England, part of the composition would have been cultivated land, but there was none here. That probably meant that slavers had been here. When slave-raiders came through a country, Sulivan knew, people could only abandon their fields. If lucky, they could hide until the hunters passed from the country. If unlucky, there came war and kidnap. In any case, crops went unplanted or rotted in the fields and livestock starved. Grass and forest reclaimed villages.

The captain and surgeon kept walking. At the far end of the valley they surprised a pair of women who ran upon seeing them. As they ran they shouted a warning to people somewhere ahead whom Sulivan and the doctor could not see. The two men followed and eventually came upon a small collection of little mud-brick houses with closed doors. The captain guessed that this was a kind of retreat; a place where the villagers felt isolated from other populations; a place too small and out-of-the-way for raiders or kidnappers. The two called out, doing their best to communicate to the hidden villagers that they were no threat, making a patient effort at explanation, conveying peace, somehow, in an alien language. Finally, a sole elderly man emerged from his house. After more effort and patience the old man eventually communicated back.

Alarm subsided, and those barred in the other little houses emerged, most of them women. They very closely examined the Englishmen, their gear, clothes, rifles. Now, still more confident, they began feeling the material of their clothes. Sulivan was unsettled at the centre of a clutch of women feeling his clothes, but did not stop them. He imagined their hands were very dirty, but stayed still. The women spoke earnestly to one another. Sulivan imagined they were stating their opinions of them. Preparing to go, Sulivan did his best to let them know that Englishmen were their friends. They seemed ultimately to understand and communicated friendship.[1]

What if Sulivan and the surgeon had stumbled upon Dr Livingstone that day? David Livingstone, after all, was not so very far away from them in the interior at that moment. Heath's squadron might have experienced a far different fate had the famous explorer's observations of East Africa been published at the beginning of their campaign.

In those same days, Livingstone was exploring the country three or four hundred miles into the continent in the Lake Nyasa region. As a younger man, Livingstone had been a typical missionary, but he had become impatient with preaching among known communities in familiar lands and left known tracts behind. To him, it seemed an army of missionaries clung to familiar beachheads until every possible convert had long since been won. Besides, he had an idea for sparking the conversion of the whole continent: by suffusing it with European influence by way of commerce. Livingstone himself would explore and identify river highways – ideally, a river that would link south-east Africa to the Nile – that would lure those with wares to sell in the interior and those who hoped to extract ivory and other rarities. The presence of traders, the attraction of 'civilised' wares, and a ready outlet for resources was supposed to allow civilisation and Christianity to flourish while undermining the slave trade both morally and economically.

While George Sulivan witnessed the waste and fear that slave raiders caused near the coast, Livingstone witnessed first-hand the slavers' murderousness. At the moment Sulivan and Dr Mortimer were exploring, Livingstone had lost contact with Britain. But he recorded his experiences in a journal published in London a few years later. He would frequently come across parties of killers and kidnappers or sometimes just their abandoned victims:

27 June 1866

Today we came upon a man dead from starvation, as he was very thin. One of our men wandered and found a number of slaves with slave-sticks [very heavy yokes] on, abandoned by their master from want of food; they were too weak to be able to speak or say where they had come from; some were quite young.

Slave raiders accepted such losses because the returns on their masters' investment were so high. An individual kidnapped for free or for some length of cotton on the mainland sold for roughly 11–14 silver dollars (£2- £3) at Zanzibar's slave market; while a child might re-sell for eight to ten times that amount in the Persian Gulf or elsewhere. The men who did the actual murder and kidnapping were often members of slaver-barons' personal armies. Alternatively, these men might visit a local ruler offering guns, alcohol, or cloth and suggest that he make war on his neighbour to produce slaves to trade, and then sit back and let them do the work.

The most valuable abductees to their masters were children who fetched the highest prices, and slave-raiders tended to invest more in keeping them healthy.

28 July 1867

Slavery is a great evil wherever I have seen it. A poor old woman and child are among the captives, the boy about three years old seems a mother's pet. His feet are sore from walking in the sun. He was [traded] for two fathoms [of cloth] and his mother for one fathom; he understood it all and cried bitterly, clinging to his mother. She had, of course, no power to help him; they were separated at Karungu afterwards.

Livingstone frequently clashed with the Europeans in his exploring party and his East African porters and guides frequently left him. Shortly after seeing the three-year-old boy taken from his mother, Livingstone himself was desperately hungry, with nothing to trade and his party fast dwindling. That is when he encountered one of the most powerful slavers of East Africa. In fact, the man probably saved his life.

Hamed bin Mohammed el Marjebi, who went by the name 'Tippu Tip', was part trader, part warlord, part agent for the sultan of Zanzibar, and fast becoming a slaver king. He was Swahili-Arab: born on Zanzibar, descended from East African and Omani forebears. After becoming a successful trader on the island, Tippu Tip plunged into East Africa with a company of mercenaries and slaves. There he murdered and battled rival strongmen; set up protection rackets and extracted tribute in ivory; hunted elephants for their tusks; bought influence with guns; and kidnapped people en masse. He began building an empire to the west and north of Zanzibar – around

Tippu Tip

today's Tanzania and Kenya – by creating and filling power vacuums, bringing ruin to countries and enslaving their people.

But he was not simply murderous, he was politically adept. When word reached him of the near-starving Scots explorer wandering and measuring the countryside he saw an opportunity to ingratiate himself with the Europeans. Not only did he give Livingstone food and tradestuff, but he invited him to stay and travel with him, which the desperate man did gratefully. And though Livingstone truly reviled Tippu Tip's slaving, he admired his regal bearing and his famous hospitality. When Livingstone left Tip's entourage, he gave the man a warm letter of introduction to the European community based on Zanzibar.[2]

Nearly all trade in the western Indian Ocean depended on the coast-skimming dhow. A large triangular sail is what made a dhow a dhow. This sail, called a 'lateen sail' hung from a yard that ran more or less straight down the length of the ship, 'fore and aft'. While this sail could be pushed by the wind, it propelled the ship fastest when it acted as an aerofoil: when wind flowed over it, that is, pulling the ship like a wing. (Most European ships, especially warships, relied on square sails, which did best when the wind was behind them.) Dhows often shared other characteristics such as a high poop in the back of the larger ones and a dramatically up-turned stern at front. But the wide lateen sail was its animating spirit. The captains of Heath's squadron called any Arab lateen-rigged ship a 'dhow' as a generic term, though the proper word for larger ones – those with multiple masts – was 'baghlah'.

The new *Amazons* – *Daphne*, *Dryad* and *Nymphe* – were well-suited to this coast because they borrowed the dhows' ancient technology. The two forward masts mainly carried square sails; while the rearmost, called the mizzenmast, tended to carry triangular sails for helping the ships sail into the face of the monsoon winds. They were a kind of hybrid.

And the monsoon ruled this ocean. From roughly November to February the prevailing winds in the ocean swept down out of the northeast, while from about April to September the winds shifted and blew out of

A sketch of a dhow, probably by Zanzibar Consul John Kirk, c. 1872

the south-west. The movement of captive East Africans depended on these winds. The pattern was for traders to bring northern wares down the East African coast in the winter months, then await the shift in the monsoon, purchase slaves at Zanzibar or Kilwa on the coast south of Zanzibar, and run for the north with their victims in the spring and summer.

In former years, when any ships were ordered to police the trade in these waters at all, they tended to be stationed at Zanzibar or patrolled its waters checking licences. But Leopold Heath decided that could not be effective since a dhow heading north from Zanzibar could simply plead that it was heading to a coastal town to the north that was within the sultan's dominions; that is, perfectly within the treaty rules. That hopeless routine was about to end.

In his study of reports and letters from former British officials based on Zanzibar and his talks with other Royal Navy officers, Heath began to develop a plan. He considered keeping his ships away from Zanzibar. Instead, he hoped that by positioning them at natural chokepoints where features of land, sea and current would force the dhows through a relatively small passage, his *Amazons* could take advantage of their barque rigs and powerful engines to descend on the slave dhows against the monsoon — while the dhows themselves would be at the mercy of wind and current forcing them into the Royal Navy's awaiting hands.

HMS *Octavia*, Zanzibar harbour, September 1868

The tall masts of HMS *Octavia* lording it over the harbour, her many commissioned officers made the short pull to the beach and the sultan's palace. Two whole goats were roasting and a lavish feast was set. The sultan sat before the array as his secretary of state personally waited on Commodore Heath.

Later, from his flagship, Heath sent a letter to his Admiralty superiors in London on the eve of launching an experiment with his new stratagem. 'For 25 years we have followed the same dull routine,' he wrote, 'capturing a few dhows here and there.' He announced that he would end the routine and commit unparalleled effort. He asked for more ships, perhaps being redirected from the West African coast where slave trade suppression was winding down. But going beyond matters over which he had responsibility, Heath also recommended an overhaul in political and diplomatic efforts against the slave trade: that permanent anti-slave trade commissions be set up in the chief ports of East Africa; that British India should police the Persian Gulf to smother the trade at the point of demand; that the government itself in London commit to finally 'erasing' all trade in humans from East Africa.

> I trust their Lordships will not think that I have given my opinion in too free a manner [he wrote] ... If I have presumed to indicate the steps which I think should be taken ... for finally attaining that object, it is because I feel that although what we have hitherto done may have annoyed and harassed the Slave Traders it has had no effect towards suppressing the Trade.

Heath would eventually learn to his cost that many in India and London indeed took exception to his free manner.

HMS *Daphne*, Zanzibar harbour, October 1868

The letter sent on its long voyage to London via the Red Sea, Heath issued orders to Sulivan, the man on the station with the most experience in East African waters: it was time to experiment with the chokepoint tactic. In October 1868, Sulivan's *Daphne* lay at single anchor in the harbour of Zanzibar. The crew scrubbed, mended and, as ever, coaled, like Sisyphus labouring under heavy bags of coal that turned to ash almost as soon he stowed them. The captain surveyed a crowded harbour. It was nearly November and the monsoon was hanging on, still blowing from the south-west. On this wind depended slavers carrying their abductees north. But the monsoon would expire soon, returning in the spring, and many of the dhows were preparing for the last northerly run.

In the coming days, Sulivan gathered what news he could find. There was a war on the African coast to the west and north. Some slavers preferred to march their captives north up the coast to some isolated landing place before boarding them so as to evade any over-zealous British captain stalking Zanzibar waters. In these days of war slavers could not march their victims here. Zanzibar and its sister island Pemba, covered with clove plantations, were particularly crowded with slaves waiting to run the blockade for the north. Some large dhows at Zanzibar, Sulivan learned, were crowded with East Africans. The dhows had licences for sailing for Lamu Island – a place within the sultan's territory. He also learned that some dhows intended to run the gauntlet for the north beyond the treaty limit, to make a run for the Arabian Sea or Persian Gulf.

Commodore Heath and Sulivan knew that most smugglers would stay in harbour with *Daphne* watching. This gave them an opportunity to run up false colours. In the next couple of days, as he moved about Zanzibar, Sulivan let slip that he had orders to sail directly for Bombay on the aged monsoon. Soon, some of the Indian merchants in the town came to ask whether he would bear some goods there. *They want to test whether we're really going there or not*, guessed Sulivan. He gladly agreed to carry their things. But he was not bound for Bombay. He would point *Daphne* conspicuously toward Bombay, but instead of heading north-east he would head north-west to the coast. The dhows, not made for the open ocean, hugged the coast all the way to their destinations in the north. At a point on the coast where they would be exposed, *Daphne* would lie in wait, her whaler, her speedy sailed cutter spread out to help corner the slave ship. The monsoon's last breezes and the current would carry the dhows into the awaiting trap whether they liked it or not, while the *Daphne* could set barque sails and raise steam to carry her into the face of the wind, leaping down on the slavers.

A few days later, and the *Daphne* was almost ready to weigh. There was a muster at quarters early in the forenoon watch, then the order for stokers to raise steam. The circling men at the capstan weighed anchor and *Daphne* edged through the traffic of the harbour in broad daylight. She pointed her head north-north-east, unmistakably for Bombay. The next day she let her boilers cool and set most sail in front of a reliable wind out of the south. To any passing craft she looked as if she were truly bound for India. Meanwhile, Sulivan had the men of the forenoon watch exercising at the great guns and the afternoon watch drilled at cutlasses.

At a point thirty miles east of the coast and out of sight of the coastal traffic, *Daphne* turned back west. Sulivan's stalking ground was near a town called Brava on the Somalian coast, a natural calling point for dhows bound north. Some small islands just off the coast formed a bottleneck here that should hem in traffic. There she stalked over several days. One late night Sulivan emerged from his cabin to have a look at things and found the midshipman on duty asleep. On a Sunday morning at single anchor Sulivan read to his crew from the Bible under bright skies and the lingering south-westerly breeze. Up boats, down boats; raise steam, bank fires.

It was a frustrating wait: nearly November, and they had yet to see one of the large dhows crammed with victims that they had seen tarrying suspiciously in Zanzibar harbour. Until, one day, after a morning of rain and cloud, the air cleared and showed a sail on the southern horizon off the starboard bow. The crew turned the clicking capstan and the stokers built steam. It was now mid-afternoon and she would have plenty of daylight for a chase. Steam up and, working against wind and current, *Daphne* began her descending run at the sail. An hour passed and the sail kept coming north, close to the shore. Another half hour's approach confirmed that she was a large dhow and George Sulivan ordered the whaler and another boat equipped and armed and the boats' crews to stand by. Soon the men hoisted out the whaler and lowered it to the sea.

The dhow, it seemed, knew then what kind of a ship *Daphne* was, but it could not easily turn and run against the five-knot current bearing it up the coast. It would not turn east and risk the open sea. Instead it turned toward the shore, slicing through large rolling seas, and ran headlong towards rock and beach. It could only mean that the captain meant to wreck, for just one terrible outcome was possible in such seas. The men on the *Daphne* could only watch since, while the slave ship was not far away now with *Daphne* steaming fast toward it, *Daphne* could not intercept it. It was about to strike. It crashed. The hull shattered. The men on the quarterdeck saw some figures immediately moving up the beach away from the disintegrating ship. The slavers, it appeared, would escape. Some captives ran before them up a hill into the tree line. Other bodies were in the water, and some were obviously trapped in the heaving, collapsing wreck.

Sulivan had no choice but to watch the dhow break on the beach, but he would not abandon the survivors to drowning as he had been forced to abandon young Orton in the cold waves under Africa. He moved, ordering the small lifeboat dropped. The waves that were pounding the dhow to fragments would also pound any boat that he sent in a rescue attempt. He would go but he would not order anyone else to go. Before he could pull away, young William Breen, only just made a midshipman, slid down the lifeline into his boat. Then the ship's carpenter, Jim Richards, slipped down. Rifles handed down, the three men in the boat pulled away.

Into the heavy waves, now, and not far from the wreck, Sulivan could see dark bodies in the water more clearly. The heaving breakers started pouring onto the lifeboat from behind. A steep wave violently flung the stern. Sulivan leapt for a line above the rudder to weigh the stern down and succeeded in keeping the boat right-side-up. Waves continued to strike the boat from behind, violently swinging at the men. But hard as the waves attacked, they also shoved the boat quickly towards the beach.

In a few minutes they were there, hurrying through the water, scrambling among wood and bamboo fragments. Bodies, many bodies, and most beyond rescue. A woman – a mother? – struggled to get a child out of the collapsing wreck of the dhow. They ran to her and found that there were other children there. They seemed too exhausted to climb out of the broken hull, to pull themselves out of the waves. The men found one who was paralysed in a balled-up position, then another; there were seven children in all, about six years in age or younger. These were the only survivors other than those whom the slavers had taken away. Captain, carpenter, midshipman worked in the waves and ruin to extract the children.

Eventually, the three men and the surviving woman carried the children to the boat. They could not stay on the beach with an uncertain number of slavers at an uncertain distance. They moved quickly to help the children in, placed doubled-up children carefully down low among the ribs. Then, where was the woman? Vanished in wave and chaos.

Suddenly, men broke out of the tree line far up the beach. Ten. Twenty. Some with guns, some with spears. Sulivan guessed they were local men drawn to the shore by the noise. With such uneven numbers, this was not time for diplomacy. He raised his rifle. He waited until they were about two hundred yards away, then aimed at a spot fifty feet in front of the leading man. He fired, and the Somalian men flung themselves to the ground. They rose, but did not take another step forward. Nor did they step backward: they would wait and see.

Sulivan turned to the boat and ordered his companions to shove off. The men pulled hard for the breakers. It was the most resolute wall of waves Sulivan had ever seen in a long career at sea. From where he had stood on the *Daphne* he could not see the see the inner face of this unyielding wall, but now he saw it for what it was. In former days he had seen seven shipmates drowned by surf less high than this, and there were miles and miles of this barricade stretching up and down the coast. When the wave drew in the water of the beach, the inhaled sea nearly left the boat aground on coral. And darkness was coming on.

But they heaved on the oars. One dash at the breakers. Repelled. A second run for it. Repelled. Behind, on the shore, the Somalian men still watched.

Haul up the boat and try to survive the night on the beach? Sulivan wondered.

Then, a slight lull in the waves. *It's now or never.*

Again, they pulled hard and aimed the bow to cut through the wall. The wave blasted the boat and poured through it stem to stern. They were through, but the children? The men counted them. They were all there. *A miracle,* Sulivan was sure.

Heath's tactic was proven. From that day, slaver after slaver was borne by wind and current into *Daphne*'s trap. She spread her ships out to coordinate in penning slavers – two cutters, the captain's gig, the broad whaler, the dinghy – even the Kroomen moving between boats in their distinctive canoe. Boats chasing in all directions. Sulivan rewarded Midshipman Breen with the captaincy of one of the boats. *Daphne* fired her monster guns to try to bring suspect dhows to. Sometimes they stopped, sometimes they darted.

Amid all of this, Sulivan worked with his trusted interpreter Jumah, his old shipmate from the *Pantaloon,* to learn about the children he and his men lifted from the wreck.

'What is your name?' Jumah asked one of the children, a small boy.

'Zangora.'

Jumah asked how long he had been marched from his home to the coast.

'From when the corn was young to when it was cut. About three moons.' His village was well inland. More questions, and Sulivan and

Jumah estimated that he had been taken off the coast at the island harbour of Kilwa, the busy slave depot.

'How many slaves were in the dhow with you?'

'A great many,' he said. 'Some were drowned.'

They had been at sea for about a week, consistent with a departure from Zanzibar. They had been packed under the deck. The entire dhow had been crammed.

Two of the children, who had seemed paralysed, had been crammed in so tightly with their heads between their knees that they could not straighten their bodies to try to save themselves from drowning in the wreck. One of the children reported that when the *Daphne* had appeared, issuing coal smoke, the slavers had told the Africans that the big ship was a cannibal ship, the fires for cooking children. They would wreck not to drown the Africans, but to save them. Once on land they should run for the trees. Sulivan and Jumah spoke with the others and heard nearly the same story. 'Fighting ... murder ... a long journey ... cruelty ... impossible ever to return to my own land.'

November, and constant activity continued: *Daphne* running down ships; the boats boarding. There were many legitimate traders and many slavers – some escaping when there were insufficient boats to chase, others running aground. Royal Navy policy stated that the slaver crews themselves must not be harmed if it could be helped; they should be offered passage to the nearest port. But naturally they always declined to spend much time on the *Daphne* among their former victims and officers who loathed them; they usually asked to be landed immediately or placed in passing dhows. Their dhows, though, were almost always burnt at sea.

One day, an experienced sub-lieutenant, William Henn, had command of one of the sailed cutters. He chased a slave ship, taking care to keep the cutter between this dhow and the shore. The dhow gave up the chase and Henn's crew boarded. The deck was clear other than the crew of ten or so, but it was a big dhow. What was below?

One of the *Amazons* attempting a rescue and
depicting the slaver running aground

Sub-Lieutenant Henn and his men looked beneath the deck. At the very bottom, along the keel, were stones laid for ballast. Crouched on these were twenty-three women and two infants. There was no room to sit upright because three feet above the keel was another deck of bamboo on which the men were held. Some few feet above them was another deck packed with over fifty children. Altogether there were 156 men, women and children squeezed into the ship.

The next day, Sulivan saw this dhow towed to the *Daphne* and hauled alongside. As the men helped the refugees on board a woman, terribly weak, came up. She held a baby, tiny, perhaps one month old. But something was terribly wrong. Jumah spoke to her and she said that the previous day, amid alarm and hurry, her newborn child had started to cry. A man had come down and struck him with a ballast stone. The man had feared, it seemed, that the approaching British would hear. The infant's heart had beat on for hours before stopping. Still, as she came on board the *Daphne* his mother held him, quiet now, beyond fear and hunger. It was a Sunday, and Sulivan almost never failed to read the Bible to the men and boys on that day, but not today. They hauled off and burnt the slave ship.

Drawing by Midshipman Frank Fauwell, "Section of a dhow showing the manner of stowing slaves on board," in his log for HMS *Forte*, 1869

More slavers caught, and more men, women and children brought on board, many starving, and many ill. A slaver made minimum investment in his captives and received a high return. He could afford to lose some to illness and starvation and against his expected return he weighed the cost of rice – usually, a handful of rice and a half-coconut shell of water per day. He weighed capture by a British cruiser – perhaps embarrassment for a master in Zanzibar or Oman – and total loss versus running aground and preserving a minority of his slaves, especially women and children who brought higher prices at northern ports. There they would be domestic slaves, sexual chattels, children trained for fighting, pearl diving, date farming, and other work. To the south, the French, Anglo-Indians, and the Madagascar Malagasy took more males for plantation labour.

One day, about noon, the masthead lookout hailed the deck. *Man in the water*. The ship was anchored two miles off the shore, but someone was swimming to her, an African, already well over a mile from shore, and he was fighting a quick current. Sulivan sent a boat to pick him up. Soon the men helped him aboard. Questioned by Jumah, he said he was of the Monhekan people and had been enslaved. He was clearly, to Sulivan's mind, a hero of a man to have attempted the feat. They called him 'Marlborough', their best transcription of his real name, which they could not manage. Marlborough was a leader, and in the coming days and weeks the officers gave him more and more responsibilities for tending to the other former slaves, keeping peace, dealing out provisions, directing duties.

Soon there were 200 refugees on board, then 300, then more. And fifteen slavers destroyed. The crew of the *Daphne* tried to make the newcomers as comfortable as possible, but the ship was a tight fit for her crew alone, let alone over 300 more. They had to shelter on the open deck, though the men rigged awnings above them. A hose was arranged to provide a shower of steam-heated water. A vast kettle boiling away in the open air provided meat stew, with Sulivan buying rice from passing merchants. The captain noted that the people tended to cluster by kindred or tribe, of which he thought some were handsome and smart, others dull and ugly.

A one-year-old with good sea legs moved about the upper deck, making it his own. The crew named him Billy and someone made him clothes, but he refused to wear anything. When the bosun's mate Tom Balmer was on duty, Billy could regularly be found in his arms. Perhaps he had left his own children far behind in England. At some point it struck Sulivan that the one-year-old adventurer never cried.

Emaciated child refugees from slavery on board
HMS *Daphne*. Photograph by George Sulivan, 1868

Dr Mortimer and his assistant Samuel were busy treating the ill. Some of the refugees were beyond help, exhausted beyond the ability to hold on to life. Some came on board suffering from dysentery; some had ulcerous wounds. Among the crowded refugees, many exposed to the virus for the first time, smallpox appeared. One morning two of the East African men died within hours and the next day a woman died. Ultimately, sixteen men, women and children succumbed to illness or to the malnutrition they suffered under the slavers. These were given a correct burial in the world of sailors, shrouded in sailcloth with an iron ball at the feet.[3]

CHAPTER 5

'IN HER PROPHETIC FURY SEW'D THE WORK'

The spiders spin their web, unaware of their own vulnerability

THE ROYAL NAVY had never struck such a blow against the slave trade as it did in late 1868. About a thousand East Africans were freed from slave ships. *Daphne* had done most of the work late in the year, though Heath sent other ships to help her as they became available after re-embarking the invasion force at Abyssinia. *Daphne*'s lying-in-wait at natural chokepoints along the coast had proved the strategy, and there was every reason to expect that 1869, with all the *Amazon*-class ships now available for duty, would be even better.

But if *Daphne* and supporting ships had intercepted a thousand, how many were slipping by to the north, or east to Madagascar, or to French-controlled islands? Heath and Sulivan could not know, but feared that they had rescued only a portion of the victims of slavers in 1868. Reckoning was difficult since the legal trade clouded the waters and made it difficult for British observers in Zanzibar to calculate the trade's scale. An East African placed on a dhow headed from Zanzibar could be headed for a port within the sultan's coastal empire a day away, or could be headed for a destination across the ocean. Still, if the rate of success was hard to calculate, it was undoubtedly unprecedented.

But what did 'success' mean and what did it mean to be 'freed' from a slave ship? What kind of success could there be for someone like Marlborough, whose town and crops were burnt, the peace of his home region overturned, his family scattered or murdered? What kind of freedom could there be for someone like young Zangora who could never go home or recapture any of his former life?

At the turn of 1869, Leopold Heath pondered these questions. So did his squadron's officers: in the months to come, George Sulivan would track down Marlborough and see what became of his life; Philip Colomb would look into the fates of some of those he removed from slave ships. On his flagship anchored at Bombay, reviewing *Daphne*'s late 1868 campaign, Commodore Heath considered the matter of freedom because someone had suggested to him that the Africans' lives as free men were no better than that promised by slavery. Freed, they would do back-breaking work in blazing Aden, the remote Seychelles, or perhaps Bombay. They would draw water as servants, or plant cane cuttings and tend to sugar boilers. Their employers would be hardly gentler or more generous than a clove plantation's foreman. Or they might struggle desperately to find work at all, even to eat.

But Heath was not ready to accept that idea, to equate slavery and bitter economic circumstances. *We're launching them into a new world*, he thought. *All is strange to them*. So it must be England's duty to educate the refugees, teach them the language, provide some training. *We're launching them into a new world*, but their status in that world still mattered to Heath. He distinguished between their physical and spiritual statuses. Physically, the people Sulivan had pulled from the slave ships were perhaps no better as struggling refugees in Aden than they would have been as slaves in Madagascar or the Persian Gulf. Yet he believed that morally, spiritually, at their essence, they were not enslaved. They entered a strange and hard world – their old world was irretrievably gone – but they entered it as free men.

In the first weeks of 1869, Heath had his three *Amazons* in Bombay harbour, and he readied them to act in unison on *Daphne*'s successful experiment.

There were constant signals between ships, signals to shore, boats zig-zagging with messages and men; coaling, stowing for a long campaign, painting. There was a squall of paperwork for Heath, along with the distractions of being in port and a lack of action to occupy the men. A deserter leapt from a ship and was arrested. Meanwhile, on his own flagship, Heath had to deal with a commander who was far too fond of the lash for the commodore's taste.

Finally, Heath was ready to send his squadron out of Bombay for the full implementation of his plan to lurk at natural chokepoints and let slavers come to him. *Daphne*, *Dryad* and Heath and his flagship would prowl strategic positions off the Horn of Africa, near the opening of the Red Sea, the Arabian coast, and near the opening of the Persian Gulf. *Nymphe* would start her patrol near Madagascar, then later in the season, with the strengthening north-running monsoon, move up to the Arabian coast too. From the perspective of those in Zanzibar, the Royal Navy would be nowhere to be seen. By the time the slave ships were half way to their northern or eastern destinations, it would be too late for them. Philip Colomb called the squadron 'spiders', and in late January 1869 these spiders began to skitter from Bombay to weave Heath's web.[1]

Even at this early point, with the squadron only just moving to implement his strategy fully, Heath was attracting hostility. Already imperial authorities in the Indian Ocean sphere were jolted by the commodore's unusual moves.

Late in 1868, the British government of India took notice of Heath's audience with the sultan of Zanzibar. Bombay had purview of East African and Arabian affairs and the governor of Bombay, Sir Seymour Fitzgerald, was the one who took unhappy notice of Heath's activities. To his mind, Heath was not acting in unison with Bombay and presumed to meddle in policy. The cotton trade, not the slave trade, was the concern of the Bombay government. And diplomacy with native princes of India, not

Zanzibar, took priority. 'Very objectionable,' he wrote on the cover sheet of a report on Heath's moves, and he forwarded it on to those up the chain of command. Bombay had charge of western Indian Ocean matters; Calcutta was capital of British India; and it was there that Fitzgerald sent his complaint.

Thus the report made its way around the tip of India and up to Bengal and Calcutta where it was also unwelcome. The head of the government of India's foreign department was Charles Aitchison, a man of powerful build and great moustache. He was devoted to two faiths: that the Lord was returning to Earth soon, and that the best way to govern was through masterly inactivity. Zanzibar's slave trade did not need new regulations, Aitchison thought, and it was totally improper of Commodore Heath to act on his own. He had exceeded his instructions. Was there a new policy declared in Calcutta? In London? No. Aitchison wrote his own objections in no uncertain terms on the cover of the report and addressed it to the India Office, Westminster. London must hear about this.[2]

In the same weeks, another complaint about Heath's new activities arrived in Bombay. Major General Sir Edward Russell was Resident at Aden, the dusty outpost above the Gate of Lament, the mouth of the Red Sea. Aden was a valuable naval base, army garrison and coal depot; but it was not a welcoming place: hot, nearly waterless, without a trace of green.

It was a hard place and it was administered by a hard man. Russell was a veteran of bitter fighting amid sage and flint in Africa, Afghanistan and India. For the moment, however, Russell had set down his sword. Now his job was to maintain the security and health of Aden, to protect and spread the *Pax Britannica*. He was to keep Aden running smoothly as an entrepôt of Indian Ocean trade and the key way-post en route to Bombay. As ever, Russell knew his duty well, and the Royal Navy was interfering with it. The boys in blue jackets were stirring up trouble, raising the ire of merchants and rulers in the Indian Ocean. Russell was receiving complaints of harassment, complaints that traders were beginning to fear the sight of British ships. When a dhow was caught transporting slaves beyond Zanzibar waters, its entire cargo was condemned. The cargo was condemned whether the ship was transporting six slaves or 300. Russell thought that was not fair, out-of-line. Many ships in these waters had slave crews; if they were all condemned, their wares forfeited, the trade in this sea would be badly hurt. And that was antithetic to his mission and the beneficent global role of the British empire.

The answer, Russell decided, was that the Royal Navy should let pass ships carrying small cargoes of slaves. That way ships with slave crews would not have to fear that their goods would be confiscated, their ships condemned. He admitted to himself that this would inevitably mean some slaves would go unliberated; but it was fairer to those carrying just a few slaves. And it would preserve the good name of Britain as a promoter of peace and trade, as a good ally.

Besides, argued Russell, was it not the case that slave masters took good care of their property? They must. They had an interest in protecting their investment in property, after all. Such were the indelible laws for free trade and private property. When the British liberated the slaves and placed them in Aden or Bombay or wherever, no one could look after them.

So Russell wrote to Bombay warning the governor of the complaints he was receiving and suggesting that Heath's squadron be ordered to limit their captures to only large slavers.[3]

These early stirrings of alarm among British officialdom in the Indian Ocean were just the beginning. Leopold Heath could not have truly grasped the forces he was prodding with his new campaign. The slave trade was integral to a vast economic network that tightly tied together India, East Africa, Arabia and the Indian Ocean Islands. It connected goods and natural resources and credit and people and politics in ways so far reaching that not even the most astute British India experts understood the scale of this network. And they probably could not grasp the sheer amount of wealth it generated for people with the savvy to exploit it and the willingness to shackle their fellow human beings.

There was Tippu Tip, who these days was extending a frontier of war and slavery, and lesser warlords in adjoining lands; but they committed their atrocities in the act of feeding this complicated market. And that market made it possible for these men to keep pushing their frontiers. The supplies that sustained and armed slave raiders and the trade goods that they used for bribes or exchange came from Zanzibar. Traders, the most predominant of whom were Indians, sold cotton cloth, guns, gunpowder, and wire to those heading into Africa. In return, they bought ivory, copal, other rarities, and of course slaves. The enslaved went to the Zanzibar market where they were re-sold. The cloves they were forced to farm went to Bombay and London; the dates some were forced to farm in Arabia were exported to the entire world.

To encourage trade, to keep traders from the US and all the world coming to Zanzibar, the Hindu Indian merchant community – with no religious prohibitions on usury – lent money at attractive rates. This kept things flowing in and out of Zanzibar harbour like a beating heart, and it kept East African captives flooding into the entrepôt, which sustained the slave labour farms on Zanzibar and nearby Pemba Island. As many as three out of four of those plantations were mortgaged to Indian lenders or were owned outright by Indians. And what was the most valuable and permanent form of 'moveable value' that borrowers could offer as collateral for loans? Their slaves.

At the top of this pyramid of finance on Zanzibar in these years was one Jairam Sewji, the Hindu Indian master of the customs house and a man of fabulous wealth. Over the 1840s to 1870s, Sewji paid the sultan of Zanzibar a fixed fee in silver each year for the privilege to extract import duties on everything entering Zanzibar. The income that Sewji made on extracting customs dramatically outstripped the fee he paid the sultan for the right; he made roughly 200,000 silver dollars (£40,000) clear profit annually in the 1860s. And that profit was only a small fraction of the total wealth he commanded. The price of ivory, meanwhile, rose each year with the rise of the American, British and European middle classes which sought out ivory for jewellery, toys, pianos, and a thousand other things. And dealers believed East African ivory some of the best for its close grain and tendency to remain white rather than yellow with time. Sewji also kept his own personal fleet of merchant dhows moving ivory and other goods between Zanzibar and Bombay; and he opened a trade and finance firm there that linked him with China and elsewhere in the wider world, and another office in London. The more the import of slave-labourers and ivory from Africa expanded, the more the import of gunpowder and cotton from India and manufactured goods from the US grew, the wealthier he became. Thus he promoted the easy availability of loans.

And the man deepest in debt to Jairam Sewji was the sultan of Zanzibar, Majid bin Said. The sultan relied on the Indian Sewji for his power, while the security of Sewji's wealth and head depended on the *Pax Britannica* as enforced by the Royal Navy. Sewji was not the sole Indian or Arab trader and financier on Zanzibar whose business linked him to India, the wider Indian Ocean, or the world; he was just the most powerful. All of them relied on the *Pax Britannica*, while the traders of Bombay and London, the cotton manufacturers of Manchester, and the ivory and clove consumers of New York and Edinburgh were in their debt too.

So what might it mean to the merchants and financiers of Zanzibar and all those of so many countries whose wealth was linked to the Indian Ocean trade network if one critical strand thereof – the slave trade and forced labour – were threatened by Heath and his squadron?[4]

Not only was Heath beginning to threaten thousands of purses at the beginning of 1869, his ally on Zanzibar, the British Consul Henry Churchill, was inviting trouble, too. Churchill's own view was that the status of slavery should be abolished, by force if necessary, in the dominions of the sultan of Zanzibar. On his own he could do no such thing; but he did think he had the right as a representative of the Crown to forbid Indians from having anything to do with the slave trade. To his mind they were subjects of the Queen, after all. Yet many of Zanzibar's Indians were slaveholders; some of Zanzibar's Indians were slave dealers; and some were linked to slaveholding by lending to slave labour operations with the enslaved named as collateral.

So Churchill acted, posting in the public places of Zanzibar notices addressed to ALL NATIVES OF INDIA IN THE DOMINIONS OF THE SULTAN OF ZANZIBAR. It promised their summary ruin, even imprisonment, if they engaged in the trade. Their domestic slaves must be registered immediately, and these would be liberated in a short time. But among the several thousand Indians on Zanzibar were natives of Kutch in western India. Their prince was allied with the British, but the Kutchees were not directly British subjects. Those on Zanzibar claimed to be beyond the prohibition of slavery among British subjects. And, beyond that, they claimed to be under the inviolable protection of the sultan of Zanzibar.

Soon after making his proclamation, a message arrived for Henry Churchill. A Kutchee man was selling slaves in the Zanzibar slave market. Churchill had him brought to the consulate and told the man that he would be tried as a slave dealer. But the Indian laughed. 'I do not deny it,' the man said. But, he added, 'I ignore your power to punish me.' Henry Churchill considered it a confession and, as promised, made summary judgment. He ordered a large fine and confinement in the sultan's fort awaiting expulsion to India.

No one was laughing now. Churchill had the attention of Zanzibar's Indians, many of them quite rich and influential. How far would he go? What business in Zanzibar did not touch, however remotely, on slave trading or slave labour? And Churchill had the attention of the sultan who relied on the taxes that the Indians generated through their ocean-spanning trade.

The sultan sent direct, sharp words to Churchill. The Kutchees were under his protection, he insisted, and Churchill must not arrest them no matter what he alleged. Anger seethed among some of the island's Indians, and on top of that the focused malice of the Persian Gulf traders who relied on Indian slave dealers. There were rumblings of riot and treason.

Into this threatening atmosphere sailed Edward Meara on HMS *Nymphe*, much to the relief of Churchill who worried for the safety of the several hundred British residents on the island and possibly the security of the sultan's throne. The timely arrival of *Nymphe*, of her 64-pound guns, of her marines, brought tranquillity for now. But Churchill's offensive against Indian slave-dealing on Zanzibar was far from decided: Bombay would soon weigh in on it.[5]

CHAPTER 6

'WITH ALL HIS MIGHT'

Edward Meara between the choices of justice and the law

EDWARD MEARA'S ORDERS were to show the flag at Zanzibar, check the slave runners who were beginning to arrive on the island before the monsoon, then proceed to Madagascar and the Mozambique Channel to hunt in earnest. From Bombay, where *Nymphe* parted from the ships that were heading for their spiders' snares off the Horn of Africa and off Arabia, the line of her track, traced in her log by a lieutenant, formed a gentle incline. Pin-pricks on the chart marked each day's progress, spaced evenly across lines of latitude. There had been some rain at the end of the voyage but it cooled the hot air a bit. And the presence of the *Nymphe* in Zanzibar harbour seemed to cool heads there, too.

Then, as February 1869 turned to March, it was time for *Nymphe* to sail south across the Mozambique Channel to Madagascar, around 800 miles distant. The story of Meara and the *Nymphe*'s next month captures so many of the bitter paradoxes of this work, of the painful contrast between personal morality and the limits of Meara's authorisation to act. The story shows a man compelled by a kind of humanity and justice that to his mind overruled any written law but was yet constrained by laws. And it shows the dangers and complications the officers of the spider squadron invited when they left the element of water for earth.

HMS *Nymphe,* north-west coast of Madagascar, March 1869

Out boats, in boats; sight dhow, chase dhow; fire blank cartridge, inspect dhow; up boat, bend sail: such were the days and nights of Meara and the *Nymphe* as she was hunting off Madagascar. Here scores of islands might hide slave depots, dhows might be honest traders or slave-runners from the nearby Mozambique coast. Any slaver here was well beyond the limit of the Zanzibar cordon of legal slave trading. The Malagasy, while permitting slavery on the island, had officially forbidden slave importation, and a treaty with the British allowed the Royal Navy to police the ban at sea. For Meara, it was open hunting.

Soon the hunt yielded a slaver carrying several captives to be sold in Madagascar. Meara allowed the crew of the huge starboard gun the pleasure of shattering the dhow, the slaver crew standing by on the *Nymphe* while their ship was transformed to airborne splinters.

After more days stalking down the coast, peering into a number of shallow bays, the *Nymphe* found the buoy before Majunga, the provincial capital of the north-west corner of Madagascar. The town stood on a stumpy promontory over a bay, placed above it was a white-walled fort and battery. Meara sent his first lieutenant, Clarke, away with the seized slavers in the cutter before he even anchored, as if to rid his ship of their presence as quickly as possible. Early in the day after arriving, a day whose heat rose high, a boat pulled away from the town for the *Nymphe*. Soon six Malagasy dignitaries were welcomed up the side. They announced themselves as emissaries of the governor of that province.

'How,' they asked, 'was the health of Queen Victoria?'

Meara returned the standard Malagasy courtesy. 'How was the health of Queen Ranavalona?'

The visitors invited Captain Meara and his lieutenants to a supper that night, and Meara accepted.

In the meantime, the *Nymphe*'s boats came and went to inspect dhows. A dhow coasted into the bay and Edward Meara chose to join one of his boats' crews to survey it, climbing down the *Nymphe*'s side and moving off in the white boat. The dhow made no sign of flying as so many did and Meara came over its side. Men on the station told stories of trouble on such occasions, but this boarding was quiet. Once on deck, Meara saw thirteen African women and four boys, clearly captives for the trade. Yet the dhow sails into harbour under the eyes of what is obviously a Royal Navy gunboat with slaves *on deck*? No running, no resistance? The dhow's captain appeared and Meara asked him for the ship's papers.

'Are there any passengers on board?' The interpreter Ali repeated.

'Yes. They are all mentioned in the papers,' the dhow captain responded.

Meara turned them over. They began, '*NAPOLEON III, Empereur des Français, à tous present et avenir, salut ...*' The dhow, stated the papers, sailed under the French flag. The kidnapped women and children were listed as *émigrés*. They were – in a grotesque fiction – legitimate passengers. An official on one of the French sugar islands had signed the paper. The interest of the French was in addressing a shortage of cheap migrant labour, whatever the means. No wonder the dhow's captain had felt secure in entering the harbour under the nose of the *Nymphe*: the papers shielded him from interference. The French would have made a major diplomatic incident out of any rashness on the part of the commander. Edward Meara could not, though, resist attempting some French on the crew, then on the 'passengers'. Of course, not a single person on the dhow could make out what he was saying in French. Ali the interpreter was able to exchange some words with the captives on the side, who told him that they had been purchased in Zanzibar's slave market.

To Meara it was a contemptible cheat. But he could only delay the dhow while he had the French papers copied. He wanted to send them to Commodore Heath. This was a bad development: if the French were selling their flag to cover the slave trade, Meara and other slaver-hunters would have no way to stop it, short of declaring war on Napoleon III and the French empire. The papers copied, he returned them to the slaver and climbed back down to his boat, while the women and boys in the dhow were left to their fate.

Rounds of entertaining followed in the coming days. Meara and his lieutenants were met by palanquins and a band on the shore below the town, then they were carried up a path lined with mango trees and scrub bushes to the gates of the fort between two cannon. There were suppers and receptions. At one, Meara asked the provincial governor about the state of the slave trade on this coast. The governor responded simply that there was none.

Dancing followed in the courtyard of the fort, a scene composed of dignified Malagasy men and elegant ladies. One of the *Nymphe*'s lieutenants danced; Edward Meara danced. Perhaps his older brother George was doing the same thing in Ireland in the ballroom of a great house. Edward Meara issued an invitation to dinner – Royal Navy dinner, an early afternoon meal – aboard the *Nymphe* the next day to the governor and the fort's senior officers.

Then he and his lieutenants made their way back down to the shore and the gig. There they came upon a commotion in the darkness: an African was in the gig and refused to be moved. On seeing the officers approach the man begged to be taken off the shore through what language he could, managing to communicate that he had been beaten by his master. Meara tried to express his regret to the man. He must not take him; the institution of slavery was legal on the island, and the gig was on the shore of that island. Whatever the captain's personal feelings on slavery, and they were categorical, Meara must not abscond with slaves because they were slaves. He must not. The gig's crew finally lifted the African from the boat and set him ashore. They pulled back into the night and the bleak-sided *Nymphe*.

The next day the Malagasy officials and officers left the shore to a salute from the *Nymphe*, with the battery above the town returning it. Meara hosted the Malagasy in his wide cabin. The dinner over at last, the round of entertaining was over. He told his guests that he would proceed down the coast the next day. It was a Sunday afternoon and the crew had few duties, and except for the standard muster at quarters in the afternoon, all was quiet.

The night too was quiet, with a hot wind blowing from over the island. In the middle of the night it shifted to blow from the sea and the temperature dropped slightly. Clouds began to obscure the stars; rain was coming. In this darkness, a noise, a man in the water, swimming for the ship. Then another man appeared paddling in a canoe. Calls, action, and the men were helped up the side. Edward Meara was summoned and discovered two Africans on the deck.

Meara recognised one of them, the slave he had removed from his gig. The other man was also fleeing from slavery. Their master tormented them, they said, and kept them half-starved. And so Meara was presented with the choice again. He understood that they were begging his personal protection; to return them to shore was certainly to condemn them. Was it different now that they had crossed the water, that he had not removed them from shore? Was it different now that they stood on the deck of a British man-of-war – was this deck the same as free English soil itself? It started to rain.

Then came a murky, wet dawn and *Nymphe* crept out of the bay under steam. She was headed for the Seychelles with the two newly freed men and the several lifted from the slave ship days earlier. A mild south-easterly leading wind was on her quarter. Within minutes of leaving the bay the watch set the lean, dart-like jibs above the pointing bowsprit, then the yardmen climbed to their positions and set the square topsails. Below these the watch set gaff mainsails on the lowest yards. *Nymphe* would soon catch the Madagascar current to help carry her north and the refugees away from this place.

Not long after this, after *Nymphe* pointed her head toward the Seychelles, Edward Meara summoned the two men to whom he had given his protection with Ali the interpreter also entering the cabin. The name of the man who had appeared in his gig two nights before they transposed to 'Malbrook', the other was called Ferejd. Malbrook spoke a Mozambican tongue and gleaning his meaning took some time, but his story slowly took shape. He had been seized across the water, placed in a boat to cross the channel, and sold to a merchant – a vicious man – in Majunga. It seemed that slavers had landed Malbrook and Ferejd not two weeks before. No slave trade to Madagascar, indeed.

The men said that slavers in two dhows had landed almost two hundred captives at the time. They could, said Malbrook, point out the very dhows, which were still anchored there. *Still anchored there*. Edward Meara immediately issued orders and, not an hour after leaving Majunga, the *Nymphe* came around with a course shaped the way she had come. Sails shifted, sails reefed. Her head was very close to the wind now and steam would have to drive her back. The rain stopped.

She was back at anchor before Majunga by noon and immediately the two freed men pointed out the pair of slave ships. Meara ordered a party of thirty formed, issued rifles and other arms. The captain dropped down with the boats and took the lead. Like the eighteen-year-old Midshipman Meara on the west coast of Africa, Commander Meara was once again marching to confront slavers. The dhows were drawn up close to the shore, so after a short pull the sailors drew the boats up on the beach. Soon a crowd formed nearby and Meara noted muskets among them, and spears. Were these the slavers themselves? If so, they made no move now, though peril was close.

Then an Arab man approached. Speaking through Ali, he confirmed that the dhows were slave ships. With that final condemnation, Meara ordered the two dhows put to the torch there and then. He dispatched a note up the hill to the governor explaining that he had been 'under the painful necessity of burning two dhows that had landed 200 slaves twelve days ago'.

Some Malagasy officers hurried to the beach and the blaze to ask what was happening.

'You have Mozambiques in your possession who were brought here by those dhows,' said Meara.

'If you meet with Mozambiques upon the high seas, then you yourselves capture them and report to your government,' replied one Malagasy officer. 'But if we meet with those who bring them across the seas to us, then we report to our government.'

At some point during the burning of the dhows, a confusion broke out down by one of the *Nymphe*'s boats. Two of Edward Meara's gig's crew were hustling the Arab informant onto the boat. The man had a hole in his clothes. Someone – never spotted – had tried to murder him in broad daylight, and the blade had passed through his robes. Soon Meara and his men returned to the *Nymphe*, and the nearly murdered man came aboard and dared not leave again.

In a few hours the captain ordered a new landing party formed, a bodyguard for Meara's visit to the governor. Twenty men and two officers armed themselves and in the middle of the afternoon they descended to their boats, pulled again for the beach, and marched up the little road to the fort. Governor Ramasy, flanked by some officers, admitted Meara. After formalities the captain demanded the captives according to the treaty between their countries that forbade the overseas slave trade.

'Twenty days ago the dhows arrived with slaves on board, and we have referred the matter to the government at Antannarivo, and are awaiting their reply as to what we must do,' said the governor. This was something the governor had failed to mention over the course of several long dinners, though he had told Meara there was no slave trade to that coast.

'I will not leave this port without those slaves,' said Meara.

'Very well. We must wait till we hear from the government.'

'How long will this take?'

'Two months.'

'My orders prevent me from waiting here so long.' He asked to count the number landed.

'We cannot tell, for this is a land full of slaves, and we cannot allow you to count them unless we hear from our government.'

'I will do what I ought to do, even if I have to fight for them.'

'You yourself know what you ought to do, but the words of the treaty say there should be no fighting between the English and Malagasy for evermore.'

'Will you give up those slaves or no?'

An officer said, again, that the matter had been referred.

'Then I go. But at midnight I will act.'

Back on the *Nymphe*, with dusk approaching, Edward Meara ordered the great 64-pounder loaded, pivoted on its track, and aimed to pass the shell about a mile clear of the fort. Fired with a shaking clap, it was like a shot across the bow.

Meara and the other captains in Leopold Heath's squadron had worked out a kind of code of conduct stating that searching for captives ashore was so perilous an act that it approached carelessness with men's lives. With uncertain ground, uncertain opposition, any captain who led his men ashore to release slaves assumed all the risk to his neck and career. In case of disaster the squadron would not defend the captain who risked it. Meara had not seen anything like a slave enclosure on shore. Could he really march on shore at midnight and expect to locate the people kidnapped from Mozambique? Locate them among all of the 'legal' slaves?

No. As outraged as he was, Edward Meara would not march his men ashore at midnight. Nor did he the next day. He kept the boat crews busy hunting the bay for more slavers. And they succeeded, his experienced lieutenants seizing another slave ship, the East Africans lifted out, bags of rice unloaded onto *Nymphe*, the slaver crew deposited on shore, and the dhow burnt.

Later that same day a boat pulled from shore. Envoys of the governor came up the side and Meara greeted them. By now they were aware of the two refugees, former slaves, on board, as well as the Arab man who had identified the slave dhows.

'Return those persons you have taken without permission,' said one of the envoys.

Meara suspected that handing over the informant constituted his death sentence.

'British sailors who escape from their respective ships to Madagascar must be delivered up to the consul or the captain of the vessel from which they escaped, if found,' the envoy went on. 'Therefore, do not carry away those persons you have seized, lest you break this treaty.'

'What you say is perfectly true,' said Meara. But, he continued, 'they are Mozambique slaves. Therefore, I retain them.'

'If you are right in seizing them, where is your commission for so doing, that we may have it in our possession?'

Meara's last vestige of diplomacy dropped away. 'I give you *my* commission.'

The next morning, at dawn, *Nymphe* left Majunga.[1]

CHAPTER 7

'IF IT PROVE LAWFUL PRIZE'

The grinding work of inspecting traders, and the question of prize money

THE DAILY LIVES of the squadron's sailors typically were marked by scenes far less dramatic than those of Meara in Majunga. More often it was a matter of running the ship, cleaning, mustering, snatching a four-hour stretch of sleep. It was by turns grindingly laborious and boring. When there was action, as in the case of a white lateen sail appearing on the horizon, the vast majority of the time the target hove to, welcoming an inspection with coffee. In these circumstances of sweaty repetition and frustration, alcohol was a tempting palliative. Every seaman of age had the right to a daily tot of rum before noon, but some sailors secreted back-alley arrack on board or, when desperate enough, raided the metal-lined spirit room.

One night not long after Orton's drowning, Sulivan found the first lieutenant, Gardner, drunk – drunk while officer of the watch. Drunkenness on any ship was no shock; Sulivan, who never used the lash, confined more than one seaman on the crossing from the Red Sea for drunkenness and other offences. But in the first lieutenant – *on watch* – who always, even before the captain, had responsibility for the fundamental details of sailing the ship? This was an enormity. Sulivan ordered his first officer confined to quarters for a whole week. At the end of that week, the captain threw his weight into a verbal lashing before releasing him.

Later Gardner was found too unsteady to stand his watch, seeking in drink a little freedom from the heat or confinement – perhaps escape from the abominations against humankind that they had all seen. Whatever it was, George Sulivan was convinced that Gardner was a hopeless alcoholic and arranged for him to be invalided and sent home from Bombay. Not disrated, not dismissed, but sent home, at least, and off his ship.

Then, as the *Daphne*'s crew were preparing their ship to depart Bombay for their patrolling grounds off Arabia – men with mallets and irons clicking and clacking as they drove long tendrils of jute into deck and hull seams, men with beeswaxed thread and iron barbs repairing sails – there was another drunken scene. Jim Richards, the ship's carpenter who had leapt into the boat with George Sulivan to defy the pounding waves of the African shore and lifted doubled-up children out of the ruins of a dhow, crashed aboard, drunk beyond containing. The marines hurried to seize him, and the officer of the watch had him locked in the cabin appointed for the purpose. Weeks before, the gunner too had careened drunkenly onto the ship.

The next day at 10 o'clock George Sulivan released Richards. But on rousing him, the marine found him still drunk. A stalwart man, but could he have been so obliteratingly drunk that he remained so for almost a day? More likely a messmate had somehow secreted the carpenter some arrack in the night. George Sulivan confined him for another twenty-four hours until he finally emerged sober the next day.

In the absence of any pharmaceutical recourse, alcohol must have been an attractive option as a chemical respite. George Sulivan's friend Dr Mortimer knew well that accidents and illness were a constant threat to sailors' health and lives. Dysentery killed three of the *Daphne*'s crew in 1869, a hernia invalided another, and injuries sent two others back to England. With men constantly climbing in all weather, falls were frequent; with men shifting guns of immense weight, drilling with swords, working through intense heat there were always accidents. Before *Daphne* parted for her place in Heath's trap, Dr Mortimer parted ways with Sulivan, his time up. One of his last duties as doctor was a desperate effort to save the life of a man whose leg had been seized by the diabolic engine's pistons and rods. But in this the surgeon had failed. A new surgeon, Dillon, a tall young man from Dublin, joined to try to stand between the men and the constant threat of maiming or worse.

Beyond the frustration of coming up empty on patrols, there was the vexation of duplicity. Slavers caught in the spider's web would often try to wriggle their way out. Colomb experienced it; so did Sulivan, as a story from early in the spider's web campaign illustrates.

HMS *Daphne*, near the Gulf of Oman, March 1869

Stocked and renewed, *Daphne* and her squadmates eased out of Bombay harbour for the north-east Arabian coast. And then the repetition of the old work: out booms, down boats; sight sail, chase; point yards, trim sails; wash clothes, holystone decks. These things were broken up at regular intervals only by the beating of the drum, mustering at divisions, and readings of the Articles of War or Bible. Day and night, the unremitting heat persisted. Ten dhows inspected. No slavers. Twenty. Forty. Fifty. No slavers. Was it still too early in the monsoon season? Were slavers being somehow informed of the trap?

So came a morning that promised nothing new, sun lighting the east over the Indian Ocean and illuminating the tall black side of the *Daphne*. Though it was already 80 degrees at dawn, at least there was more than the usual insipid, dribbling wind leaking out of the Persian Gulf: today it moved with intent out of the south-west. *Daphne* soon worked to stay at her station in the wind, dropping anchor and watching the south-west horizon for dhows coming up from Zanzibar or a coastal slave pen. Then there were three large triangular dhows' sails close together. The signal flashed to the boiler room below: up steam. Orders to the men at the capstan: weigh anchor.

So the chase began. It would take an hour – two? – to catch the dhows. On seeing what *Daphne* really was, the dhows scattered. They appeared to be working together to maximise the chance of escape, but two of the *Daphne*'s boats were out, and she and the boats coordinated their movements so as to keep the dhows from running ashore.

It took two hours of hard work in a wind that grew harder, though the sky never darkened. *Daphne* overtook one dhow, and the long white whaler and cutter each brought in one. One of these three was a slaver; but it was not the floating nightmare of crushed captives, but another sort common on these seas, a slaver with just a few abductees aboard. A Zanzibari slaveholder might want to rid him or herself of a disobedient slave, or a dhow captain who had unloaded a cargo from the north and was returning there with little else might invest in a few victims as his own side-business. Sometimes a dhow captain might not have the money to buy a slave for resale at a northern market, instead simply kidnapping someone, often a child for ease and the high price she would catch, on the eve of sailing.

Sulivan and Jumah interviewed the East Africans. Among them were a man and a child, a father and his son. The man said that they had been slaves in a house on Zanzibar, but were one day taken to the slave market where these men had purchased them not long ago. He understood that he and his child were being taken to another market. Could he have dared to hope that he and his son would remain together through another sale? *These men*, Sulivan thought, *don't just steal souls and bodies, but hope.*

Darkness fell quickly and the wind shifting to come off of Arabia was hot. Stars appearing above the blast were unobscured, but it was very dark. Sulivan summoned the captain of the dhow that had carried the handful of captives. The man's ship was forfeit, he told him, but he would land him and his crew at a convenient place. Sulivan thought hanging a better fate for this man and all slavers, but the choice was not his, nor his commodore's, nor that of the Lords of the Admiralty. It was written somewhere else; in a treaty or in some book – on a piece of paper that stated that pirates should be hanged but slavers carried to a nearby port. Stealing property from a ship meant death; yet making property of a human being did not.

Later in the darkness came a report: the slave dhow was gone. It had cut lose in the night, quietly. The other two, it seemed, had been trying to draw *Daphne* away from the real slaver. The dhow captain still on the *Daphne* was not the dhow's captain. He was a crewmember pretending. Another decoy.[1]

Given the boredom, danger and frustration experienced by men on this station, what motivated them? For ordinary seamen it probably was not a question of motivation; hard work and frequently misery was the simple reality of their lives. Besides, running and risking the lash or worse was not a good option 4,000 miles from home, though some took that risk. And yet there was some attraction to this duty: the bounties they received for each slave ship caught and each African saved.

Bounties, or 'head money', meant as a special reward for gruelling service in malarial waters, were a holdover from the previous generation of suppression efforts on the west coast of Africa. The British government credited a Royal Navy crew £5 for every liberated African out of a budget set aside for that purpose, plus about £1 per ton of the ship ('tonnage' was actually a measure of the ship's volume). Alternatively, if a ship carried few or no slaves but was otherwise implicated in the trade by carrying slave trade supplies and gear or on the basis of testimony, the crew received £4 per ton. In both cases, the capturing crew might keep the proceeds of the sale of other goods the slaver carried. A proven slave ship must always be burnt or broken up – in past years slave ships, once sold, were often put right back into the slave trade only to be re-captured.

The way a ship's crew actually received their reward – eventually – was like this: first the senior officer on the spot must judge whether the ship was truly a slaver, not always easy if a ship was not carrying victims at the moment (a story from Colomb's work will illustrate this). Then, along with a senior officer, he must calculate the volume of the slave ship, also not easy when dhows were not simple rectangular shapes. The slaver was then usually burnt because dhows were hard for the inexperienced to handle and because towing a condemned ship – bound to be destroyed anyway – into port in Zanzibar or Aden or Cape Town would have meant the slaver-hunter abandoned the hunt. Then the captain and officers must get an official decree from a senior official in the nearest British community – often the consul at Zanzibar or Aden – that the condemnation was justified (this was called a Vice-Admiralty court). Then a captain sent receipts, certificates and accounts by any available ship to London, to the office of a professional ship's agent.

This agent wrote a claim against the bounty budget, handled on behalf of the British government by the Treasury. The Treasury, by ancient custom, sought to limit the ebb from Britain's coffers by seeking any errors, irregularities, or extravagances in the claim; the agent earned his commission by anticipating and fighting this. Capturing crews sometimes tried to plump up the volume of their capture by around 10% because it was an article of faith that the Treasury regularly deleted 10% of a slaver's volume (a charge for which there is some evidence).

If the ship's agent successfully advocated his clients' claim, the spoils were widely distributed. First the agent extracted his costs for making the case before the Treasury. Then he took a 2.5% commission; then 5% went to an Admiralty budget for expenses; then 5% went to the Greenwich hospital for sailors. After these were paid, 3% went to the station's commodore or admiral and 10% to the ship's captain. The remaining money for a ship like the *Amazons* with a crew of 130–140 was divided into 1,000 shares. The lowest ranking member of the crew, the lowly ship's boy, received one share; servants and ordinary seamen received two; the able seaman received four. The lowest level officers received 7–12 and highest 20–45.

What amounts did crewmembers in the spider squadron actually receive in this campaign? A lucky ship in 1868–1869 might earn £2,000, with the captain taking home £170 and the crew sharing £1,500. The ship's boys received £1.5 and the ordinary seaman who did the real toiling, £3. But what did £3 signify in 1869? A trained worker in London might make

£25–75 per year in that period. A post-apprenticeship ironworker in a London workshop, for example, might make 30 shillings a week; a worker in a textile factory 10 shillings plus lodging.

So £3 for an ordinary seaman and £6 for able bodied was no doubt a delightful thing, but not life-changing, and not obviously worth risking one's life for. For some, the attractions of the many ports between Zanzibar and London probably coaxed away their rewards rather quickly.

Even with the bounties, it seems slaver-hunting did not have a reputation within the Royal Navy as a way to get rich quick. With its hardships and frustrations, the difficulties in extracting rewards, and the danger of liability, most captains on the duty found the bounties welcome but not a significant inducement. The £170 a captain might earn in an extraordinary year was far more significant, but he also incurred a lot of risk. If he authorised the burning of a suspected slaver or the sale of its goods and later the Vice-Admiralty court or Treasury denied his claim he was personally liable for paying back the ship's owner, sometimes at great expense.[2]

HMS *Nymphe*, east coast of Africa south of Zanzibar, March 1869

This was something that happened to one of Heath's captains, though at the moment of the capture he did not suspect he would later incur the wrath of the squadron's civilian overseers.

Forced to leave hundreds of Mozambican victims in the hands of slaveholders in Madagascar, Edward Meara and the *Nymphe* crossed the Mozambique Channel to Africa and now moved up the coast followed by a light but reliable south and south-westerly breeze. As always, it was already hot at sunrise. The crew spread canvas high – mainsails, topsails, topgallant sails – to try to catch the entire breeze and leave the engines cool to preserve coal.

The *Nymphe*'s navigating lieutenant aimed her for the mouth of the wide Rovuma River whose length spread deep into unknown parts of Africa, and on whose back slavers carried their captures to the coast. Mid-morning, the ship arrived at a Mozambican bay south of the Rovuma called Keonga. It was small, but relatively deep and fractured, and lined with overgrown islands, places shadowy and secret. This was a favoured landscape of slavers, where they could lie in dark places while deals were made, their victims smothered in dark places, awaiting a crossing to a market. *Nymphe* hove to and the watch swung out the cutter and the whaler. Meara made Lieutenant Norman Clarke – a slaver-hunter of solid experience, though young – captain of this two-boat team.

Clarke received the usual orders: inspect all dhows and if they are suspicious, take the opinion of the interpreter, the midshipman. If agreed it is a slaver, condemn and tow it to the ship forty miles to the north, while the slave dhows' crew may come to the ship or land immediately. If wind, current, or condition of the dhow prevent towing in time to make the rendezvous with the *Nymphe* the next day, burn it. The *Nymphe* set her sails and pointed north, leaving Clarke's raiding party to begin its search. It was Good Friday, and on the last leg to the Rovuma Edward Meara spoke the old words for the Christian calendar from the quarterdeck. The old story: a man was seized, marched, bound, and spent his last moments in agony.

The next afternoon, *Nymphe* stalking the coast around the mouth of the Rovuma River, the cutter and whaler returned from the south. The crews came up the side and soon afterwards Norman Clarke reported on their work in Keonga Bay. Yesterday they had come upon a Portuguese ship and boarded as usual with no problem. She was an innocent Bombay trader, but her crew told of slavers operating in the nearby bay. One had passed out from it yesterday full of slaves, but another was awaiting a shipment and was there still. Clarke and his boats hurried to the spot and a dhow was indeed anchored near the shore. Men moved about, some work was going on, a sail was being mended or was drying on land nearby, while a canoe moved between the beach and ship.

Clarke approached and boarded with Midshipman Reynard, the coxswain, and interpreter Ali. On seeing them, a man on board drew a dagger.

Through Ali, Clarke managed to talk the man out of making a try with his blade; he proved to be the captain's brother. The ship had four enslaved men on board who appeared to be serving as crew. The sailors managed to have a look at the dhow's papers. It was a slaver – a legal slaver – licensed to traffic humans between the mainland and the market at Zanzibar; but the licence was out of date. Clarke made further inquiries through Ali, speaking to the dhow's captain, who gave some inconsistent replies to questions. He claimed that at the moment they were merely fishing, not transporting slaves. For the next two hours Clarke surveyed the ship. Given the expired pass and the presence of four slaves, plus the discovery of large pots and large water tanks on board – typical of slavers – Clarke felt confident in condemning the dhow. He received a confirming nod from the midshipman, then declared the dhow forfeit.

The dhow captain begged Clarke not to burn the dhow. It was not his; it belonged to a rich man at a distant port. But the judgment had been made and Clarke believed that the crews of his two boats were not fit to sail the dhow up the coast. The freed Africans climbed down in the Royal Navy boats, while the dhow's crew descended into their canoes, carrying their things, and Clarke told the coxswain Allen to set fire to the dhow. But as the flames built, the captain's brother remained on deck clutching his dagger and refused to move. Allen finally managed to wrestle the man into the sea before he could be overcome by smoke and flame. A scramble, clutching, and he was lifted out of the water and placed in a canoe with the rest of his crew. And the dhow was consumed.

Four men were released from slavery, but time would show this to be an ill-fated episode.

The *Nymphe* then continued up the coast slowly heading for Zanzibar, hunting all the way. Most of her officers manned the boat fleet, going in and out, peering up rivers and creeks, creeping around mangroves. Meara joined the work on one of the boats, though it was the work of younger men. Younger, as Meara had been when he had ascended the rivers of West Africa, always exposed to the sun, or constant wet, exposed to mosquitos which sometimes descended on these rivers in clouds on the evening land breeze. Some of the men on the station fashioned themselves jumpers with hoods and long sleeves and hid within them from sundown to sunrise while in the boats. A little barrel was modified by the blacksmith for a stove to cook on – perhaps some fish – and they had ship's biscuit, quinine and sherry or rum. Each man had his canvas ditty bag for a pillow and a boat's plank seat for a bed since sleeping on shore risked fever and other dangers. Meanwhile, an unexpected wave might overturn the boat or an unexpected skirmish with surprised villagers might end in blood.

While her captain was away and *Nymphe* was lying at anchor as mother ship to the boats, a dhow came into a bay in which she was lurking. A small crew manned the white whaler, led by a young officer, and pulled for the dhow immediately. They came up the side of the dhow, meeting no resistance, to find about forty souls on board, among whom there were six slaves. The dhow's captain offered no objection to returning to the *Nymphe* with the sailors to await Captain Meara's return from stalking some creek.

Returned the next day, Edward Meara and the interpreter made their own inspection of the dhow and interviewed the captain. The dhow was owned by a Mombasa man, and he had let it out to be chartered. She was just out of Zanzibar, headed for the small port of Lindi, a place to the south that the *Nymphe* had passed in recent days. The dhow's captain had sold cloth and powder up the coast and had other goods for Lindi. The swirling winds had slowed their passage and they needed water so had put into the bay with the clear little river.

Meara and the interpreter looked at the dhow's papers. Old ones, the interpreter said, that showed that in years past she had been a slaver licensed by the sultan of Zanzibar. They turned to the enslaved Africans on board and the interpreter spoke to them. They were treated cruelly, they said, and used in shameful ways. They said, too, that the cargo on board was for the purpose of trading for more slaves.

Edward Meara told them they were to be released. And so followed expressions of happiness, in the languages of their homes. The *Nymphe* found them room on board among the many others lifted from dhow hulls in recent days.

The *Nymphe*'s crew had its own reasons to be pleased. The next morning, before dawn, some of the morning watch unloaded valuable cargo from the dhow onto the deck of the *Nymphe*: bales and boxes. Meara having condemned the dhow as a slaver, its goods were all forfeit. The men would share in a small bounty paid for each African released, a bounty based on the cubic measurement of the condemned dhow, and a share of the proceeds of these items once sold at Zanzibar.

At five bells of the morning watch, around sunrise, the dhow's crew was set onshore at their request and the dhow burned, a spectacle familiar, by now, to the crew of the *Nymphe*. The forenoon watch relieved the morning watch, and the stokers made up steam to sidle out of the bay. In a few days they would be in Zanzibar. They set all plain sail to catch a light but regular south wind, the same wind that should strengthen soon to bear the northern slave traders into Leopold Heath's spider's web.[3]

CHAPTER 8

'OF MOVING ACCIDENTS BY FLOOD AND FIELD'

Dryad *and* Daphne *continue the hunt, meeting success and near disaster*

THE MONSOON HAVING STARTED, work began in earnest for the crew of the *Dryad*, which moved from Bombay to its place in Heath's web. Commander Philip Colomb took a characteristic approach to the problem of trapping his prey, employing technology and a rational procedure.

HMS *Dryad*, off the north-east Arabian coast, April 1869

HMS *Dryad* was poised off Ras Madraka, Oman, at the north-east corner of the Arabian peninsula. It was April now, and Philip Colomb noticed wind and tide becoming steadier, coming up the coast of Arabia – still light, but steadier. In recent days they had met dhows from Zanzibar, pushed by the new monsoon, but they had been legal traders. The slavers must follow close behind, and it was time to prepare his corner of the trap.

It was a corner, Colomb hoped, from which the *Dryad* might see the slavers before they saw her. Much of this coast was open, sandy beach – exposed. But today he was inspecting a place that might hide *Dryad* from wind, tide and north-bound dhows, a cape, a peak of reddish-brown stone, around 400 feet high, that stood out into the sea. Just beyond this point was a small, low rocky island. Under steam, the *Dryad* approached cautiously,

Dryad (Colomb's ship) making a capture

not knowing exactly where the bottom was. The leadsman dropped his line frequently to find it. It was deep here, he learned.

A dhow sailing up the coast should pass close and should be visible from the peak above, Colomb thought. A man there should see at least twenty miles. Further, behind the peak was a good anchorage for the ship. A man in the masthead could even keep an eye on a small horizon of sea between the point and the island, the ship remaining hidden. There were good hiding spots for boats around the fractured little island off the point, too.

Colomb was satisfied, and he could feel the drift of the crew's mood, the shared sense that there was an enemy nearby, a monstrous thing, and they were eager to hunt it. One hundred and thirty-five minds were bent on the game.

Colomb continued to scheme. What if he could place some men on the top of the promontory permanently as look-outs? They might signal to *Dryad* and the boats below when a dhow was in sight, perhaps even signal details of number and direction using the signalling techniques Colomb had demonstrated years before in the Admiralty's test.[1]

So Philip Colomb worked out a rudimentary system of signals to pass between the *Dryad* and her boats and a lookout he would post on the peak above, with flags by day, flashes by night. He saw that the boats were stocked with rifles, pistols, provisions, water; in the pinnace was stowed powder and shell for the breech-loaded gun at the stern. Then the captain selected twenty-six men for two boats and sent them off to lie under the shadow of the island, ready to chase. After that Philip Colomb sent his first lieutenant Henry Walker to reconnoitre the little island. Walker and his group had two orders: first, to make sure there was no one on it to cause them trouble – a *musket volley from the surrounding rocks,* Colomb thought, *might be unsatisfactory*; then, to drag one of the island's little inlets for fresh fish.

Captain Colomb himself climbed down into his gig with his coxswain, boat's crew and interpreter Saleh bin Moosa. They pulled for the base of the peak above them. Soon they saw ten or fifteen armed men on the rocks that bordered a white sand beach, but these figures disappeared inland before the boat touched ground. Colomb turned to John Pitcher, his coxswain, by ancient tradition a captain's capable hand. Follow them, he ordered. Make friends, but don't take risks, don't go too far. And take Bin Moosa to interpret.

With that, the captain and a few men searched for a way up the dry promontory. It was the perennial temperature of 85 degrees and the red rocks over which they walked and crawled seemed burnt. Finally they found the way up and arrived at a little plateau standing above the earth and sea. *Glorious,* thought Colomb, a great sweep of creation below him. He could see the entire island to the east, with red-brown rock fringing white sand in its middle. And they could also see far inland to the west. A lookout and signal party stationed here could defend the plateau with ease. In case of dire emergency they could easily retreat to the island, fording just a narrow channel.

The day, the climb, the view lifted Colomb's spirits and he and his junior officers scampered back down from their new fort. Leaving the gig's crew to await the return of John Pitcher and Bin Moosa, Colomb and the younger men swam, crossing the channel to the island boy-like, with a sense of some bygone summer's day.

Colomb and his officers arrived at the island's beach to find the fishing party happy and successful, with piles of fish already on the beach. Colomb appeared in time to lend a hand in tailing on to the net, the water churning as the net approached the shore. Fish, large fish, began to jump and twist; two great ones escaped the net and the captain took it upon himself to chase them down. They swam and twisted into a little side pool where he jumped and scrabbled until he was on hands and knees trying to grab them. One of them jabbed him with a spine then escaped through his legs. The other Colomb was able to seize by the gills and, after a fight, land on the beach amid the sailors' shouts and laughs.

Then they saw one of the captain's gig crew hurrying from the opposite beach. He was shouting, but they could not make out the words. Something was wrong.[2]

The story of the spider squadron stands for many kinds of complexities and paradoxes, but perhaps no single member of that squadron embodied paradox more directly than Saleh bin Moosa, slaver turned slaver-hunter.

In these early days of still getting to know his ship and shipmates, Philip Colomb came upon the *Dryad*'s interpreter one morning. Saleh bin Moosa returned a greeting, raising his small red skullcap. He was willowy, but graceful, not bony; fine-featured, open-faced, with a gentle look and usually a smile. His simple white robe contrasted with dark skin.

'Well, Moosa, think we shall catch a slaver today?' It was trifling talk: there was really no chance at this time of year and in these waters.

'Oh, suppose slaver come, we catch him.' He touched the breech of the great gun next to him – the immemorial rite of sailors, touching wood to invoke luck.

In such chatter were the beginnings of a kind of understanding, later esteem. True understanding was beyond overcoming rank and national and religious prejudice, yet it was a kind of understanding. Trifling talk turned to more substantive talk over the long passage over the Indian Ocean, longer days in the harbour, and sailing and steaming to the Arabian coast.

Over these days Philip Colomb learned that Saleh bin Moosa was born on the island of Johanna, off the north-west coast of Madagascar. Upon reaching adulthood – Bin Moosa looked young, but was probably older than he appeared – he set out to be a trader in cattle and moved about markets on the Comoro Islands and Madagascar. He succeeded, married, and became a father. But one day there was some trouble with the Portuguese in Mozambique, the source of his cattle. They confiscated his stock and sentenced him to flogging. Ruined, he determined to rebuild. He changed professions, managing to charter a dhow and buying slaves from a middleman in Mozambique. Wedging them inside, he boarded and set sail for Madagascar. Then followed a short crossing of the Mozambique Channel.

After the brief passage, Madagascar's Boyanna Bay was dead ahead. Bin Moosa thanked God for his success as a headland loomed between the dhow and the bay's landing spot. Arcing over it and turning south for the beach, Bin Moosa saw the trap too late: a British cruiser was already leaping for him and there was no escaping the bay.

God had not delivered him success in slaving, but instead delivered Bin Moosa into chains. It was as if God had allowed him to read from the book of time itself, so that he knew the trade in man was abhorred by God. Saleh bin Moosa concluded that he was now enthralled to the trade's destruction. Blessed he was that God made his will known, for God would surely punish all those who persisted in the slave trade. As an Indian Ocean trader he had picked up some Portuguese, some Malagasy, some English. Added to his Arabic and Swahili tongue and letters, and he had the makings of an interpreter. And so he began to serve God's sentence on board British cruisers.

One day Bin Moosa told Philip Colomb of the disapproval he sometimes met in Arab ports when he walked among his British shipmates (though some shipmates were West African, Chinese, Ceylonese).

'"You eat pork on board that ship – Englishmen all eat pork – you eat pork, too!"' Bin Moosa related. 'They say, "You drink grog – you smoke!"'

But Bin Moosa abjured the forbidden things, studied his Koran, prayed five times daily.

'Oh, I say, "Englishman all same."' Saleh bin Moosa paused. 'Yes, all same God.'[3]

A man hurried from the opposite beach, shouting. Saleh bin Moosa was taken. The coxswain had escaped.

'They's been and fired on him, sir. Four shots.' It was Williams of the gig's crew. He poured out a disjointed story. 'Pitcher only saved hisself by running under the rocks.'

Colomb collected rifles, then sent off the crewmen with the nets and haul of fish to *Dryad*. He and his gig's crew were soon rowing for the shore near where Bin Moosa was taken. They found Pitcher there and he described what had happened. 'Well, sir, there was a lot of 'em on the hill. Then Aggis,' he used the men's name for Bin Moosa, a bastardisation of the word *eggs*, which the interpreter mispronounced, 'he said they was a callin' of him to come. And I says, "we's far enough from the boat." But he says it was alright.' The Arabs then surrounded them with spears and daggers.

'Then they had no muskets?' Colomb was relieved. Williams' tale might have been a bit overstated.

'No, sir, I seen no firearms.' He went on. 'They shows their spears and swords, and makes motions of cuttin' our throats. And then they makes Aggis sing a song.' Next, Bin Moosa had told Pitcher to hand over his hat ribbon, then told him the men were going to take them to their king. Finally, the interpreter told Pitcher that he could go back to the boat, for he would make it all right.

Colomb and the men next pulled towards the place the coxswain pointed out until the boat touched the beach. Just then Bin Moosa emerged, coming down from the rocks flanked by two Omani men. He wore his most amiable face. His escorts, though, were dour.

Philip Colomb approached them, acting as if his men had never been threatened or seized. Through Bin Moosa, he spoke as if he were delighted to make their acquaintance, shaking hands innocently. There followed smiling chat, the promise of trade for biscuit and cloth, and a kind of treaty was struck.

Later, as the party pulled back for the *Dryad*, Bin Moosa told his story. The Omanis had summoned him and Pitcher with very real threats. He thought it was finally his fated day to die. It seemed the men thought Bin Moosa an apostate. So he had quoted the Koran – the 'singing' heard by Pitcher. Then they ordered Bin Moosa to send Pitcher away. When they asked what the *Dryad* was doing there, Bin Moosa had said they were gathering water – a successful lie.[4]

HMS *Daphne*, off the south-central Arabian coast, April 1869

In the same days as Colomb was hunting off the north-east coast of the Arabian peninsula, Sulivan moved to the south-east. Near her post above the entrance to the Red Sea stood Mukalla, a white city that clung to the edge of the sea, rocky cliffs rising hard behind it. Before Mukalla was a shallow bay, sheltered from the northern monsoon, and behind her a pointed mountain peak. The peak was like a lighthouse that summoned the trade of the whole Indian Ocean, the trade of the Red Sea, India, Abyssinia – and the slave trade from Zanzibar.

George Sulivan knew that some East Africans were sold into slavery here. He also knew many more were off-loaded to await favourable winds for the ports of the Persian Gulf. The captain went into the town to invite the sultan of Mukalla to visit the ship.

Sulivan arriving before him, the sultan's welcome was strained, as if he thought that the British gunboat might be there for no good. But when the sultan boarded the *Daphne* the next day there was a practised amiability. And when *Daphne*'s 64-pounder fired, it was for the sultan's amusement – and away from the port. Sulivan went through the spoken pantomime of asking whether slaves were transshipped here, and the sultan went through the pantomime of replying that he knew nothing of the slave trade.

The winds were light and turning, but most often south of east; the monsoon had been slowly manifesting and with it the traffic from Zanzibar waters. The cutter, whaler and long galley swarmed over the local coast. *Daphne* herself moved east, out to sea, to get the weather gauge of dhows coming up the Arabian coast, the wind at her back instead of her face.

One clear, hot afternoon, with only a breath of an east wind to work with, *Daphne* was springing on dhows under steam, blasting her titanic guns to bring the dhows to, and sending a lieutenant in the whaler to board. Then, in one of the dhows, the boarding party found two boys. They brought them back to the ship where George Sulivan and Jumah interviewed them. They were crying, terrified that they would be returned to the dhow; they begged, fearful to the point of physical pain. They had been kidnapped along the African coast by the captain of the dhow about a month earlier. Sulivan knew the gambit: the dhow captain on the eve of heading north kidnapped one or two young victims, paid no slaver middleman, but turned a profit, almost a perfect profit – depending on how much he bothered to feed his captives – at some Persian Gulf market. This dhow was condemned and taken in tow, yet the boys could never go home.

Later that same day, word came that one of the cutters was bringing in a dhow. Lieutenant George Loch, who had replaced the alcoholic Gardner at Bombay, had made the capture. In time, he reported to George Sulivan that upon boarding there had been some snarls, some half-drawn weapons; it was a dangerous situation. But as the cutter crew mounted up and up on the dhow, the situation looked hopeless to the slaver's crew. They edged back and surrendered. Sixty Africans, most women and children, were crowded on the deck. There were no papers and no flag on the slaver.

Normally Sulivan would have summarily condemned such ships there and then and burnt or exploded them. They were difficult things for the inexperienced to keep afloat, and he did not want to leave his station for the purpose of towing a pair of dhows to a Vice-Admiralty court for what he assumed was a trial with a foregone conclusion. But he was now close to Aden and its consular bureaucracy; he could hardly justify not towing them in. Besides, he could hunt in Aden waters too.

The dhows properly condemned at Aden some days later, the *Daphne* pointed for the Seychelles. It was time to land the scores of people who had no more home now than *Daphne*'s sun-bleached deck. On most nights the East Africans danced to contrived drums and sang. Sometimes *Daphne*'s engine lent its own rhythm. At those times they danced under a light cloud of coal smoke and steam. Other times they danced under flashing lightning. Other times under stars, while a young officer found *Daphne*'s position by Alpha Centauri and Vega.

The music had no appeal for George Sulivan. *Monotonous*, he thought. But he believed that the Africans' music and dancing were a sign of at least some kind of relief, and he was glad that these were not the walking or even paralysed skeletons that he had sometimes carried aboard *Daphne*.

On a Sunday, not long after George Sulivan read the Bible to the collected men, *Daphne* steamed into Port Victoria, Mahé, Seychelles. She navigated the complicated approach and moored. The next morning boats moved between the ship and shore. They carried men, women and children born East Africans, then made slaves, then freed by *Daphne*, then transmuted again upon stepping foot on dry land. They were now *Seychellois*.

.   .   .

Were the slavers' victims better off landed on the Seychelles than they would have been landed in the Persian Gulf or Madagascar? This was debated by many in the Indian Ocean diplomatic establishment, the ministerial bureaucracy in London, and Commodore Heath and his officers. And it was a question that George Sulivan, though he had no doubts about the evil nature of slavery itself, investigated in spring 1869.

While he gave leave on the island of Mahé to the *Daphne*'s crew, 146 sea creatures finding their land legs, Sulivan and a few of his officers sought out some other new *Seychellois*. They learned that some more of the *Daphne*'s refugees had died of smallpox after their arrival on the island, the virus burning through those with no previous exposure, totalling fifty. After this sobering start to their inquiries they came upon a neat little house and there called upon the mighty Marlborough, the man who had swum almost a mile against the current to reach the *Daphne*, then became a kind of deputy officer on board. And with him was his wife, another refugee from *Daphne*. Next they called upon another little home and Peggy, noted for her gracefulness while on board the *Daphne*, and her husband Jim. *They made the best they could of a world that had treated them so badly*, thought Sulivan. To him, the couples communicated some kind of contentment. If there was no fairytale ending, he thought that, at least, *they shared their miseries together*.[5]

CHAPTER 9

'DESTINY UNSHUNNABLE, LIKE DEATH'

The courtroom on the Dryad *and the battle in Zanzibar harbour*

TWO SCENES FROM APRIL 1869 characterise some of the extremes of the squadron's anti-slave trade work, while conforming to the personalities of the two captains that they feature. Philip Colomb was performing scrupulous examinations of dhow crews in order to condemn or absolve the ships he snared. If he were to condemn a ship he sought a watertight case however laborious the process. Edward Meara, on the other hand, ordered an assault on a slave ship, rifles flashing. Meara himself was some distance away from the fight; by ancient custom the captain let his lieutenant lead the mission in the hopes that he would win garlands and promotion. But as ever in this campaign, violence seemed to hover closest to Meara.

HMS *Dryad*, north-east Arabian coast, April 1869

Night-time, and *Dryad* was anchored in her hiding spot behind the peak off Ras Madraka. Philip Colomb was playing whist with his three senior officers in his great cabin. He played poorly, letting down his partner while his attention wandered to his hunting. He rose, left his lieutenants to the game, exited his cabin and climbed the steps to the poop above it where he found the seaman assigned to watch the sea space between the island

and the mainland. The moon illuminated the sea, the island and the peak above the ship. The wind was light but told of the maturing youth of the south-west monsoon. He had with him his night glass and spotted the boats in their places near the small island.

'A fine clear night,' to the officer of the watch.

He had begun to head back to his cabin to take more punishment at whist when something on the island drew his attention: a white tent … a white tent that moved slowly to the left. No, a sail. Then another, and another.

'Signal the boats. Quick, now.'

The signalman hurried to parcel out gunpowder in little piles so that it would ignite in flashes. Lighting them, five dazzling bursts, the signal was made to the boats in the distance.

Now Philip Colomb counted eight dhows passing beyond the island. *For all we know every one of them might be running a full cargo of slaves.*

The boats lurking under the island were moving off almost instantly after the flashes. More boats from the *Dryad* were being lowered and manned within moments. Frederick Brown, the *Dryad*'s chief engineer, was soon at Colomb's elbow, reporting that he had already warned his division below to be prepared to raise steam. Living coals were already banked in the boiler room, ready to be pulled under the boilers, awoken, and spurred to whip up a greater flame.

The engineer did not have to wait long for the order. 'Draw the fires forward and up steam as fast as you can.'

Brown darted off and soon the sound of shovels biting into the great hoards of coal echoed sharply up from the stoke hole.

'Hands, up anchor!'

In time, far out at sea before the *Dryad*, Philip Colomb saw flashes: the pinnace's gun. More flashes: rifle fire. Shots across bows.

Colomb imagined what was going through the minds of the dhows' crews. Did they imagine pirates? Murderous rivals? They must have been bewildered, at least. The question of whether to heave to or to run. When *Dryad* arrived on the scene in under an hour, Colomb guessed it settled the minds of the dhows' captains. This was not rapine or murder but, as Colomb imagined them thinking, *only those eccentric Englishmen slave-hunting again*. The dhows, seven in total, surrendered, the coordination between *Dryad* and her boats a success, even in the dark.

Dryad and her boat fleet laboured for the next two hours against a strengthening monsoon current to tow the dhows back to the shelter under the peak. It was well after midnight before all was quiet again. Inspection would have to wait for the light of dawn.

The prayers of the Muslim faithful on the dhows greeted dawn. Not long after, Philip Colomb read Christian prayers to his assembled men, though they were far from all Christian.

Then Colomb assembled a little courtroom, taking a seat at the round table in the centre of his great cabin, flanked by his two senior lieutenants. Saleh bin Moosa stood by as interpreter, adopting an uncharacteristically grave face.

Bin Moosa began ushering the dhow captains in one by one from the quarterdeck, and so the long day began. Questions about the dhows' owners, origins, routes, cargo; a search for inconsistencies, deceptions. Colomb conducted close inspections of papers, too. By the light of day, it was clear none were slavers on any significant scale. Some of the dhows had African crewmembers, but Colomb did not find they were being held against their wishes; nor did they seem abductees nabbed for a quick sale at a northern market. One by one, Colomb permitted the dhows to go on their way, giving them certificates indicating they had been passed by him in case another of the squadron stopped them.

Next, Saleh bin Moosa led in a wiry middle-aged man, followed by an African boy of about ten. Through the interpreter Colomb asked the boy to wait outside. The dhow captain's eyes darted around the room, then he handed Bin Moosa his papers, knelt, and thrust his balled hands into his cheeks to wait, still, but for those eyes. Among his papers was a form from the sultan of Zanzibar certifying the dhow as a legitimate merchant. One of the other captains in Heath's squadron had shown Colomb an example of one in Bombay. Cross-examination followed. The dhow was supposed to have been from Sur, the great trading centre, up and round the Arabian coast to the north-west. The ship had left Zanzibar about a month earlier, sold grain at Mukalla, and was heading to Sur with the proceeds.

Then Bin Moosa and the man spoke more loudly in quick exchanges ending in apparent appeals to heaven.

'What is the matter, Moosa?'

Turning, planting his finger on the round table. 'This Arab man speak lie.'

Colomb dismissed the dhow captain and Bin Moosa led in the boy. He was at least not starved, even healthy. Colomb observed him closely: so little emotion from him, wooden. Philip Colomb imagined that misery and helplessness must dull the senses of captives like this boy. But the captain also shared the common prejudice that such an African acceded to his fate because he did not share the Englishman's innate love of liberty. Love of freedom, he imagined, was inborn in British blood, not so in most other – to his mind, lesser – races.

Bin Moosa turned and pronounced the boy an obvious slave.

'Very well, now ask him where he came from.'

There was further exchange in Swahili. 'Come from Angoche – Zanzibar – in a dhow.' Angoche, the stronghold of slavers in the Portuguese sphere that a seventeen-year-old George Sulivan had attacked without success.

'Ask him if any more slaves came up with him.'

None.

'Ask him if he can speak Arabic.'

He could not. To Colomb's mind, this fact was key in distinguishing between an East African who signed on to a dhow for wages and a captive.

Colomb dismissed the child to a corner of the *Dryad* away from the dhow's crew, and soon summoned the dhow captain again.

'Moosa, ask him how many slaves he brought from Zanzibar.'

An exchange in Arabic, becoming loud, ending in a sort of sob out of the man's mouth. He denied that he had any slaves on board. The boy was an orphan from Sur, had travelled to Zanzibar, and was now returning home.

Colomb had a member of the dhow's crew brought in, including an Arab boy, not too much older than the East African child. Bin Moosa questioned him and the boy, calm and without hesitation, said that the African boy had come on at Zanzibar. Two other crewmembers cited two different Arabian towns as the boy's original home.

Colomb had the dhow captain and child brought in together.

'Now, Moosa, you tell him I must take his dhow.'

The small man wept. He put a question to Bin Moosa. Could the captain take the boy and let him go?

'No, Moosa, tell him I cannot do that. Tell him I must burn the dhow. But ask him where he got that boy.'

More crying. He had bought him at Zanzibar for fourteen silver Maria Theresa dollars. He expected to sell him for thirty at Sur. Meanwhile, he transported 200 silver dollars on the ship, which would now go in a strongbox on the *Dryad*.

Colomb felt two chief sources of satisfaction: that he had tried the case scrupulously and so that the dhow captain was cornered into a confession; and that when this man next visited the slave market at Zanzibar he would remember the time he had lost his or his master's ship and silver for the sake of a single small boy. On the other hand, though he sensed it was an improper thought, Philip Colomb believed that the punishment exceeded the crime; one African boy's life was not worth 200 silver dollars (£40) and the price of a ship.[1]

HMS *Nymphe*, Zanzibar harbour, April 1869

While *Dryad* was springing her trap off the north-east Arabian peninsula, Edward Meara and the *Nymphe* hunted along the East African coast on her way to Zanzibar until she came to rest in its harbour. The crew was not at rest, but Edward Meara did not bother to send out the boats since it was unlikely a slaver would depart with *Nymphe* watching. Collect their victims on shore, smother them on slave decks beneath the waterline, yes; but it was something else to run out under the eyes of a known slaver-hunter – and one with a growing reputation. The crew washed and mended, made repairs, cleaned the holds, stocked fresh food, reorganised. The black sloop would soon leave to take its place in the spider's web to the north.

Night brought little relief from the day's heat – nearly 90 degrees even under clouds that day, perhaps 5 degrees cooler after dark, while the wind barely moved. About an hour after midnight Edward Meara received a note. A man carried a message from the island's British consul and pleaded that the captain might read it immediately.

So Meara read how the British consulate had received information from a source who must remain secret but who was perfectly trustworthy: slavers from the north were loading a dhow with slaves under cover of darkness not far away. Not far, in fact, from the British consulate itself which fronted on the shore. Meara could be perfectly assured that these were illegal slavers – not those permitted to move slaves within the sultan's dominion by the terms of his treaty with Britain. Would Commander Meara investigate?

A rush of activity followed as Meara ordered Lieutenant Norman Clarke to lead the two cutters on a raid. Clarke had boarded countless dhows around Madagascar and along the African coast – had even gone ashore and tried to track slavers' captives inland, a dangerous thing. He was something like Meara, a son of gentry in the back of the line to be lord of his father's manor. Today was Clarke's twenty-fourth birthday and this mission could make his name.

The crew of the *Nymphe* swung the cutters out over the water and lowered them, manned and armed the boats, and raised their masts and ran up their sails. Clarke and his men crossed the harbour in the dark and found the large dhow where it was promised to be loading. It was only about twenty yards from shore, held off it by a stern line, while there was

The crew of the *Nymphe* boarding a dhow in Zanzibar

busy movement on shore close by. Clarke gave the order to board and the boats' crews climbed the ship's sides. Immediately the dhow's crew began jumping from the ship, splashing and swimming toward the beach.

There were Africans on deck, more apparently below: a full slaver. A crewmember – the captain? – began cutting the stern line, apparently hoping the ship would drift on the breeze to shore where the men on the beach might then be able to retake the dhow from the boarders.

Now came a shot from the shore. Now perhaps thirty muskets firing on the raiding party. Clarke returned fire with his revolver and his men with their rifles. But beyond the muzzle flashes, their targets on the beach were hard to see: they could only fire into darkness at the flashes. Still, Clarke expended his revolver. Then he drew his dirk and rushed a man in the stern who was hacking at the cable tethering the ship. The man turned, holding a spear. Clarke cut, striking the man's arm, but he fought on, thrusting his spear low. The point entered Clarke's thigh and came bloodily out of the other side. By now the man was long since the last defender of the dhow. With Clarke wounded, he leapt overboard to join his men on shore, but he was shot by one of the *Nymphe*'s crew and never reached it.

Firing continued, and it seemed the slavers on the shore had a far better view of the dhow and the sailors against the sea and horizon. Musket balls zipped past Clarke and his boarders. A bullet passed through Clark's cap like an unrealistic scene in a penny dreadful. Then more blood, as a bullet burst out of the hand of Sub-Lieutenant Tom Hodgson. It had entered his elbow, burrowed down his arm, irrupted from his hand and flown on. Then able seaman William Mitchell was hit in the thigh: a dangerous wound – blood was leaving him quickly.

Norman Clarke ordered that the dhow be tethered to one of the cutters as musket balls continued to rip through the air. He ordered Sub-Lieutenant Hodgson on board the other cutter, while some boatmates helped the heavily bleeding William Mitchell onto it. It cast off and hurried for *Nymphe*.

Though outnumbered, the *Nymphe* crewmen on board the dhow and the remaining cutter did their best to cover for the retreating boat with their rifles. Pull back the hammer half way – flip open breech block – pull the extractor back a bit to free the empty case – flip the rifle to drop the case – slide in a heavy cartridge – flip breech block closed – pull the block back to fully cocked – aim and pull the trigger. An echoing pop and a little cloud of dark smoke. Repeat. Ten shots a minute, a terrifically quicker rate of fire than that of the muskets. Fifteen minutes of fighting passed. Beside the man dead in the water, it was unclear how many slavers were shot. Another fifteen minutes. The men on shore began to break rank until, before another quarter hour passed, the firing from the shore stopped. Then Clarke and the remaining boat's crew hauled off the dhow and headed out for *Nymphe*.

On the ship, Meara had heard the storm of firing within half an hour of his boats' departure across the harbour. First he saw one cutter return with Tom Hodgson bleeding, William Mitchell bleeding far worse. Then, finally, life finished pouring out of William Mitchell, whose twenty-fifth year proved his last.

Then forty-five minutes later the second cutter returned, towing a dhow covered with freed captives, 136 men, women and children. The British consul came up the side of the *Nymphe* soon after that, still well before dawn. He spoke Swahili and began asking the East Africans where they had come from and who their captors had been.

Then came dawn, came distant thunder, but little wind, and what rain fell did not cool the air. It was Sunday, but no awning was spread for Bible text and prayers. Throughout the afternoon, the hands cleaned the slave ship lashed alongside. Then shortly after four in the afternoon, twelve hours after he had died, young William Mitchell was lowered into one of the boats. Meara descended with other officers and sailors.

The boats pulled for a little coral island just outside the harbour to the north-west, a narrow islet, uninhabited; a green, pleasant place that the sultan had reserved for Christian burials. The boats touched shore, the first dry land Mitchell had occupied in some time. They took him to his place, they lowered him down, said the words over him. As darkness came on, Edward Meara and the others left the island. And William Mitchell was alone when night came.[2]

CHAPTER 10

'MOST DISASTROUS CHANCES'

*The daring of the Kroomen,
the success of the spider's web
tactic, and the cost in lives*

THIS STORY BEGAN on the shadowed deck of a slave ship, where Kiada, Aminha, Bakaat, Mabluk, Masumamhe and Masuk crouched, desperately hungry. What happened next to them?

HMS *Forte*, off the mid-Arabian coast, May 1869

At the height of the spider's web ploy, Leopold Heath was in his position on the mid-Arabian coast on his flagship *Forte,* having crossed from Bombay. *Forte* had a long bow, a great, reaching bowsprit, and rigidly upright masts that made her look matronly when moored near the *Amazons* with their rakish masts. *Forte* was a different thing from the sisters *Daphne, Nymphe* and *Dryad*. She was a frigate of twenty-eight guns on two decks and a crew of over 500 compared to the sloop's four guns and 140 hands. Her engines struggled to move her bulk, while the sloops were relatively speedy. Heath inhabited a sweeping great cabin, forty-five feet wide, twenty-five feet long, seven feet high, punctuated by large gunports. It was a great room by any standard, and an expansive ballroom by naval standards. From here, with the aid of his clerk, he directed the squadron's business.

Forte had a middle position in the trap. *Dryad* was north of her, near the western turn toward the Persian Gulf, *Daphne* was south of her, closer to the Red Sea, while *Nymphe* stalked still further south. The south-west monsoon was now tirelessly carrying the Indian Ocean trade north on its back.

On this morning, still before dawn, coal smoke was coming from *Forte*'s funnel. It was nearly 90 degrees even without the sun. Bows pointed into the south-west wind and current, with very little sail abroad, she hugged the coast as close as she dared, trying to stay between the land and dhows coming from the south. Trying to prevent the horror of a dhow running on land, smashing and drowning, she crept.

Then there was a sail on the lightening horizon, dead ahead. *Forte* stayed quiet, with no boat lowered, no change in course. The flagship was nearly bare of sail, and the hands had even lowered the royal yards from the tops of each mast so that she had very little silhouette from the perspective of the sea. Now *Forte* needed to get between the sail and land; she needed to close the distance before announcing herself, so she waited and an hour passed.

It was a dhow. Now, a guncrew loaded blank cartridge into one of the guns. And then fire and thunder. A second gun five minutes later. Except for the heaviest sleepers, the sleep of the foregone middle watch was exploded.

In that dhow were eighty men, women and children squeezed in a space forty feet long and not twenty-five wide. They were in the dark, under a bamboo deck, in airless heat – bent, crouched, huddled. The meagre hull moved north along the coast. Above it was dawn. But dark, always, under the deck. In that dark were Kiada, Aminha, Bakaat, Mabluk, Masumamhe, Masuk. Then a noise like thunder, but not thunder. As loud as thunder, but sudden, then gone. Popping. Something was happening.

On the *Forte* there remained the question whether the sail would heave to. Two rockets followed the guns. The dhow to the south had three choices, try to skirt *Forte* to seaward, dodge her and dash for shore, or heave to. And the choice had to be made now.

She hove to, the great triangular sail lowering. *Forte* disengaged her engines and lowered her cutter, manned and armed. It crossed the short distance. It was only a forty-foot dhow, with just a crew of five to work her, but eighty human beings were found jammed under her deck. The cutter crew brought the dhow up to the ship, and the hands began the work of helping the East African men, women and children up the side and under the open sky again.

And so Leopold Heath saw them. Ten young men, two women, forty boys, twenty-eight girls. One was an infant. Naked all – many were only something like human forms, but attenuated, pared down beyond human likeness. Many of the figures could not be straightened from the positions they had been folded into under the dhow's deck. The slavers came up too, and were placed on a dhow that passed a few hours later.

Heath and the crew began the work of trying to revive the East Africans on board with some food, some warm water to wash impliable, brittle bodies, and some extemporised clothes. No one could say whose was the infant as none of the women were capable of nursing her. Charles Peters, the bosun, soon had a cradle rigged for the baby, and not long after fitted out a mechanism for the baby girl to suck food. She lived on.

The interpreter went to work questioning those who could respond. Most of the people were taken from around Lake Nyasa. War had come to their land and they had been abducted and marched to the sea; others were kidnapped more recently from Kilwa or Zanzibar.

As darkness approached, the slave dhow was cast off. The watch reported to quarters for gunnery practice. Solid shot, case shot, exploding shells – a barrage of over twenty concussions aimed at the dhow.[1]

HMS *Dryad*, north-east Arabian coast, May 1869

The climax of *Dryad*'s work in the web meant defeat, disaster and death, though Philip Colomb did not know it when his eyes opened earlier than usual in the last minutes before dawn one May morning. He lay in the sleeping space adjoining his large cabin on a naked plank – for him it was too hot to be cocooned in a canvas hammock. He rose and laid his hand on his telescope, then went out of the cabin – it was windy out here – past the marine sentry on the quarterdeck, then up the steps to the poop where the watch's signalman stood. By then the eastern horizon was just lightening, though this first light was filtered through mist and squalls in the direction of India. He swept his telescope up. With the coming of daylight the signalmen ought to be at their place atop the peak, but they were not there. He waited with the impatience of a hunter who felt there must be a game afoot but that he was too late or in the wrong position.

To his mind he was a hunter. Not a philanthropist, nor an abolitionist crusader. He admitted to himself that his primary impulse was the challenge, the excitement that accompanied sport hunting. He knew that it would be a better thing in him if he were stirred by the righteous ghost of Wilberforce; but he looked within and found no ghost, nor better angels. In him there was sympathy for the enslaved, yes; hatred of the slaver, certainly; duty, at the foremost. But the days and nights were hot and long and brutally sapping. He had been exhausted, he gauged, since his third week on the station. So to power the unceasing inspections of the unceasing train of dhows – so very often in vain – he drew upon the exhilaration of the hunt. It was, he imagined, this sense that caused him to wake early that very morning.

And it was this sense that made him fume at the tardy signal party that should now be on the peak above him. The signalman next to him became uneasy at his commander's conspicuous impatience and shifted his attention elsewhere. Then Colomb barked and the signalman jumped back to attention. Flags from the peak had appeared in his telescope: *one large dhow, S.S.E.* Then, *four dhows S.W.*

To the signalman: 'Signal the boats!'

The flag signal made, Colomb spied the men on the island off the point hurrying to get underway in the cutters, then turned his telescope to the narrow gap between the little island and the mainland. He soon saw the first sail, moving fast from right to left, while his officers appeared on the poop deck, the sense among them that the boats should be able to cut the dhow off.

A few minutes later Philip Colomb saw movement again through the gap, something that he had not seen in over a week stationed here: a sail moving from left to right – the same sail. Quickly, he guessed the terrible meaning of the left-to-right sail.

'Tell the chief engineer to have steam as fast as he can. Let the carpenter rig the capstan. Ask the first lieutenant to shorten-in cable at once.'

He was sure that the dhow meant to wreck. It carried treasures of some kind, or its owner would suffer politically if she were seized, or the slavers hoped the wreck's survivors would cut his losses having been marched overland to some slave market. More orders as the men finished turning the capstan: anchor up; set main- and topsails.

Dryad moved from her lair and, as she cleared the cliff and island, the strong wind washed over her. She turned closer to the south-west monsoon. More orders, new sails to bend. The jib was run out on its stay, the yard of the gaff mainsail hauled up, the spanker hauled out, aided by the wind, to serve like a rudder in the oncoming breeze. This was the suit of sails for pointing closer to the wind. That breeze, now carrying mist, was soon blowing a growing cloud of coal smoke aft of *Dryad*.

It took some time for the ship to build speed, and now on the open sea the dhow could not be seen from the iron bridge or mast. Still, Colomb believed that he could catch the dhow before it committed murder. The shore towards which it ran was rocky; if the dhow ran onto it she would implode and her captain and crew possibly shatter with their victims. *It would be too mad,* he thought.

There was, though, a sandy beach some distance south beyond the rocky stretch, a place where the crew could escape and hope for a good number of surviving captives to round up. But the dhow was fighting wind and current and Colomb could not believe that she could make it. And even on the slim chance she did, the interior of this country was sun-blasted rock, with few springs – those salty, and with fierce local people. She would heave to and surrender before risking it.

Steam building in three boilers, barque sails being drawn on by the strengthening monsoon as she sailed close hauled to the wind, and speed increasing, still they did not see the dhow from *Dryad*'s quarterdeck. There were many indentations on the coast and the dhow could have ducked into one, dropped her great lateen sail, and now be hiding out, perhaps hoping that the British cruiser would miss her. Philip Colomb had a choice to sail either close in or far from shore. Staying away meant a better view of the coast's narrow coves and bays, but it increased the risk that *Dryad* would come upon the slaver with the dhow between him and the shore, ready to dash for it. Staying close to shore lessened this risk, but increased that of scraping on rock, or even total disaster.

Then the nearby signalman reported to his captain. Signal station back on the peak communicating, *Dhow gone on shore*. The signalmen on the red peak could be seen from here? After all this time, over two weeks, only now did Philip Colomb learn that their signalmen were visible from the sea to the south. It was a wonder that they had surprised as many dhows as they had, and a lucky thing that the signalmen had been late in climbing to their post this morning. Only in finally doing their duty – late – had they alerted the slaver. Colomb had placed unjustified faith in his plan and he knew it in this instant.

And now this. *Gone on shore?* How could they not see her, though the station could? The crew scanned and focused. Philip Colomb was sure that he saw the dhow, was disappointed; was sure that he saw her again, was disappointed. He ordered one of the giant 64-pounders loaded and swung on its tracks to point more closely ahead and at the shore. He wanted to be ready to fire across her bow when they found the dhow. Filled with enough powder, it could reach three miles. And, in case they came upon a wreck and survivors, he ordered two boats armed and equipped with plenty of line and other life-saving gear. It had been an hour since the sail had first appeared. Warm mist turned to rain.

'There she is!' called many voices.

The *Dryad* had just passed a projecting rock behind which the dhow had hidden. The slave ship was anchored, not ruined. It had reached the end of the rocky coast and found the spot at which it became sandy. The slaver seemed to be hedging his bets: hide, hope the British missed him, but stand ready to run for the beach – only two hundred yards to run. The crew would weather the landing, and a good many of their African victims might, too.

The dhow had seen *Dryad* almost the moment that *Dryad* had seen her, and the dhow's crew cut its anchor, ran up its sail and immediately started moving for the beach through a heavy surf.

'Give her a shot, now. Right over her,' ordered Colomb.

An explosive clap, and the ball flew only yards over the dhow's mast. It burrowed into the sand of the beach beyond. If he could have sent it through the dhow's captain, Colomb decided, he would have, rather than let the dhow reach the beach. But he had not the power. The dhow sprinted and *Dryad* chased.

Then the dhow heeled unnaturally, like a wounded animal: it had struck. At this distance, Philip Colomb could not make out details, but what he saw brought to mind a stream, a dark stream of bodies, struggling limbs, the living and the dying. He felt it as much as he saw it.

Colomb took pride in his coolness, congratulated himself on a lack of sentimentality, was sure that black and white were different in essence, that he must not imagine the African suffering from captivity the way a free-born Englishman would. He drew motivation from the hunt, from duty, disgust at the slaver, rather than drawing a human link between the slavers' victims and himself. But at this instant, just for those moments, Philip Colomb was losing himself in the tumbling, pouring dark limbs; lost to indignation and bitterness. *That horrible outpouring,* he thought, *is formed of men, women, and children like ourselves.* In this moment, at least, it was not about hunting, duty, or bounties.

The *Dryad* hurried toward land until the last safe moment and beyond, then dropped anchor. Colomb wanted to save those he could from the wreck and the beach. A quick word then with his first lieutenant: yes, it was worth the risk of heavy surf and desperate slavers. Then the bosun, gunner and a junior lieutenant were summoned and a plan quickly worked out. The two gigs would land while the cutter would hang off the land and provide covering fire as necessary while receiving Africans ferried off the beach by the gigs. The order given, the boats dropped, and men hurried down to take the oars. Saleh bin Moosa joined, a party of Kroomen joined, and they pulled hard and fast as the cutter sailed.

Colomb watched: on the beach he could see groups of survivors forming into clumps. The slavers appeared to be about to force them into the scorched hinterland and a desperate march towards some far-off slave market. The captain ordered the great gun loaded with the maximum charge of powder and pointed over the heads of the slavers and captives on the beach. He meant to show that fleeing promised death. It fired, and rocks shattered not far inland. Then an explosive shell was loaded and fired, and there was a burst perhaps half a mile off. Another shot, and there was a distant burst of yellow dust.

Now the *Dryad*'s landing party had reached shore and through the eyepiece of his telescope Colomb could see one of the gigs pulled up close to the heeled-over dhow, using it as a kind of breakwater from the large waves. Four sailors leapt out, Saleh bin Moosa among them, splashing out of the water toward the survivors on the beach.

Colomb searched for the second gig, but did not see it at first. Then there it was, swinging in the surf, low – far too low – in the water. It had swamped. Now he saw a few men – boys, really – leaping from the cutter in the direction of the swamped boat. Their speed conveyed desperation. Reaching the wallowing gig they thrashed and searched and finally drew something out of the water: a body. It was a pale body in white canvas slops, one of the crew. As they carried him to the beach the desperation was gone from them. Even from the ship, Philip Colomb could tell the spirit was gone from the body they lifted. Still, for some reason he willed the boys to lay the body on the sand gently.

Work on the beach continued as three, four children were lifted from the broken dhow and laid in the gig. Colomb could see clearly the strong bosun pulling from the beach by himself with the children in the bottom of the gig, aiming the boat for the awaiting cutter. He succeeded in passing them over, then returned to the beach for more survivors. Meanwhile, William Henn was moving up the beach away from the sea with six others to try to find survivors who had fled for the rocks.

But now came a report of several more dhows being sighted on the horizon. Colomb changed focus and saw that the sails were moving in *Dryad*'s direction. As he scrutinised them his mind was working on the likelihood of the boats still left at the island station intercepting them. While he was doing this one of the new sails turned for the shore.

Quick orders, followed by raising the anchor, and *Dryad* began her turn. The boats on shore were on their own, for now. Colomb ordered the signal made to the shore party insisting that they not go too far inland in pursuit of the slavers and their victims. It was far too dangerous. Two of the three furnaces in the belly of the ship were now blazing and in minutes the *Dryad* was speeding to intercept. At that moment, Philip Colomb felt he had the advantage and could place himself between the slaver and the shore. The dhow was in range and he ordered a gun loaded. *Dryad* had to yaw a bit to aim – though it could be swivelled, the gun could not be pointed perfectly straight ahead – and then the gun crew had a good target. The shot flew over the slaver. *Dryad* then had to straighten her course to intercept.

'Put a shot under her bows. That may stop her,' the captain soon ordered.

Guns sponged to douse any embers in the barrel, in went a cartridge of gunpowder, then ball or shell pushed down the muzzle, a wad rammed in to make sure the ball did not roll out. Then men pulled hard on the tackles to run the heavy gun and elm truck out until it rested on the bulwark. A long pin thrust down the touchhole to pierce the gunpowder cartridge, and fine priming powder poured in. A friction tube inserted in the touchhole, a kind of match, a lanyard connected to this. Gun sited and gun crew warned to stand back. The lanyard pulled, friction tube sparked, a titanic hammering and leaping gun.

When the smoke cleared Colomb could see that the ball had landed so close to the dhow that the splash almost reached it. But she fled on, and now as he angled toward the shore Colomb had to worry about where the ground was beneath his ship. A bump at this speed could crack his keel, bend his propeller, or worse. The chase stretched on, and before long Colomb was far less certain of his ability to cut off the slaver.

He considered, and considered something desperate. The shore toward which the dhow ran was rocky, and these parts of Arabia extremely harsh. The captives on the dhow faced either drowning in a wreck or a forced overland march that meant death to most. *Things cannot be worse than they are for them,* he concluded.

'Try and hit her. A shot through her sail may stop them.'

Fired. Missed.

And now, as the captain feared, the dhow crossed *Dryad*'s path until it cut through the surf. Then it cracked on the rocks and Colomb and his officers saw the dark bodies falling out. It looked to Colomb like oozing blood, and though he wanted to stop the wound he had no boat left, and he had insufficient men to do the work if there had been a boat. The officers watched the scene as if it were their duty while the dhow rolled and broke. Deck, mast, spar, tumbled and fell in on itself, fell apart. They saw it transform into an inchoate thing of ruin as they kept vigil. Unseen, the slavers on the deck presumably leapt for the beach and headed inland with what survivors they could gather.

Colomb and his crew saw it done, then turned and set the fore and aft square sails to run roughly before the wind. They returned to their shipmates up the shore where Colomb expected to find the cutter full of rescuees outside the breakers awaiting their return; expected to see one of the gigs ferrying more out towards her; expected to see the swamped gig bailed out and at work too. But he found only trouble when they reached the spot. The cutter was labouring towards them, creeping heavily under greater wind and growing waves. He saw the beached dhow rolled almost to nothing. He saw the swamped gig an irremediable ruin; of the other gig he saw nothing. At a distance beyond all this he saw twenty of his crew stranded on the beach.

The cutter made it to the ship's side and it was hard work in heaving waves to bring the East Africans on board, fifty-nine men, women and children. His men came up and Colomb heard the news: the slavers had disappeared into the interior. The man pulled lifeless onto the beach was young Francis Treblecock, ordinary seaman. Though he had been ordered to stay in the gig, he had seemed to see some trouble or danger on shore and wanted to help his shipmates. He had slung on a cork jacket, lifted his rifle above his head and stepped out; but he had misjudged the bottom and the jacket had failed him. Weighed down, he could not reach the surface in time. Without him aboard to keep the boat aimed into the waves, they poured in and the gig swamped.

In the cutter had been Krooman Jim George, who had volunteered to swim back through the high surf from the cutter to the beach with a rope. With this, the men in the anchored sail boat could pull the smaller gig through the rollers to safety. George had succeeded, and began helping the survivors off the beach into the boat. The bosun, meanwhile, had done good work in ferrying former slaves off the beach. Once, twice, three times the gig made the dangerous journey through rising surf to the awaiting cutter. Twenty-eight feet long, six wide, the boat already held eighteen sailors – and now three dozen East Africans.

Then came the final trip with all of the remaining sailors and refugees. The gig was heavy, but the men judged that, with the waves rising, it was now or never to get off that beach. The sailors pulled mightily, and they were almost beyond the breakers when a high wave broke on top of them, filled the gig, and sent it like a stone to the sea floor. Under the swirling water it cracked. In this final boat there had been Kroomen Jim George and Peter Warman, powerful swimmers who managed to pluck up two children from the water, save their shipmates, and haul them up the beach.

Excellent men, thought Colomb of the Kroomen.

But they could only do so much. Henry Blake, not yet twenty years old, never reappeared. Neither did three of the East Africans. *The sea and gallows*, went a saying of the day, *refuse none.*

Having heard the story, Colomb needed to concentrate on matters at hand; there were still men on that beach, and they had lost their food, water and rifles in the sunken gig. There was a slaver crew on shore – perhaps two crews – not far off, and they might have preserved their guns. Darkness would fall in a few hours.

Kroomen Coffee and Wheel volunteered to load their canoe with guns and provisions and run the gauntlet of the high waves for the shore. *The Englishman goes to the devil, the Krooman goes with him.* Colomb believed the situation desperate enough to allow the risk. In the canoe the West African men carefully stowed a few rifles and ammunition, some biscuit, a keg of water, and some instructions for the shore party. The canoe lowered, Coffee and Wheel climbed in. In addition to swimming, the Kroomen were renowned for their ability to work a canoe and Colomb saw their obvious skill as they darted off. He watched as the canoe approached the breakers and was whirled by the first roller like a toy. Then it disappeared from view.

And now what? Dusk was coming on, wind and surf rising. And there were no more boats or canoes. Fifteen fearful minutes passed, until finally rifle fire came from the shore. Two shots, and fear lessened. The note to the shore party ordered them to fire two shots if the Kroomen reached them. Coffee and his partner had somehow dragged the swamped canoe ashore.

And so the *Dryad* hovered off the shore all through a night of ever strengthening wind and climbing seas. In the early morning the captain saw the shore party through his telescope. Relief spread among the men. He ordered a signal, *March.* There was no choice but to send his men and the African refugees overland to the *Dryad*'s base ten miles back up the coast. Soon the people on shore began their walk and Colomb pictured the party ambushed by the enraged and desperate slavers, saw them captured by the local people. The group had to pass through an unknown land, risk blind chasms. But *Dryad* must head back north to her base.

A little over six hours later, *Dryad* back at her home under the red peak, the shore party arrived, safe. Colomb soon received their report. It had been rough going, but the released captives had acted courageously, collecting firewood and water on the night of their camp ashore when the seamen had been exhausted. Not long after setting off in the morning the party had come upon several local Arabs in the stony land. The men said they were friends, and turned out to be some of those whom Bin Moosa had met under tense circumstances. They guided the sailors and refugees to a spring, then showed them the way through the hills to their ship.

In time, Philip Colomb reflected on the deaths of his men. They were from his gig's crew, his coxswain's select men. And he reflected on those East Africans who had survived the wrecks. They had been forced inland to make the same desperate walk that his own men had made, but perhaps many, many times longer, with no friends around, and with what food and water? And so Colomb reached his characteristic conclusion: that for all the sacrifice of life, the fate of most of the slaves that had been stowed in those ships was many times worse now than if the *Dryad* had never found them.[2]

HMS *Nymphe*, Mahé, Seychelles, May 1869

Meanwhile, far to the south-east, the *Nymphe* wound its way into the complicated entrance to the harbour of Port Victoria, Mahé, Seychelles. Poles painted like barber's poles guided the way through a channel past reefs, while white sand under the shallow water lit the sea emerald. Above the port of about 10,000 souls, a cone of rock sprang up many thousands of feet, sometimes reaching above the clouds.

Anchoring, Edward Meara and the crew of the *Nymphe* then landed scores of former slaves, most of whom had been taken from the dhow cut out in Zanzibar harbour in a storm of lead balls. The refugees came under the charge of the chief magistrate, a representative from Mauritius. The men and women headed for their separate houses, and homes were sought out for the young children without parents. There, too, landed young Hodgson, whose arm had been ruined in the fight. There he must await return to England, his work over.

And there Edward Meara gave his crew general leave. Within just a few hundred feet of the beach they found limes, oranges, pineapples, bananas, mangoes, red lychees, all growing semi-wild. The Seychelles merchants, selling eggs and steak, beer and wine, practically leapt at the sight of the seamen. Surgeon John Noble was soon certain that the men had enjoyed themselves only too well since not long after this period, the men started to come to him complaining of spots in places where they regretted finding them. Some of the women landed there by the Royal Navy made their living through prostitution. Amid all of this, ordinary seaman Henry Rogers and marine private Patrick Doyle took the opportunity of a Sunday afternoon leave to desert.

Two weeks later, *Nymphe* was heading for her rendezvous with most of the squadron at Aden at the bottom of the Arabian peninsula. The monsoon wind and current was at full force now, so that in the absence of magically refilling coal holds, the *Amazons* were under the same inexorable power of the monsoon as the dhows. The spiders could no longer perch motionless in their places, especially since at certain places on the ocean the web itself – the current-borne sea – moved. It was time for them to report, compare tactics, and work out a new plan for the second half of the year.

So under overcast skies, the *Nymphe* was moving north towards the squadron rendezvous at an easy pace, Africa not far off to port, before a steady wind. To make the greatest use of it, Meara sent the topmen up the masts high above ship and sea to let out all of the reefs of the topsail; then they mounted higher, crossed the lithe topgallant yards and furled topgallant sails. Their work done, he ordered a slight increase to engine speed and the *Nymphe* quickened.

Then, in the middle of the afternoon watch, a man spotted a sail almost directly behind them to the south. Captain Meara ordered a stop and *Nymphe* hove to and swung round to face the sail. It proved to be a dhow riding up the coast and he ordered a cutter dropped. Lieutenant Hodgson was invalided and Clarke was recovering from a spear wound, so Meara had to send a twenty-one-year-old sub-lieutenant, one primarily concerned with navigation, to captain the cutter. And this young officer, Charles Hopkins, had to keep the cutter between the dhow and shore or invite calamity.

Soon the cutter and dhow converged, Hopkins managing to keep it from running ashore, and in about an hour the cutter and dhow were sailing toward the *Nymphe*. Before long the crew could see that its deck was covered with Africans. Lines were thrown between the *Nymphe* and the dhow, the men warped it alongside, then helped up no fewer than 266 Africans.

Almost before this dhow finished burning, a second one was spotted and the entire scene was repeated, so that before dusk there were 419 released East Africans on board, over twice as many former slaves as sailors.

From then on it was a difficult passage around the Horn of Africa to Aden. Surgeon John Noble saw the worst of it. In another repeated scene, he struggled to save the lives of the sick and starving. Two days after they came on board, two girls died. Dr Noble lost another patient the day after that, then another. Until finally, the next day at dusk, the overladen *Nymphe* steamed into Aden harbour. Over these four days Edward Meara had rarely allowed her speed to drop below eight knots.

The dawn after arriving, a hot morning as always, the boats shuttled the refugees to an island in the harbour, a place of bare sun-blasted rock, a far different place from the green Seychelles. For the African arrivals awaited long open barracks where food and water were provided, but little else. Work was scarce for them in Aden, and many were transported on to Bombay. India offered no promises of opportunity or contentment, but the refugees stood a better chance there. The luckiest went to the Seychelles or Mauritius where there was more work to be had.

Having hurried, the *Nymphe* was the first of the squadron to arrive at the rendezvous at Aden. Then came in the *Dryad* and Philip Colomb. Then arrived the *Forte* and Leopold Heath and the smaller auxiliary, HMS *Star*. Sulivan and *Daphne* were at the Seychelles having already reported at Aden two weeks before. The ships' crews helped their African refugees to the quarantine station while others were busy with restocking and refitting.

The officers compared tracks, logs, experiences. As Edward Meara and Philip Colomb discussed their capture, Meara had to admit his luck, relating how two full slave dhows essentially tripped over him in the final days of his mission. It was, he said, as if the slavers sailed up to him and politely asked, 'which side they were to come up for discharging their cargoes'.

At Aden there was a Vice-Admiralty court judge, and in the coming days he declared official the squadron's condemnations and issued prize money, bounties for the slave ships and for each African released. And one by one the captains emerged from the consulate happily carrying claims from the Treasury for thousands of pounds.

In May 1869, the spider's web stratagem met its greatest successes; Heath's web had worked the way it was meant to. Including the totals from *Daphne* the squadron had destroyed thirteen dhows that April and May alone: 967 men, women and children freed from their captors. In under two months, the squadron had released almost as many captives as it had in the entire year of 1868, and that had been a comparatively good year because of Sulivan's work. The squadron released over twice as many people from slave holds in just two months of the spider's web than had the Royal Navy on the east coast annually in the previous decade. In the minds of Heath and Consul Churchill the sense of success was heavily tempered by some well-known and unshakeable figures: the customs house scribes on Zanzibar recorded collecting taxes on around 17,000 trafficked humans to that island annually – 'legally' trafficked: they were meant for the slave labour farms of Zanzibar, neighbouring Pemba, or the sultan's coastal domains. The fact that his squadron intercepted so many slavers convinced Heath that the trade was larger than he had imagined; given the limits of the ocean his squadron could cover, some vast majority must be slipping by him. Still, the squadron's web represented a revolutionary overturning of past practice and results.[3]

PART II

'A dangerous sea'

CHAPTER 11

'TOO TRUE AN EVIL'

Forces array against the squadron while Daphne *approaches the realm of a slaver king*

TROUBLE WAS BREWING for the squadron. While they were facing heat, disease, boredom and slavers' guns and spears, the squadron's most powerful opponents were beginning to muster. Between late 1868 and mid-1869, first India then London took notice of the threat of Heath and his new methods – the threat to their economic and political arrangements, not the squadron's threat to slavers.

Britain's relationship with the Zanzibar sultanate was the province of both the Foreign Office in London and the British Indian government in Calcutta, capital of the eastern half of the British empire, a sort of Constantinople to London's Rome. ('Why, this is London!,' Kipling wrote of the city on the Hooghly, 'This is Imperial.') Calcutta and its sub-administrations, Bombay and Madras, concerned themselves with Britain and India's relationship with China, with administering the vast province of Burma, with piracy in the Straits and beyond that threatened trade to Singapore and points beyond; they worried about the threat of imperial Russia near its northern borders, about difficult relationships with Afghanistan and Indian princes beyond Britain's direct rule. High on the list of concerns was keeping tradeways open through the Persian Gulf, out of which flowed a stream of pearls and dates and other luxury goods, a place of simmering dynastic and national rivalries. Also high on the list was keeping the paths between Zanzibar and Bombay open and active. Zanzibar meant ivory and copal, chiefly; and it represented a market for cotton textiles and other trade goods and source of cash remittances from its successful Indian merchant community back to India.

For the British Indian administration, the goal of order and the flow of trade through the Indian Ocean did not jibe with zealously fighting the slave trade. The Viceroy in Calcutta, the Earl of Mayo, was in fact reported to think the slave trade question an annoying diversion from his sprawling tasks. The Indian government had never concerned itself too closely with outlawing domestic slavery in the Raj. It was technically illegal from 1843, but under the theory that it should honour local custom to avoid disrupting things, the government looked the other way unless a slave managed to find a British official and plead for release.

Keeping trade moving freely and quickly – and towards India, and not Marseilles or New York – meant keeping Swahili and Arabian rulers and Indian mercantile colonies happy and secure. To this end, India had to keep one place in particular sedate: the port capital of the Omani sultanate, Muscat, which sat right at the opening of the Persian Gulf. The sultans of Oman and Zanzibar were brothers, their father having built an empire that stretched down the East African coast similar to many European empires – a string of colonial ports for extracting the riches of the interior. When the sultan of Oman died, his eldest son claimed Muscat and the younger, Majid bin Said, claimed richer Zanzibar. A dynastic war on the high seas of the Indian Ocean loomed. Trouble in Muscat waters would have meant trouble for all trade coming out of the Gulf toward Bombay and beyond. In order to avoid chaos on the shipping lanes and in the markets, Indian officials brokered a treaty in which the Zanzibar sultanate paid the Omani sultanate an annual subsidy in acknowledgement of its richer inheritance. Zanzibar's most reliable source of income for the paying of that subsidy was the tax it collected on imported humans.

Meanwhile, a major component of the economy in the Oman region was the illegal importation of slaves from Zanzibar by blockade runners. One prince in the Gulf of Oman said that for the mere price of twenty baskets of dates bought on credit, one of his subjects could buy twenty slaves in Zanzibar whom he could then sell back in the Gulf for 1,000 silver dollars. With peace at the gate of the Persian Gulf depending on careful political arrangements – in turn, dependent on the success of the slave trade, the Bombay government made clear that it did not want any disruptions to the status quo.

Heath and his captains were doing just that, and the British Resident at Aden at the southern tip of Arabia was the first to warn Bombay. Starting with Sulivan and the *Daphne* at the end of 1868, then in even greater volume in the spring of 1869, shipload after shipload of refugees appeared in Aden's harbour. With so many, Sir Edward Russell suspected that Heath's captains must be overstepping, overzealous. This, he believed, risked wrecking long-cultivated British relationships with the princes of the Arabian coasts and Indian Ocean. Writing to Bombay and copying in Leopold Heath, the Resident warned that the squadron was condemning ships if they had *any* slaves on board, even a handful, even if they were the personal slaves of passengers or enslaved crewmembers. By that threshold of guilt, the squadron might burn half the shipping in this ocean, so many native merchants carried a few personal slaves. Instead, only large 'cargoes' of slaves should be stopped. Yes, he wrote, those carrying small numbers of slaves for sale might then be able to 'escape …, but on the other hand a great injustice is avoided, and I am of opinion that if the wholesale destruction of dhows is permitted, the British name will be abhorred, and the minds of the Chiefs and natives will be turned decidedly against us'.

The governor of Bombay himself then approached Heath while the squadron awaited its late March 1868 launch from Bombay. He shared Russell's concerns and told Heath that he was referring the question of what constituted a legitimate slaver to Bombay's attorney general. He was also referring the question to the India Office in London.

At the moment this seemed a squall, not a hurricane to Heath's mind. He believed that his squadron's instructions were clear. They were the same that had governed the West African squadron in which he had served as a younger man, that had choked the trade to the Americas. A ship carrying slaves on the open sea was forfeit, the status of the slaves did not matter. They could be domestic servants, sailors, or solely carried for sale. Besides, Heath knew that the slaves, whatever their status, could always be sold. It was nearly inconceivable that the squadron should let pass ships because they were only carrying, say, half a dozen victims. If the instructions changed to set a certain threshold below which a slaver could pass, the obvious result would be that every ship on the African and Arabian coasts would carry this many, knowing that the British could not touch them. *The heartburn of the Resident at Aden would cease,* imagined Leopold Heath, *but at the cost of practically legalising the slave trade.*

A month later, Heath received a letter from Bombay stating that it was the opinion of the Bombay government's attorney that the squadron's captains must have proof that any slaves on board were being carried expressly for the purpose of being sold. Ships carrying slaves must be presumed innocent of slave-*trading*. And so the barometer tilted left again, towards RAIN, but Heath still believed that he had his longstanding instructions on his side, whatever the view of Bombay. He also had evidence in his possession – letters taken from a captured dhow – showing that slave owners sometimes sent their victims to work on a dhow during a passage overseas with the intention of then selling that slave once that dhow reached port. He forwarded these to the Admiralty; slaves that served as crewmen could also be headed for sale, and they didn't have to just take Heath's word for it.

HMS *Forte*, Aden harbour, June 1869

On arriving in Aden for his rendezvous with the squadron after the spider's web campaign, Leopold Heath found a letter from the Admiralty in London. It instructed him to tell his captains to tow captures to port or send them in under prize crews. Captures should, it read, be investigated by authorities in Aden, Bombay or Cape Town before official condemnation. And suspected slaver captains should be given passage to port so they might defend themselves in Vice-Admiralty court. Only if it proved impossible to reach port should dhows be burnt on the spot, and in such cases the officer must carefully detail his justification in doing so in a report to the commodore and these forwarded to the Admiralty for review. And so the barometer dropped, again.

His squadron had just completed its most successful campaign ever. That success rested on a greater focus than had ever been shown by the station and rested on a strategy of lying in wait for slavers driven before the monsoon. If his ships had to return to far-off Aden towing a delicate dhow and bearing its captain every time a cruiser made a capture, they would be constantly off their positions and slavers would slip through the web. Simply put, the strategy would fall apart.

Among the documents enclosed with the Admiralty instructions there was a complaint from the sultan of Zanzibar that his people's dhows had been burnt by *Daphne* solely for carrying slave sailors or because they carried fittings suitable for bearing slaves over the sea. It was a natural defence of the sultan's merchant subjects, to be expected. And Heath saw that the consul at Zanzibar, Henry Churchill, had answered the sultan defending the squadron. The squadron did not act arbitrarily, he said, but always took care to distinguish slavers from honest traders. Churchill's support was a good sign. But Heath came to another letter in the bundle, clearly the one that prompted the new instructions from the Admiralty. It was from Whitehall, the Foreign Office. Bombay's communications with London had indeed attracted attention, it seemed – and had indeed been convincing, it seemed. The Foreign Office wanted assurances that the squadron was only condemning ships on the basis of 'ample evidence' and that they were really in violation of treaties. And so it had asked for the new instructions ordering the slaver-hunters to tow their captures into port. Complaints coming from varied corners, from influential offices: it might be a sign that a real storm loomed beyond the horizon.[1]

CHAPTER 12

'THE WIND HATH SPOKE ALOUD AT LAND'

As word of the squadron's 'zealotry' spreads, so does alarm in official circles

IN LATE SPRING 1869, Leopold Heath ordered George Sulivan and the *Daphne* south to the Mozambican coast. It was here that a young Midshipman Sulivan had raided a pirate nest with the boats of the *Castor* twenty years earlier. In those days, and as recently as the late 1850s, this coast had been haunted by European, American and Brazilian slave-dealers taking abductees to the Caribbean and South America. Now, Arab, Swahili and French ships took them to Madagascar or sugar plantation islands.

The Portuguese had been involved in what is today called Mozambique since shortly after Vasco da Gama sailed around the southern tip of Africa in 1498. They found a thriving trade centre on an island off this coast, an independent sultanate of one Ali Mussa Mbiki, who subsequently lent his name to the region. Over the centuries, the Portuguese wrested the island from his dynasty and poached or built other trade sites at the mouths of East African rivers. Mozambique Island became a fortress, dockyard, destination for ivory and gold dust, Jesuit headquarters, and slave market. Indeed, in times when trade was good, merchant households typically held twenty slave labourers so that the enslaved outnumbered the free on the island. The Portuguese went on to become the world's foremost slave carriers measured by voyages, and about 8% of those carried across the Atlantic to the New World were taken from these south-eastern lands.

What the Portuguese could not manage to do over the centuries was create a stable territorial empire in the Mozambique region. Wealth was made at the coast, trading the ivory that came down from the hinterlands, serving the ships that passed on their way to Goa, dealing in slaves, extracting customs from African, Arab and Indian traders; the upriver regions, meanwhile, had a reputation for malaria and war. Governors sent out from Portugal had a reputation for seeing their time there as a chance to make personal fortunes instead of working towards inland settlement.

There were some few who saw the interior as a place to make their fortune, on the other hand, people like Tippu Tip in the lands to the north. Colonial militia captains received licences to create inland fiefdoms in exchange for planting the Portuguese flag and enforcing the emperor's peace. But peace was not very profitable; peace did not generate captives for the slave trade.

One part-Portuguese, part-African dynasty knew this lesson well and used outright warmaking as its favourite mode of production. The Mariannos' was probably the most persistent and depraved slave duchy in the colonial period. It was begun by a half-Portuguese colonel, Paulo Marianno, who defeated his rivals and then built a vast slave labour operation and personal army. Europeans who encountered him said he had an unhurried air, and would survey his personal empire from a high balcony in his makeshift palace while smoking cigars.

But his princes had reputations for wild violence. Paolo Marianno II made a new name for himself and his father's dynasty when, fetching a spear, he ordered forty men, captured fighters for one of his rivals in the river region, assembled before him. He approached the first and thrust the spear into him, then repeated this a total of forty times. Marianno could have made money on these prisoners; after all, his brother-in-law was the chief supplier to the French of slave labour – technically 'indentured' labour – for their Indian Ocean sugar plantations. Marianno could have had these men marched to the coast, but either his legendary temper forbade it or he meant to send a message to his Portuguese and African enemies: fear Marianno, tremble at his coming. In personally murdering forty men, he made a name that Marianno would pass down to his heir and grandson: *Matekenya*: he who makes men quake.

Matekenya built a new fortress on the Shire River as a seat for his slaving empire, a double-rowed stockade, pierced by musket loopholes and positions for four cannon, protecting a town for his followers and slave army. The war captives too young to serve in his personal army worked in the fields to feed it. His brick manor house with its tiled roof stood in the middle of the fort and fields, comfortably furnished in a European manner. His wife, meanwhile, they called a queen. The enslaved sang a song about Matekenya's aunt Maria who always dressed in Indian fashion as if she came directly from Portuguese India, though she was African. 'I have no mother/I have no father/I have no mother to nurse me/My mother is Maria.'

Matekenya's brother, *Bonga,* the wildcat, was his top general, while Matekenya's brother-in-law, Antonio, sent guns to Bonga, who would march into the hinterlands and trade them to the region's chiefs for war captives. Rulers would take the guns and raid their rivals to pay for them. And Bonga and his men spread their own terror, too, burning and murdering, in order to kidnap refugees themselves. Bonga marched the captives to the sea in chains and Antonio sold them to the French, who would declare them 'free emigrants' and transport them to their Indian Ocean plantations. Antonio used the revenue to buy more guns, and so a decades-long cycle, a fire of war and kidnap, spread across the region.

Livingstone and his party had seen their handiwork first hand a few years before, had seen bodies floating down the Zambezi River, massacred by the wars of the Mariannos and war's skeletal shadow, famine. George Sulivan's friend, a missionary, had heard the people of the Zambezi River lands sing songs of the wars and evils of Matekenya. English and French travellers returned from the interior telling how Matekenya once made a sport of shooting all the Africans he could see from the door of his fine brick house.[1]

HMS *Daphne*, Mozambique Island, July 1869

It was early summer 1869, and *Daphne* was about to depart Zanzibar for Mozambique Island. While the men finished stowing supplies ferried across the harbour from French Charlie's saloon, *Daphne*'s new surgeon reported. William Dillon was a seasoned doctor though younger than Sulivan, an Irishman, tall and athletic. He told Sulivan that Tom Hurrex, a Suffolk-man who had joined the ship straight out of a prison two years before, had died of dysentery. And, Dillon reported, he had more cases below in the sick berth.

Some days later the *Daphne* was at sea east of Mozambique Island, with the eastern horizon just beginning to lighten behind her, showing a sky dotted with cloud. The watch set jibs, set *Daphne*'s wide gaff sails. The wind blew only moderately, but steadily, coming almost directly abeam as *Daphne* sailed west, and drawing the air of the southern latitudes to cool the morning. Before long land was sighted, the Mozambique coast.

Later they raised Mozambique Island, a place a little over a mile long and very narrow, sitting in a bay into which three African rivers poured. Another slight turn of the wheel, up steam and down sails as the current resisted *Daphne*. The ship steamed into the small harbour slowly and sounded often, since the sea here hid coral all around. The pier of sixty or seventy yards came in sight and soon the men of the afternoon watch dropped anchor.

At the northern point of the small island a Portuguese fort had stood for centuries. The population of the island was about ten or twelve thousand, comprised mainly of slaves, the rest Africans, Arabs, Indians, Portuguese, and combinations thereof. It was from here that the Portuguese ruled their Mozambican territory, or were supposed to rule – George Sulivan had seen little evidence of Portuguese control beyond this fortress. As a seventeen-year-old he had fought a losing battle at the river Angoche with slavers and pirates precisely because the Portuguese could not drive them out themselves. There was another fort at Ibo Island to the north; there were posts here and there along the coast, mainly for attempting to extract customs dues; and to the south there was a garrison at the town of Quelimane at another coastal river mouth.

Other than the fort at Mozambique, Sulivan considered all of these places pathetic. The Portuguese might claim to hold the entire coast, thought Sulivan, *but by what right or authority? Certainly it is not by right of conquest, since they have not yet conquered it.* There were Mozambican Arab towns just across the bay from the Island of Mozambique that scoffed at Portuguese authority. Sulivan soon learned that the slave king Matekenya's brother, called Bonga, had in recent months slaughtered a Portuguese expedition sent to tame him. And there was some fear that Bonga might put Quelimane itself to the torch to teach his supposed masters a lesson.

George Sulivan entered Mozambique Town. Everywhere were signs of former wealth and activity with its wide streets, a large palace, hospital and convent. On these streets were many white-turbaned Indian traders and crowds of East African slaves, but it was a place that had been decaying for a long time. Sulivan soon sensed that there was something unusual going on here, perceived agitation or dread. *Daphne*'s interpreter Jumah made inquiries and reported.

It seemed that an enslaved man – defiant or indifferent or runaway – had been publicly whipped so brutally and long that he had died. The majority slave population was terrorised. The minority slaveholders were, in turn, fearful and more vicious so that more atrocities followed. Sulivan thought death by whipping would have surprised him in nearly any other place, but not on this abominable island. He and Jumah returned to the ship.

Night fell with the barest sliver of moon under broken clouds. Some time after darkness set in completely, word was passed to the captain: a man had swum from the pier and scrambled aboard. He was a runaway from slavery, and George Sulivan had the man brought before him. He questioned him with the help of the interpreter, and the man showed Sulivan recent wounds.

So it continued for the next few days. By day, the crew of the *Daphne* could see Africans hiding under the pier, hiding along the shore, waiting for darkness and an opportunity to try the swim to the ship. Some came from across the bay in canoes from the Arab towns there.

Sulivan questioned them. Most came originally from the interior of the country, sold and bought in Mozambique Town or one of the towns ringing the bay. They would point to a wound, a bloody stripe on the back. One showed him an inch-thick iron bar that had been affixed to his leg, wrapped around it twice, soldered there. It dug into him, even pressed directly against the bone. His master, the man said through Jumah, had hammered it there as a punishment. The *Daphne*'s blacksmith, John Letten, worked gingerly to saw it off.

Soon there were ten refugees on board, then a dozen, then more. The evening before *Daphne* was to depart to hunt to the south, a Portuguese man of uncertain office came up the accommodation ladder. Young William Breen, who once struggled on the beach with his captain to save children from drowning, was summoned since he could understand Portuguese.

The official did not seem pleased. He had a newspaper clutched under his arm. He produced it and Breen read: *Several free negroes are aboard* 'Daphne.'

'We have no such on board. Those which we have are slaves,' said Sulivan.

The man spoke in Portuguese. 'They are not slaves, but free,' Breen translated.

'If so, they had a right to come on board,' said Sulivan.

'No! They require passports.'

Not only would they be flogged, perhaps to death, if I returned them, thought the captain, *but it would be a disgrace to the flag and dishonourable.*

'They are slaves. They came on board the ship for protection,' responded Sulivan. 'I refuse to surrender them.'

Sulivan could not have known the official trouble – further trouble – he had brought on himself and his squadron.[2]

The British empire's preoccupation with the Persian Gulf started before there was much of an empire to speak about. It began there the same way it began in India: with the seventeenth-century East India Company searching out trade opportunities and opportunities to drive off their Portuguese and other European rivals. And so, from small beachheads British influence inched inland by winning more and more concessions from local rulers, often in exchange for the services of the Honourable Company's navy, until by 1869, with the East India Company replaced by the Raj in Calcutta, the Gulf was firmly under British naval dominion. From a sprawling colonnaded Residency in Bushire, Persia, the Indian government enforced a maritime truce hammered out with difficulty between princedoms for whom corsairing and raiding had been a way of life. It also enforced treaties against the foreign slave trade in Gulf waters and policed piracy. Meanwhile, it watched jealously the manoeuvres of the French in the Persian court and, even more so, the Russians – who might very much like a friend on the western frontier of India.

As in the Indian Ocean, various Hindu and Muslim Indian merchant communities followed the spread of British influence and established themselves in the chief ports. Under British protection they grew in influence until, as in Zanzibar, the customs of Muscat in the eastern Gulf were collected by an Indian firm. While at the western end of the Gulf, exports of pearls – the most important luxury export of the region – were in control of Hindu merchants who sent them to Bombay, whence they fed a hungry world market. That pearl industry depended on many thousands of slave divers.

·   ·   ·

There was a row in the Persian Gulf. Lewis Pelly was Britain's chief diplomat to Persia and tasked generally with keeping the peace in the Persian Gulf. He had spent years getting the myriad coastal powers from Muscat to Basra to observe a maritime truce, shuttling between courts, even getting a new telegraph line extended in the region to help him collect and react to news. And the news was that the Royal Navy were the ones setting fires, not adventuring Arab or Persian corsairs.

In spring 1869, at the height of the spider's web campaign, Lewis Pelly received some alarming messages. The Persian governor of a Gulf port wrote angrily to accuse HMS *Dryad* of arbitrarily seizing a trading ship returning there from Dubai having sold a cargo of dates. *Dryad* had stolen the captain's trade proceeds, he wrote, and burned the ship – all the while within sovereign Persian territorial waters. The governor threatened to go to coastal leaders and summon a raiding party to retaliate. Pelly suspected that the Russian and French delegations in the Persian Court at Tehran would soon fan the flames of this controversy, if they hadn't already.

Pelly wrote to his superiors in Bombay to ask that if any of Heath's squadron should enter the Gulf in pursuit of slavers that they first call at a Persian port to allow a Persian official to come on board to oversee things. Persia had outlawed the overseas slave trade in 1848, but the Royal Navy had no right to search for slaves in Persian waters. Only if Heath's ships carried the right Persian official would it be legal for them to board and seize a slaver. Furthermore, Pelly should be informed of her sailing orders should any of Heath's ships come hunting in the Gulf.[3]

HMS *Dryad*, Trincomalee harbour, Ceylon, June 1869

The alarmed Bombay government wrote to Heath who was giving the crew of the *Forte* some rest at Ceylon in company with Colomb and the *Dryad*.

Philip Colomb had not seen such living greenness as Ceylon's in about four months. On the coasts of Arabia and Persia he and the crew had seen little more than some stunted palms; but when they steamed slowly into Trincomalee harbour, they saw carpeted layers of the colour, with trees over-hanging still waters multiplying the effect. Colomb had last visited the place as a boy on one of his first ships and this, he felt, was something like coming home again. He sensed happiness spreading aboard *Dryad*.

The crew needed it – crew and ship, both. Tropic-worn, both, with rotting ropes and sun-blasted canvas, empty storerooms, and withering men. The hands seemed harried and exhausted with ten men in the sick berth. Colomb himself had not felt whole for a long time.

And so followed a month of recovery, restocking and restoring; leaves for the crew, welcomed quiet for Colomb who a year before had agonised from boredom on a P&O steamer. The naval dockyard at Trincomalee was small, but neat, well-built, well-stocked. *Homely*, thought Colomb. There was special lodging for officers, but the commander-in-chief of the dockyard made his sprawling bungalow available to visiting captains when he could. The house was laid out like a man of war, with a captain's great cabin, a ward room, a line of lesser cabins and a stern gallery overlooking the harbour. Here Colomb spent many nights talking with the commodore and other officers on the station.

There were rides in the country, hunting, cricket, rockets on Coronation Day. It was hot here – the highlight of one hunting trip was long hours spent cooling in a clear stream – but the heat was less brutalising here where at least there was shadow to be seen. Philip Colomb visited some of the ancient irrigation works of the island; some of their reservoirs drew wild menageries, and he saw elephant, boar, buffalo, apes, pelicans and cranes.

But with the complaints of the Persian Gulf diplomat and Bombay, Colomb could not rest the entire time; Heath ordered him to draw up a formal response to the Persian charges. Colomb wrote a statement explaining that there had been a boy obviously trafficked for sale on the ship in question. And that ship, in fact, flew no colours – Persian or otherwise – and had no papers. It was taken three miles from shore, not close to Persian territorial waters. It was burned, but its burning was judged legal after the fact by the Vice-Admiralty court in Aden. He drew a chart showing the location of the capture, collected affidavits from his officers testifying the same, and swore a statement before the Trincomalee justice of the peace. He collected all of these and delivered them to Heath, who dictated his own backing of Colomb and sent the packet on.

Weeks passed and between leaves the hands cleared, cleaned, white-washed, restored and stowed. Rattled down and re-rigged; caulked, scraped, painted, watered and coaled. After these weeks, Colomb received orders from the flagship. *You are to proceed to Tamatave and place yourself in communication with Mr. Pakenham, Her Majesty's Consul for Madagascar. It appears from a communication from that gentleman that there has been some misunderstanding between Commander Meara of the* 'Nymphe' *and the Commandant at Majunga.*

Not long after, late on a warm afternoon with rumbles of thunder and threats of squalls, the *Dryad* steamed out of Trincomalee harbour pointed south for Madagascar at the other end of the ocean. Philip Colomb would see what his old shipmate Edward Meara had stirred up in Madagascar.[4]

HMS *Forte*, Trincomalee harbour, Ceylon, July 1869

In these same weeks, in green Ceylon, Leopold Heath received a folder from the Zanzibar Residency. The ally of the squadron, Consul Henry Churchill, was in England recuperating from a tropical ailment. His temporary replacement was Dr John Kirk, a physician, botanist and explorer well-known as a long-time companion of Dr Livingstone. He had more knowledge of the interior of this coast than nearly any other Englishman (or, as he was, Scotsman). Kirk worried for his colleague Dr Livingstone, still somewhere in East Africa looking for the source of the Nile. Rumoured to be murdered, rumoured to be found, supposedly murdered again. Kirk and Livingstone shared a faith: they believed that the slave trade could be ended, and all East Africans uplifted, through commerce. The Nile or another great African river must be mapped and commercial ports planted. This would tie East Africa into the market of the British empire, a market that demanded ivory, maize and cotton, not slaves. So went the hymn of Free Trade. Onward, Christian soldiers.

In the packet was a copy of a complaint from Dr Kirk to the Bombay government about the interpreters sailing with the squadron. They were incompetent, he said, at best; scoundrels at worst. Kirk claimed an incompetent, perhaps even illiterate, interpreter on board *Nymphe* led Commander Meara to burn an innocent dhow at Keonga on the east coast. The interpreter, Kirk wrote, could not have made out the dhow's papers. The Indian authorities agreed with Kirk.

Then a complaint had arrived from the chief British representative at Madagascar, Conolly Pakenham. Again, a charge of over-zealousness, a threat to Britain's relationships with Indian Ocean kingdoms. The consul relayed Malagasy authorities' complaints that Edward Meara and the *Nymphe* had more or less made personal war on the town of Majunga, even raided the town for slaves, hurried them on board, and fired a shot at it. The diplomat was not ready to believe such a tale in its details, he wrote; but he insisted that the captains of the squadron should appeal to him if they thought a treaty was being violated before jumping headlong into the middle of international relationships.

Such a tale Heath had to investigate. If true, if Meara really had fired upon the town, the diplomatic consequences would be dire, could easily lead to the French stealing a diplomatic march on the British there.

First Heath ordered Colomb and the *Dryad* to Madagascar to ascertain things. Heath sent along a message for the consul: whatever his complaints of overstepping, Pakenham could not deny that the illegal trade in his sphere of responsibility was as active as ever. And it was only Commander Meara acting on duty and conscience that led to the discovery of the illegal importation of Mozambicans, and decidedly *not* the conscience of authorities at Majunga who never mentioned it to Meara until he discovered it himself on the information of two runaway slaves.

Then Heath ordered *Forte* to ready for sea. He would go to the Seychelles to speak to the escapees from Madagascar whom Meara had landed. On the flagship's broad quarterdeck the officer of the watch directed *Forte*'s departure from Trincomalee. In mid-afternoon the men turned the capstan as a wind began picking up which would hurry their way. But on the wind came clouds.[5]

< >

CHAPTER 13

'SWELL HIS SAIL WITH THINE OWN POWERFUL BREATH'

Sulivan, Meara and Heath work to expose hypocrisy, and Daphne *tries to outrun a curse*

FRANCE ABOLISHED the slave trading in its empire between 1818 and 1826 and outlawed the institution itself in 1848. First the ban on trafficking, and then elimination of the status itself, left French colonies in the Indian Ocean short of labour to work their sugar operations. Thus, one day in spring 1843 a French captain crossed from the Isle de Réunion, just east of Madagascar, to Zanzibar bearing a letter to the sultan from the French colony's governor. He asked that the French be permitted to seek indentured labourers, or *engagés*, on Zanzibar and the sultan's coastal territory from among the free African population there. These 'contract labourers' would owe their employers fourteen years of work in exchange for their passage across the Mozambique Channel to the expanding sphere of influence in the southern Indian Ocean: the islands of Réunion, Mayotta and Nosi Be. The sultan agreed, and so began a new kind of slave trade by another name.

There were very few free Africans on Zanzibar; instead, dealers in *engagés* bought slaves, both at the Zanzibar market and at coastal depots. This was carried on under the conceit that the dealers were in fact freeing the captives and offering them an opportunity for work. Yet David Livingstone reported seeing a boatload of 'free' *engagés* in chains as they awaited passage to a French colony. Others reported a scene of unctuous theatre that occurred each time *engagés* dealers forced their 'clients' on board their ships for passage: a colonial official would meet the Africans as they boarded and ask them in French whether they came of their own volition. An interpreter would then purport to translate the question into Arabic or Swahili for those boarding. There is no recorded instance of the 'free labourers' ever responding negatively.

The French soon made arrangements, too, with Portuguese to the south of the sultan's dominion. It was a lucrative scheme for them: a person exchanged for the price of a length of cotton in the interior by the likes of Matekenya was sold at the coast to a middleman for about 20 silver dollars; the coastal Portuguese officials collected as much as 12–18 dollars in finding fees when the *engagés* dealer bought them for 35–45. Roughly 2,500–3,000 East Africans were carried to the French colonies from the Mozambique coast annually under this falsehood.[1]

HMS *Daphne*, Mafamede Island, south of Mozambique, July 1869

Before departing Mozambique Island with the refugees who had swum aboard *Daphne*, George Sulivan received word that there was a ship flying French colours gathering slaves at the mouth of River Antonio not far to the south on the coast. If Sulivan could take her and, as reported, she truly did not have documents showing that she was a 'legal' carrier of *engagée* labour, it would show that the direct slave trade itself was carried on under the French flag. Such proof would be an international thunderclap. Sulivan would have to be careful, sending out boats to investigate, staying out of sight of the coast by day; he lacked the advantage of a spider's trap. His lunge at such a French dhow would have to be decisive and overwhelming.

So Sulivan needed a place to lie in wait. He remembered a coral island on this part of the coast he had seen as a youngster in the *Castor* covered with tall wispy pines. *Daphne*'s masts would blend in with them. Seven miles from the mouth of the River Antonio, the ship should be under the horizon from the shore.

Picking carefully through a coral halo that surrounded the low island, the *Daphne* arrived there from Mozambique Island and Sulivan sent the crew ashore in groups. They had not had leave in the disturbed Portuguese capital, and besides, he wanted to give some of the men target practice – no idle pastime since more than one boat crew on the squadron had come under fire from slavers in recent months and many slavers carried significant arsenals. Under floating white clouds Sulivan too crossed to the island where he soon saw three figures in the distance. He and his men approached them until the strangers made a noise as if startled, one of them suddenly heading for the water. Sulivan saw, then, that it was a seal. The others were two eagles, huge things with wings spreading almost six feet. This he should take as a specimen and he levelled his rifle and shot.

In the dark the next morning came the moment to send two boats across the seven miles to the river's mouth in the hope of catching the French slaver in the act. A large party filled the white whaler and cutter and the moved off into the blackness. This was dangerous work. Boat work could always end in disaster: sailors were exposed and often outnumbered by those they encountered. Not far from this very spot, during Sulivan's last mission on this coast, a boat crew from HMS *Lyra* disappeared. And this coast was in turmoil with the Portuguese accusing the Arab settlements here of treason and with the conflict between Bonga, the Marianno strongman, and his supposed Portuguese masters still smouldering.

After a tense day of waiting, Sulivan keeping himself and the crew busy with a long list of chores, the boats returned at dusk, working against the wind. The landing party reported that they had heard that the supposed slaver was said to be upriver and would run for Madagascar either tomorrow or the next day. Its destination was supposed to be Cape St Andrew, a point on Madagascar's west coast that jutted into the Mozambique Channel. Running for Madagascar – the rumours appeared true. Could Sulivan capture the slaver and implicate the French?

So followed two days of hunting, with *Daphne* hung off the coast, for she must not take the slaver within gunshot of the shore or risk political complications with the Portuguese. East and west, off and on, up sail and down. More than one watch sighted sails, but never one likely to be the slaver under French colours.

The captain ordered a course set for Madagascar and *Daphne* hurried. There she stalked off Cape St Andrew and boat parties boarded several dhows, but none were slavers. Some ships both here and on the African coast escaped close inspection altogether by virtue of a French flag at the mast, but from their looks they were not candidates as slavers.

After a few days of frustration, *Daphne* pointed back towards Africa and crossed the Mozambique Channel with a heavy swell from the south rolling under her awkwardly. There George Sulivan ordered the two cutters lowered, armed, men chosen. They were to head back up the River Antonio to investigate. At dusk, after a day of passing showers, they made the crossing from the island to the coast. Another expedition sent into the volatile land, another long wait for those remaining on the *Daphne*.

After dark, finally, an intense blue pyrotechnic light shone on the horizon. Quickly, *Daphne* lit one in response. Then two lights from shore: both cutters signalled home. Only after midnight did both boats find their mother *Daphne* and the officer of the expedition give his report. The boats had made the crossing without incident and moved up the River Antonio to make inquiries. But upon approaching a settlement, they were surprised by a well-armed force of the local population on the banks. Things might have gone very badly, but the interpreter Jumah had managed to communicate with the strangers. The local men had thought them a Portuguese force, expecting that they brought retribution for the Arab 'revolt' or were hunting for the rebel Bonga. The townspeople had seen Portuguese troops passing this way in recent times. Once they were established as Englishmen, the leaders of the band relaxed, talked, even came aboard the boats. But there was no word of the French slaver that had loaded on the river.

George Sulivan finally conceded, then, that the French ship had somehow skirted his blockade in the dark or passed under his nose under the
French flag in a ship that looked nothing like a slaver, and so an unknown
number had been delivered into slavery.

The next day dawned perfectly clear, cloud and thunder having passed
away in the night, with the air warm but not hot. George Sulivan read the
Bible and led prayers, a quiet beginning to Sunday. But all was not well in
the sick berth. Dr Dillon reported that he now had fifteen men under his
care, many with the same dysentery that had killed Hurrex a few weeks
before. The multiplication of cases meant that his usual medicine against
flux was dwindling. George Sulivan wasted no time, immediately decid-
ing to head for the French colony on the island of Mayotta, a far more
healthful place than this coast, where they would have the medicine the
doctor needed and some fresh food. Sulivan remembered all too well how,
based at almost this exact spot as a young officer in 1850, dysentery had
completely overpowered his ship with 113 men entering the sick list and
many dying. The greatest danger to his ship's crew – to any Royal Navy
crew – was still sickness.

Daphne turned north-east toward the island that sat astride the north
end of the Mozambique Channel. A providential wind blew almost directly
over her beam and Sulivan ordered a mass of sail. When the wind backed a
little astern of the ship, Sulivan had the stunsails set, sails set on extended
spars that hung far out over the sea. So now *Daphne* appeared to throw
out wings, tying to out-sail the sickness in her own belly.[2]

The wind was light but steady and coming neatly abeam, gathered
by sails reaching to the topgallants. The captain led the men in extra
prayers as *Daphne* hurried to Mayotta for medicine. But sickness outran
her. On a cloudy morning, two hours after sunrise, Jumah died. The

squadron's most veteran interpreter, he had served Sulivan on the *Pantaloon*, worked on the gunboat *Star*, and had rejoined Sulivan, whom he called 'master', on the new *Daphne*. A favourite among the men, he was known in the squadron and among Vice-Admiralty courts for his skill and honesty.

The law of the Muslim devout and the Royal Navy were of one mind in burying the body as soon as possible. So before noon, wrapped in white sailcloth with a 64-pound shell at his feet, Jumah was committed to the deep. Above him, as he sunk in the quiet, his messmates glided onward without him, pointed north-east, their paths forever diverging.

A few days later, at dusk, the *Daphne* arrived at the French sugar island of Mayotta. She was welcomed by banging salute, but immediately placed in quarantine. The next day was Assumption Day, an important holiday in Catholic France, and the ecumenical Sulivan ordered the ship draped with signal flags, the French tricolour at the mainmast.

After that, the French governor released *Daphne* from quarantine. The commissary-general laid his bounteous blessings upon them and Dr Dillon, with a fresh supply of medicine, went to work. Fresh food was taken on and bullocks hoisted over the side, along with extra coal. George Sulivan entertained the captain of a French gunboat also in port, and received a brief visit on board from the governor of the island, General Columb, with whom Sulivan diplomatically broached the matter of the multiplication of French flags flying over dhows in the Mozambique Channel – a flag that, he felt certain but did not charge out loud, protected the slave trade in those waters. The governor evaded.

Over the course of the next week the sick berth began to clear, the men saved, perhaps, by the aid of a slave labour island's officials. Over those days, Sulivan and his senior officers happily glimpsed the memorable daughter of the kindly commissary-general. Until, on a windless afternoon, the stokers raised steam to ease out of Mayotta's harbour and resume hunting.[3]

HMS *Nymphe*, north-west coast of Madagascar, August 1869

While *Daphne* was patrolling the west side of the Mozambique Channel in August 1869, *Nymphe* was patrolling the east. One day, five months after Edward Meara had left the place, the *Nymphe* sailed into Majunga harbour on Madagascar's north-west coast. For five months, the fates of just under 200 East Africans hung in the balance. The governor of the province had promised to refer the matter to his capital in the centre of the island and Meara intended to find out how the capital responded. What excuse could the capital offer for holding them? That they were free *engagés* labourers? The provincial governor could offer no such proof the last time Meara was here.

Not long after arriving, Captain Meara was informed of visitors, officers from the fort above the harbour. He received them and all was politeness and civility, in contrast to Meara's departure that spring. They bore an invitation to sit with the governor.

The next day Edward Meara crossed to the beach where he had summarily burnt the two ships an eyewitness fingered as slavers. Then up to the fort to meet Governor Ramasy, up a path framed by fruit trees among coarse grasses, and to a rough stockade above a deep ditch. Two guns framed the fort's entrance gate, within which lay the large square where Meara and some lieutenants were entertained in the spring with music and dancing. There was another civil reception and eventually Meara put the question to the governor. Had he received an answer from the Queen's Court?

Yes, he had. He was ordered to keep the slaves and await further instructions from the capital.

Meara then asked how many Africans there were.

'There were one hundred and seventy-four slaves landed, fifteen of whom died very shortly after they were landed. Twenty-six have died since.' The governor said that the Africans were distributed about the households of Majunga.

And so, unless he and his men turned the town upside down, Edward
Meara still could not release the East Africans. Still, Meara managed – this
time – to leave in politeness. Just after nightfall, Meara was presented with
a bullock and chickens on board the *Nymphe*.

At dawn the ship left the harbour for the south. The *Nymphe* was
due in Zanzibar soon, but Edward Meara intended to search some more
bays for the slavers he believed must be landing on this coast. Soon the
Nymphe hovered outside a suspicious bay and the boats moved out. Before
long word came that two Africans on shore reported having seen slavers
recently. Meara and the interpreter Ali rowed to interview them. A dhow,
they said, had landed slaves at this place ten days before, while a second
had taken 120 slaves to Majunga – to the harbour the *Nymphe* had just left.

Connivers, wrote Meara in a letter to Commodore Heath. *These
Malagasy do trade in slaves. They conspire in silence.*[4]

HMS *Forte*, Port Victoria, Mahé, Seychelles, August 1869

At that moment, Leopold Heath and HMS *Forte* were to the north-east at
Port Victoria, Seychelles. The commodore was investigating the Malagasy
claims – sent through the British consul there – that Edward Meara had
raided a port and carried off slaves. He found freed men, but only two –
Ferejd and Malbrook – who had swum on board Meara's sloop. Through
an interpreter he interviewed them and had them swear over a deposition
that they had fled of their own free will. *And once on board, the deck of
a British man-of-war being British territory*, thought Heath, *they became
ipso-facto free.*

Had Meara really fired a warning shot over the town in order to rattle
the local governor into releasing many scores of captives? Unclear, and
Heath would not know until he caught up with the *Nymphe* somewhere in
this vast ocean, but he would hardly condemn Meara for it, given that a
show of force, as he thought of it, might have been called for in securing the

freedom of people undoubtedly brought there in violation of Madagascar's own treaty with Britain. And, bewildering to Heath, they insisted on holding the Africans hostage until they heard from their capital. Heath sent the depositions to Consul Packenham at Madagascar and hoped he had won some vindication for his squadron.[5]

CHAPTER 14

'STAND UPON THE FOAMING SHORE'

Philip Colomb tries to win the release of hundreds of kidnapped Mozambicans

As August turned to September 1869, Philip Colomb and the *Dryad* arrived at Madagascar from Ceylon. First he called on the British consul who was headquartered on the eastern side of the island and received a long-sought-after letter bearing the seal of the Queen of Madagascar – one that Colomb would later relish handing the governor at Majunga – then he crossed over to the western side and the port of Majunga where nearly 200 East Africans were still being held.

HMS *Dryad*, Majunga, Madagascar, September 1869

It was Colomb's first time there and, as he saw the town from the quarter-deck, its low stone buildings on undulating ground, its patches of woods, memories of Irish towns came to mind. And tomorrow's breakfast came to mind. It had been a long crossing from Ceylon, and now that he was in relatively cooler waters he could think of something other than the heat – like enjoying food. So, sending off a boat to the shore, he imagined what the stewards might forage for in the morning.

The captain was not the only unhappy man on the *Dryad* the next morning. Everyone found the worn old sea breakfast dished up. The word was that the breakfast expedition had encountered only closed doors and rejection. The local authorities, it seemed, had ordered that no provisions be sold to the British: *Dryad* was under breakfast embargo. It was an inauspicious start.

A little after noon, a boat pulled from shore bearing an official deputation and the group came up the side. Their leaders wore refined white suits and simple but elegant straw hats. One of these, who also carried a walking stick, introduced himself as Rakotovao, the son of the governor.

'How is Queen Victoria?' asked Rakotovao with such earnestness and concern that it was as if Her Highness might have lain ill in the sick berth below.

Philip Colomb replied courteously and, trying to muster the same tone of immediate concern, asked, 'How is the health of Queen Ranavalona?'

Pleasantries and introductions continued, interpreted. Colomb was struck with the beautiful sound of the Malagasy language. Most words ended in a vowel and sounded like Italian, he thought, with an even better kind of flow and melody. Colomb took a liking to Rakotovao, who was lighter of skin than most around him. Though he couldn't understand a word the man said, Colomb judged him a civilised person, and intelligent. For the sake of Rakotovao, the captain forgave the town of Majunga for denying him a decent breakfast.

That afternoon, Philip Colomb and three officers pulled themselves across the water to the beach. First they were served coffee in the fine stone house of a successful Indian merchant, his large entertaining room hung with many mirrors. Then it was up to the fort borne on palanquins and surrounded by drummers and musicians. Soon the body entered the square within the palisade, lined by soldiers, a tall spear planted in front of each, and each shouldering a musket. On a dais at the opposite end of the square stood the governor, who wore a black coat over white trousers and a crimson hat, and carried a very great scimitar. There was some ceremony performed before the governor even looked at the sailors. The details of its elements escaped Colomb, beside the conspicuous flashing of the governor's scimitar. Colomb, always measuring races against the

British model, judged the reception very much overdone and chalked it up to a mere mimicry of the more civilised.

A barked salute to Queens Victoria and Ranavalona completed, there was a salute to Colomb, and finally the governor took the captain by the hand and led him and his men into a hall. There a long white-clothed table, a bottle of French spirits, water and glasses stood ready. A group of courtiers or officials joined and they sat.

'I am very glad to see the governor looking so well,' said Colomb. He told him how honoured he was with the reception. The interpreter translated.

'The Queen and Prime Minister enjoy good health and spirits,' responded the governor. It seemed the interpreter had kindly corrected Philip Colomb's misstep and had had asked after the health of the Queen and Prime Minister of Madagascar, per etiquette. 'How is Queen Victoria? I hope she is pretty well. How is everything in Europe? What is the news?'

'Queen Victoria is very well. The Prime Minister is very well. Everybody in Europe is generally very well. There is no news, but every-one is always glad to hear good news of the Queen of Madagascar.' The interpreter translated. Colomb added, 'I am very sorry to disturb the governor on Sunday, but time presses.'

'Very much pleased to see an English captain. Man-of-war. Englishmen generally.'

Colomb asked whether any slaves had been landed recently. The governor said – contrary to the evidence gathered by Meara just weeks before – they had not. Colomb asked whether the governor had received any messages from the British consul in the capital. The governor said he had not.

Colomb had a surprise for the governor, the letter bearing the seal of the Queen of Madagascar that he had carried from Consul Packenham at Tamatave. Colomb handed it to him and the governor handed it to a sec-retary in a blue coat. The man pulled out great brass spectacles with green shades on their sides and read, whispering to the governor. The governor whispered to the interpreter. The interpreter paraphrased. For some reason he, too, whispered to Colomb. It was a royal order to release, finally, the trafficked Mozambicans.

The governor said that the slaves could not be gathered now and that it was not possible to speak openly, but the Africans would be gathered soon.

Why did the governor and his interpreter whisper, saying that he could not speak openly? Perhaps it was simply because he would need to surprise the town's slaveholders if there were any hope of removing the kidnapped East Africans. But it was also true that in carrying out the demands of the British, the governor was acting against powerful interests. Madagascar's economy was based on slave labour, after all, and central government officials themselves held as many as 3,000 slave labourers. The wealthiest families in Majunga also depended on the persistence of the slave trade. As in Zanzibar, a set of Indian families financed the local market, providing the loans that bought the trade-goods, that bought luxuries and the enslaved on the Mozambique coast. They provided mortgages for slave labour farms, even slave ships. Like Jairam Sewji in Zanzibar, with whom they worked, they ran – even built – the customs house in Majunga. This circulation of money fed, and was fed by, the trafficking of up to 8,000 East Africans to Madagascar each year, with around half those being trafficked again to the French islands.[1]

The next day the trustworthy liberty men enjoyed leave on the shore under bright skies and benign warmth. Colomb, too, was able to do some exploring with some of his officers. They walked under mango trees, one titan that appeared to have a hundred-foot canopy. They walked around manioc beds and rice paddies. And they delighted in the apple of the cashew tree, while carefully avoiding the noxious skin of the nut itself that clung to it.

To the captain and to others of the crew who went ashore it was obvious that the African slaves in the town were hoping that they had come to free them, or at least that they might be able to jump into their boats when they left the shore. The people made furtive signs, pleading looks, and some few even ran for the boats but were seized by Malagasy soldiers. Other times, though it chafed them, the crew had to lift Africans who had managed to reach a landed boat out of it. *Against our grain,* thought Colomb. But a boat on the beach was in Madagascar, and the British had no treaty right to free slaves in Madagascar. Edward Meara had known it, however much it rankled; Philip Colomb knew it.

In his patrolling the coast of Arabia, visits to Muscat at the mouth of the Persian Gulf, even at Zanzibar, Philip Colomb believed that he did not see among the enslaved Africans such desperate faces or eyes watching for the opportunity to dash. He chalked this up to the essence of the African; certain Africans had their virtues – he greatly honoured his Kroomen's bravery and ability, after all – but the love of freedom, so strong in the Englishman, was not most African's, he thought. But these desperate men and women – these Mozambicans, most of them – frustrated such easy reckoning. Even for Colomb, so self-assured, his racial certainties were now celestial objects that would not stay still in his sextant glass.

In the early afternoon, Colomb and every officer that could be spared from the *Dryad* were borne up the hill in much the same way as the day before, received in much the same way at the fort, entered the same hall and gathered around the same table. And here were the same dignitaries as yesterday. The governor's secretary, he of the great brass spectacles, was there, carrying a great scimitar slung from three belts and wearing impressive Hessian boots. The governor's son Rakotovao joined. Bottles of ruby Medoc already arrayed along the table, all sat and toasts to the Queens of the two islands commenced.

Toasts completed, the food flowed: curries, kabobs, rice, roast beef, sausage, a kind of crêpe, duck. Rakotovao carved, as if the men were friends or brothers. Near the end of this copious feast, one of the *Dryad's* officers drew the attention of the others to Midshipman Gerard Brooke, nineteen. Somehow, after all this food, the boy was in the act of devouring half a goose by himself. Colomb and the others laughed.

Of course, Colomb knew that he must return the courtesy and at the end of the night issued an invitation to the governor and his entourage to join him in his great cabin soon. With polite sounds, the men took their leave and were borne back down the hill.

Finally, late the next afternoon, the illegally landed East Africans were assembled on the beach and ferried to the *Dryad*, her boats plying to and from the shore with 140 men, women and children. Philip Colomb's mission was accomplished, and Edward Meara's cause.

Not long after this the governor and his entourage came aboard for a late supper. They had adopted more military dress for the occasion. One man in a red frock coat and epaulettes communicated with Colomb an interest in having a missionary sent to the town. The captain tried to communicate something concurring and managed to find a Bible on hand to offer him.

Just before the meal commenced, late by naval standards, a message came for the captain: a dhow had been seen leaving the shore at dusk. The gig was dispatched per routine to check her papers. The crew of the ship, Colomb heard, had drawn its weapons when the unarmed inspection party approached, then the ship had run. It was not only highly suspicious, but a violation of the treaty between Britain and Madagascar granting the Royal Navy the right to search, and Colomb then issued orders to arm and dispatch one of the cutters in chase.

The meal now being served, the captain apprised his guests of goings-on in the bay. Later, another message came describing the state of the chase as monitored through a telescope, and Colomb relayed the news to his guests as they ate. With the same breath with which he poured courtesies, he reported on his efforts to catch his guests in conspiring to deceive him. Written on the face of the governor was a burning desire to be off the *Dryad*.

Finally came the report that the dhow had run ashore when it was obvious it could not escape. This was proof enough for the captain that it

had been smuggling slaves out of Majunga. The dinner ground to an end
and the governor and his entourage parted under the echoes of a deafening
five-gun salute from the *Dryad*.

The next day as the crew cleaned, cared for their new passengers, shifted
sails, and prepared for departure to Mauritius, several Africans were helped
up the side of the ship: runaways who had somehow evaded capture on the
beach and canoed or swum across the small harbour. A repeat of Meara's
experience, it was Colomb's first though he had anticipated it. A council
of the captain and his senior officers had already determined that, while
they could not be so rash as to take escapees off the beach, it was a different
matter if they made it to the teak deck of the *Dryad*. The ship, they agreed,
was British territory, and successful runaways would not be sent back. And
so, when the inevitable embassy of Malagasy officers arrived to recover the
runaways, Philip Colomb was prepared. According to treaty, they argued,
the British must not remove Malagasy subjects without a passport.

'No slave is a subject,' replied Colomb. He summoned the men to
appear before the officials. Did they argue that these men were not slaves?

No, they did not but, with diplomacy, they asked to take them ashore.

Philip Colomb, with diplomacy, declined.

The next day, the day of departure, was Sunday, and Colomb and several officers had accepted an invitation to attend church in the town before
sailing. The escort arrived on shore and they all ascended to the fort where
they entered a narrow long hall within its walls lined with windows, white
mats on the walls, and at one end a raised platform where a large Bible
translated into the native language sat open on a small table. As the crew
entered, the congregation was singing a hymn in four parts, sung with
precision though it was unplaceable to Colomb, though faintly familiar.
Different individuals took turns at reading from the Malagasy Bible, leading
prayers. While among them Colomb noted some who had pled the day
before to take away in chains several men now safe on the *Dryad*.

Throughout this, Philip Colomb, prince of an isolated kingdom popu-
lated only by men, felt the magnetic current centred on the young Malagasy

women in the congregation, with their pure white wraps, their elegantly braided hair.

By noon, Colomb and his senior officers were back on the ship. Up steam in one boiler, hands to the capstan, up anchor, engage the screw, and the *Dryad* departed the harbour, bearing over 140 people formerly enslaved. And as he had before back on the P&O steamer, he thought about the functions of the market in slaves. They had, Colomb hoped, struck a blow against that market: a slave was a bad investment if an erratic British man-of-war's captain could bear him and hundreds of others away at a single stroke.[2]

CHAPTER 15

'TRAITORS ENSTEEP'D TO CLOG THE GUILTLESS KEEL'

The squadron sails into political trouble

Westminster, July 1869

THERE WAS A SLAVE TRADE bureaucracy within the British government in London. In other words, there was a network of offices and individuals centred on slave trade issues. It originated in the need to enforce Acts for regulating Britain's own slave trade from the 1780s, grew after the 1807 ban on that trade, and grew again after the 1833 Emancipation Act and the expansion of the West African slave trade suppression squadron. The Admiralty, Foreign Office, Treasury and other ministries monitored their citizens' and other countries compliance with slaving bans and treaties, gathered intelligence sent in by consular agents or Royal Navy stations, published reports for parliament, administered slave trade suppression budgets, and presided over claims for bounties and paid them. A slave trade department grew in the Foreign Office until, by the 1860s, four permanent specialists (out of a Foreign Office complement of only forty civil servants) spent their days working on slave suppression matters alone.

The five most influential figures in this system were the Prime Minister, the Foreign Secretary, his superintendent of the Slave Trade Department, the First Sea Lord, and the Treasury's slave trade advisor. The Prime Minister determined the priority and tone of Britain's anti-slavery effort, which ranged from the crusading and bluff Palmerston (in office 1855–65) to the far more restrained and ambivalent Gladstone (1868–74, 1880–6,

1892–4). The Foreign Secretary took his cues from his Prime Minister, viewed the entire question through the lens of relationships with foreign powers, and led his corps of diplomats across the globe accordingly. The chief of the slave trade department, of course, took his direction from his master the Foreign Secretary but like any lieutenant shaped things himself depending on the degree and direction of his diligence. The First Lord of the Admiralty was important in implementing national slave suppression policy since he was ultimately responsible for which officers and ships did the work, suppression strategy, and how budgets were spent. But it was in a difficult position, only as effective as allowed by its budget and the shifting level of enthusiasm of the government of the day; blamed when suppression work was going poorly, blamed when it was going too well. The Treasury's slave trade advisor was an attorney who was tasked with making sure that the government and Admiralty were following British law and international treaty in their suppression work. He also, practically speaking, defended the nation's slave bounty budget from inaccurate or illegitimate claims by Royal Navy officers.

In 1869, the slave trade department was led by William Wylde, a thirty-year veteran of the Foreign Office. For most of that time his work focused on slavery suppression politics and enforcement, whether scrutinising the illicit trade from the west coast of Africa, struggling with the Cubans to enforce their own prohibitions, or investigating the trade carried on under American colours. He was diligent in his duties and truly had no love for slavers, but for Wylde the work of stopping the slave trade must be gradual and temperate. The first rule of his masters in the Foreign Office was to keep the peace; and from this followed corollary rules: maintain friendly relations, extinguish fires – do not start them, employ the carrot – not the stick. So, Wylde gathered intelligence, rewarded cooperation from foreign governments when possible, and waited. The benevolent hand of commerce, he believed, must ultimately eliminate the supply of slaves from hinterland Africa. Make local rulers and overlords capitalists and they will have a vested interest in peace; make taxes from ore exports, not slave exports; make a man more valuable as a worker than as a slave. Wylde saw a role for the Royal Navy, too. They should show the flag, enforce existing treaty rules, maintain a small fleet in slave waters. Yet they, too, should wait.

But in July 1869 he was quite unhappy with the Royal Navy, his alarm growing since word had come some months before from the diplomatic personnel in the Indian Ocean. The Royal Navy was badly overstepping; they were starting fires. Indeed, to Wylde's mind, they were practically renegade and threatened to unravel Britain's carefully maintained relations with multiple crowns.

He reported to the Foreign Secretary who before long ordered Wylde to take steps to rein in the Royal Navy. He was to convene a committee of the Foreign Office, Admiralty and Treasury to rewrite the rules governing Leopold Heath's squadron before it did too much damage.[1]

HMS *Forte*, Zanzibar harbour, August 1869

Leopold Heath, meanwhile, crossed west from the Seychelles to Zanzibar, the wide flagship lumbering heavily into the wind and repeatedly doused by squalls over a ten-day crawl. Anchoring, *Forte* boomed out a 21-gun salute to the sultan's flag and a boat pulled from the nearby shore under the echoes. The new consul at Zanzibar, Dr Kirk, companion of the great Livingstone, was coming to the flagship, and soon he, too, was greeted with his own salute from the guns.

The consul up the side, the formalities of the welcome were completed, and the commodore and Dr Kirk spoke. Dr Kirk agreed with those diplomats and Foreign Office officials who believed that the squadron had been overzealous in their pursuit of slavers in the previous year. And the consul believed that summary condemnation and burning at sea was the root of the problem, giving Britain a bad name, making her navy look piratical, angering the sultan whose cooperation Kirk was always at pains to court. That spring, the Admiralty had written to Heath telling him to advise his captains to tow slave ships into Zanzibar or Aden unless strictly impossible; Heath obeyed, but responded that doing so would practically halt his anti-slaving work. Dr Kirk suggested that he understood the commodore's objections: the time lost away from the hunt, the way that dhows tended to swamp in the hands of those unfamiliar with them, the coal expenditure. So he had a plan to propose: why not, he asked the commodore, have your captains tow the suspect ships to the nearest port within the coastal dominions of the sultan? Leave the ships there in the hands of the local governor and return to the ships' hunting grounds. Then, when the season was over, try the cases with him in Zanzibar as Vice-Admiralty judge. If Heath's captains could prove their cases, prove that the seized ships were truly slavers, the sultan would order his governor to hand over the ship for condemnation. And – good news – Kirk had already raised the plan with the sultan who had agreed. Leopold Heath did not bother to hide his scepticism; the consul's plan meant posting foxes to police the henhouse.

Dr Kirk then told Heath that he had recently ruled against Edward Meara and the *Nymphe*. In his role as Vice-Admiralty judge, he had just ruled that a condemnation – a burning – by the *Nymphe* off the Keonga River on the coast was illegal. The dhow, while it had equipment on board that could be used in the trade, while it had some slaves on board, while its pass to transship slaves was well out of date, was not condemnable. The slaves on board said that they were being shipped for sale, but to Kirk's mind they were not reliable witnesses – they were slaves, after all, falsely claiming they were being taken to sale so that they might be freed. So judged Kirk.

Heath told the consul that Commander Meara should fight him in court, appeal the case to London. In England, Heath said, Kirk's judgment would be reversed.

But the consul's judgment was official and final. It only remained for Edward Meara and the *Nymphe* to put in to Zanzibar, then Kirk would order Meara to pay the dhow's owner the price of the burned ship, reimburse him for the condemned goods that had been sold off, and restore the dhow owner's other property – the slaves themselves.

By now Leopold Heath could not have mistaken the loom of a serious storm on the horizon. There were Kirk's moves against the squadron, and there was ongoing pressure being placed on the Admiralty by the Foreign Office. The growing sense from that ministry was that, as officials in Aden and Bombay argued, only ships fully laden with Africans should be deemed forfeit by the squadron's captains, while ships carrying fewer should be stopped but presumed innocent of shipping Africans for sale.

Heath wrote to the Admiralty that Kirk did not understand the trade, either on the East African coast in Zanzibar waters or to Madagascar and the French-held islands. He insisted that the instructions by which his squadron operated authorised it to condemn ships that carried even a few slaves on board when there was any chance that they could be sold at the next port and that he had proof that it was a common practice on the coast for captains to ship a few captives as a side investment. Heath wrote that if the critics of his squadron had their way, only a minority of slavers would be caught.

Given all this, he concluded by stating that he had come to believe in a new solution to the problem of slavery in this ocean. More strength and more numbers in the squadron, yes; but it was also time to close the slave market at Zanzibar. He dictated, 'the most efficient step that England could take in this matter would be the purchase of the sovereignty of Zanzibar'.

Heath prepared to dispatch his response to Suez and beyond, but he had other important news to enclose for London. A caravan of Arab merchants arrived on the coast and crossed to Zanzibar shortly before *Forte* left the harbour. The travellers carried word of David Livingstone. The famous explorer, long feared dead, was alive.[2]

CHAPTER 16

'VOUCH WITH ME, HEAVEN'

Sulivan tests the depths of hypocrisy while Colomb examines the fate of the African refugees

THE PORTUGUESE CROWN decreed a ban on slave trafficking by its subjects in 1836, though few took notice in Mozambique. There followed a decree in February 1869 – only made public in Mozambique in July 1869 – that called for the end of the status of slavery throughout the Portuguese colonial empire. In late summer 1869, George Sulivan witnessed just how effective was Portugal's abolition declaration. Even if Portuguese officials in Mozambique Town had truly wanted to halt the traffic in humans in the Mozambican interior, it is doubtful that they would have had the influence to do so, Portuguese power being so weak outside the main ports. Besides, for colonial officials, a posting to one of Portugal's colonies on the East African coast had few attractions, but the opportunity to make money by abetting the trade in *engagés* was one. For their 'services' Portuguese officials, including the governor, the attorney general, the head of customs and the governor of the port of embarkation, each received their share of *engagés* dealers' fees. Other Portuguese merchants became contract pro-curers for the French – one entered into and fulfilled a record contract for 1,500 'free labourers' one year – and they in turn stoked the local economy by employing subcontractors and purchasing vast amounts of food and trade goods.

HMS *Daphne*, off the Mozambique coast, September 1869

George Sulivan was back on the Mozambican coast where he found news
that Portugal had recently officially abolished the slave trade in its colonies.
It remained to be seen what such words meant in this abominable place.

The *Daphne* was anchored off a small island hiding place, not seven
miles from the Mozambican coast, with tall pines crowding over white
sand. It was a morning of clouds in blue sky and fresh breezes, but not a
peaceful morning as *Daphne*'s great guns were pounding away. The crew
was exercising at quarters for battle, with the marines, the gunner and his
mates, bosun, gun crews, lieutenants and midshipman arrayed in their
places. They hurled 64-pound shells, 7-inch, 22 pound shells, shattering
case shot, and exploding percussion shells, aiming at the trees as if they
were masts.

Not long after the exercise began, a lookout sighted a vessel to the south
moving north up the coast towards them before a southerly wind. Not a
high-prowed dhow, and no fat lateen sail, within about twenty minutes it
showed itself a schooner. The gunnery exercise still going, Sulivan ordered
one of the cutters manned and dispatched to perform the routine inspection. The cutter beat into the wind to intercept the schooner, which did
not flee, and not long after the ship, bearing a Portuguese flag, was alongside. Sulivan examined the people on board with the interpreter Abdalla,
the former assistant of the deceased Jumah. The ship was recently out of
Quelimane, the Portuguese fort near the Zambesi River, and was bound
for Mozambique Island. The crew was mostly Portuguese, but some men
on board were Indian, born in the British territories of India, but now
trading out of Mozambique Island.

On the ship Sulivan saw eight African children aged perhaps four to ten.
Questioning some of them in Swahili, Abdalla repeated familiar stories.
'Stolen … dragged … sold … brought in a vessel from the mainland …
beaten.' Sulivan and the interpreter eventually came to a clutch of the
youngest of the children, boys and girls, who had holes in their lips and

ears where there were once ornaments. Abdalla put the usual questions to them, but the children showed no sign of recognising Swahili, the lingua franca of the region. No one on board the *Daphne* or the Portuguese ship could understand them. *They have recently been brought from the interior,* thought Sulivan – so far in from these lands that they did not speak Swahili.

Questioned, the captain of the schooner said that none of the Africans on board were slaves. They were, using the Portuguese jargon, 'free negroes'. He had passports for them all, purchased at the customs house on Mozambique Island. One of the men from British India kept the passports for the four small children who did not know Swahili. They were Portuguese subjects, he claimed, and were migrant labourers.

Sulivan knew that Arab slavers took the blame for the trade across the Mozambique Channel when in fact the trade was fed by the Portuguese and their allies. And it was sometimes carried on by them in this piecemeal way, a handful of victims at a time. Portuguese ship captains or owners trading up and down the Mozambican coast would make small trades for a handful of captives along with their other cargo. These they would take to the island of Mozambique. A quiet sale, then, either to dhow captains running for Madagascar, or to a private buyer on the island, or to *engagés* dealers. An open slave market like the one at Zanzibar was illegal on Mozambique, illegal even before the recent declaration of emancipation made in Lisbon. But shadowy market there was.

To Sulivan's mind it was unjust that the Portuguese escaped blame. But, he thought, here was a perfect chance to expose the trade carried on by the Portuguese themselves. Now he could put their hypocrisy on display. Now he had four children with tales of kidnap and sale, and four small children who could speak no known language, who could never be claimed to be selling their labour freely. Yes, the men on the schooner held passports for them, but Sulivan was certain that he had these Portuguese caught.

So he had a choice: he could take the crew and children on board the *Daphne* and tow or burn the schooner, defending his action later in the Vice-Admiralty court at the Cape of Good Hope. But there was a risk that the court would accept the sham passport system. He knew that the squadron was under heightened scrutiny from civilians. Who knew how far it went? A less risky choice, he believed, was to escort the schooner into the harbour of Mozambique Island itself. Surely the governor there could not claim that these children were mere passengers who had bought passage to Mozambique Island, migrant workers. The schooner must be condemned.[1]

After a short passage north over flashing bright seas, the *Daphne* lay at anchor in the wide harbour of Mozambique Island, her prize, a Portuguese schooner, lay not far away. Having busied his people with rattling down rigging, scraping and preparing to paint, George Sulivan crossed to the pier, went down it and into the town to find the governor, Fernando da Costa Leal. That schooner, he expected, would soon be condemned and burnt, the African children borne to the Seychelles or Mauritius or perhaps to Bishop Tozer's small school on Zanzibar. Past the flat-roofed houses and the cathedral, once grand, but wearing badly under the tropical sun, he headed for the governor's mansion, plastered pink.

Sulivan eventually found him and an interview followed. After pleasantries Sulivan and Da Costa Leal came to the matter of the passports, properly signed by the appropriate authority in Quelimane. The governor judged these all in order, and came to a decision. He told Sulivan, assured him, that the children were *not at all* slaves but 'free negroes', as proved by the passports. Still, as he spoke, the governor slipped, saying that the children legally 'belonged' to the Indian merchant on board. He caught himself up: they were not property, they did not 'belong' to anyone. The schooner, he concluded, was a perfectly legal trader and honest transporter of free labourers.

Sulivan had not expected this depth of hypocrisy. He thought the entire institution of Portuguese colonialism on this coast a kind of fraud, thought their protestations against the slave trade were cheap, affected piety, but he had not truly believed this was possible. Yet it happened, Governor Da Costa Leal had solemnly declared the sun the moon. The children on that schooner who could not speak Swahili, let alone

Portuguese, had somehow travelled to the coast of their own volition to contract with an Indian merchant for labour services and transport of their own free will.

And so now Captain Sulivan was left two bad choices: abandon those children to lives as slaves – lives, including for the girls among them, in which their bodies were forfeit to the whim of a master's appetites; or place a prize crew on that schooner, run for the Cape and plead for a successful condemnation in the Vice-Admiralty prize court. And at the same time detonating, most likely, a diplomatic bomb since the governor here had given a clear ruling as to the legality of the passports.

Probably madness, but still he considered it. Finally, though, he decided what he could only decide given the existence of the papers, the judgment of the governor: the children were lost to captivity.[2]

Also in late summer 1869, the squadron – or one of its allies – suffered another blow that displayed the gap between officials' pious words and deeds. Consul Henry Churchill, before he left for England to recover from illness, had tried to break Zanzibar's main Indian community of their slavery habit. These Indians, many of them subjects of the Rao of Kutch and not immediately British subjects, kept slaves and Churchill suspected them of dealing in slaves alongside their other trade in ivory and copal – trades that could hardly be unlinked since revenues from one fed the other, goods traded to supply one supplied the other. Churchill had threatened the local Indians with arrest if they did not stop, had even arrested one man who had laughed off his authority to do so. But since then Dr John Kirk had taken over the consulship.

And now the government of Bombay spoke. It feared abolition would drive the Kutchees and other Indians into the arms of the sultan beyond the influence of the British. So Bombay renounced the plan, declaring that the Indians of Zanzibar, though they should not partake in the trade, should continue to hold slaves for their personal use.

Meanwhile, a rumour circulated through the small British community at Zanzibar that suggested the sultan would not or could not prosecute those who smuggled captives illegally to foreign shores. Either he did not care about those who ran the blockade, or was too financially beholden to those who profited from that trade, or feared reprisal from the perpetrators. It seemed that the piratical Omani Arabs that had battled the boats of the *Nymphe* in Zanzibar harbour that bloody night had never been arrested. Word was that their tribe, their quarters, their very identities were known. But they had walked freely in the town after the incident; indeed had spent over a month on Zanzibar before embarking in a dhow for the north. The sultan had promised the British consul he would arrest them.[3]

HMS *Dryad*, at sea bound for Mauritius, September 1869

If Philp Colomb's racial views were deeply prejudiced, though challenged or complicated by his experiences on the squadron, what were those of the squadron's other sailors? Of course those, too, would have been complicated and varied, but the scene on the *Dryad* as she carried the 140 East Africans freed from Madagascar provides some clues.

The ship rounded the north side of Madagascar, then worked its way east towards Mauritius, called Isle de France when the grandfathers of these sailors took it from Napoleon. A stiff wind blew broad on the starboard bow and the sea sometimes heaved.

Philip Colomb thought of himself as particularly dispassionate or, as he considered himself, *practical*. He consciously watched himself for creeping sentimentalism of abolitionists, whom he tended to think maudlin. When such emotion appeared, as it had when he watched slavers' victims drowning, it was rare and fleeting. He believed that he did not need to draw on sentiment to motivate him to take action against the slave trade in any case. He rejected sentimental conventions about Royal Navy seaman too. He knew that the popular mind held the foremast blue-jacket to be 'a jolly tar': simple, but brave and inherently good. Colomb knew better; he knew them in their complicated detail, ranging from ignorant, drunken devils to the almost saintly.

But as he watched his men with the Mozambicans taken from Madagascan captivity, he could not help but slip in his feelings towards the men. They were to a man gentle. Having 140 additional souls meant extra cleaning, extra feeding, meant working around the bewildered and ungainly, meant all kinds of disruptions. Bin Moosa, for example, had constant extra work to make the crew understood by the refugees. But the men were patient, often cheerful, helping to doctor the hurt, sharing out bits from their mess, mother-henning. Colomb sensed a common feeling of pity among the men, so much so that when one of their passengers got in the way they would not even speak in the tone they would use with a wayward boy in England.

If the East Africans represented nothing but a bonus payday to most sailors, the scene would not have been one of mother-henning. And Philip Colomb, who above all the captains in the squadron viewed the question of the slave trade through the lens of hard-headed economics, would have been the first to interpret the men's little generosities as 'preserving their investment' or the like. Instead, in Colomb's and others' descriptions, the sailors tended to display a simple sympathy, if perhaps it had the flavour of paternalistic 'handling' of stereotyped 'unfortunate creatures'.

There were two or three meals of rice or grain per day, and the men fitted hoses to the fire pumps on the deck to provide a daily shower with water warmed by the boilers. The first instance was confusing at best for the East Africans, but in subsequent days the shower seemed to be enjoyed, the women preserving modesty beneath wrapped undergarments. The Africans sang and clapped at night, a music Colomb found maddeningly repetitive, and he congratulated himself on his indulgence in letting it go on.

Whatever his esteem for his West African Kroomen, Colomb clearly did not consider these East Africans his equals and was quick to identify the ways they were uncivilised. He was appalled at what he deemed his passengers' poor toilet habits, and shocked when he came upon a man and woman having sex. (Neither Colomb nor the other officers on the squadron left word whether the sailors and refugees ever had sex, but they did note that the men had their obvious favourites among them.)

On a day of beautifully moderate warmth, the *Dryad* steamed into Port Louis, Mauritius, and moored head and stern. *The most pleasant spot on this ocean*, he thought. Not just for the green and relative cool, but for the sense it gave him as European, prosperous, organised, well-governed.[4]

As George Sulivan did months earlier, Philip Colomb now had a look at the conditions under which he would leave the *Dryad*'s refugees. Most of the adults, he soon learned, would become indentured labourers. British observers, including Sulivan, railed against what they viewed as Portuguese and French hypocrisy for calling themselves anti-slavery but participating in the *engagés* trade, but was that fair given the British use of indentured servitude in the Indian Ocean in the same years? Like the French on Réunion and Mayotta, British growers on Mauritius and the Seychelles were perennially short of cheap labour to plant, harvest and process sugar and other crops. In both places, during French and British colonial rule up to 1833, that had meant slave labour; afterward, it meant indentured servitude and importing labour that, if not slave labour, was not free.

The first unfree labour on Mauritius, as in much of the British Caribbean, was the system of so-called 'apprenticeship' that lasted for six years after the abolition of slavery there. This was really an accommodation for slaveholders and their gradualist sympathisers, meant to ease the transition from slave to free labour to lessen their economic pain. Over 600,000 formerly enslaved people in the empire above the age of six were forced to remain on their plantations and work for their former masters for forty-five hours per week for six years. Many abolitionists called it hypocrisy for the British to declare themselves liberators then deliver the supposedly emancipated into forced labour, and between their protests and those of the formerly enslaved, the apprenticeship system was halted two years early.

After those years, many former captives naturally left their captors behind and made their own way; hence the shortage of labour on plantations. First, the growers on Mauritius hoped to 'recruit' labour from East Africa, paying rulers on that coast 'fees' for the privilege, in exactly the same way that the French came to do, thereby encouraging slave-trading. The Colonial Office refused to allow it in 1840. The big growers then turned to the solution of drawing far more labourers from India, who came mostly from the north-east or south, often from a slave caste, and entered into the contracts for five years in exchange for wages, food and clothing. They were attracted by wages advertised at two to three times local rates and sometimes could receive advances that allowed them to buy themselves and others out of slavery. By the mid 1840s there were almost 40,000 Indian indentured labourers on Mauritius. By the 1860s, for every one person of free background, there were three formerly enslaved and eight indentured or free Indians in a population of over 300,000.

Though often motivated by economic desperation, at the moment of signing the contracts they did so of their own free will; this is the key difference between what the French and Portuguese were doing and what the British did. But having done so, these Indian workers had limited freedom. They were required to spend every day but Sunday on their employers' fields. And it seems they frequently were not aware of all the handicaps embodied in their contracts. If they chose to run from their planting operations, they were often hunted down as if they were refugee slaves, subjected to savage violence. Yet they were not legally subject to any whim of their masters and were liable to be tortured or raped as a slave might be. They might also sue their employers for non-payment or other failures to meet their contract; almost 10% of indentured workers did so on Mauritius, winning their cases over 70% of the time.

In the 1860s and up until 1872 the Royal Navy brought about 2,500 African refugees to the Seychelles where they were welcomed by existing

planters and merchants, who thought their islands under-populated and
their economy in need of labour and consumers. In Mauritius the total
number is lost, but official letters indicate they were sought after there too.
This is in contrast to Aden, where at least in this period, Edward Russell
did not like to see refugees dropped off; he complained that it was too
hard to find them work. In Mauritius and the Seychelles, some refugees
entered into a contract for five years of weekly labour in return for wages
and food, while others laboured on their own terms, especially in the
Seychelles where there was less industrial farming. Afterwards their fates
were mixed. Some became sharecroppers, others bought their own land;
others experienced poverty and limited prospects.

The East African refugees had not freely entered into a contract, of
course, as had the Indian indentured immigrants. They could no sooner
chose the destination of the *Nymphe* or *Dryad* than walk on water. Yet
even had they been able to choose the destination, they could not have
gone home. The *engagés* contractors or slavers would have laughed at
their fortune as they re-abducted them at any port at which they might
land. And in the unlikely event that the refugees reached their homelands,
chances were those places had been over-swept by fire or famine when
the victims were originally seized. Of course the British could not have
forcibly escorted the refugees to their homes in Zanzibari or (semi-)
Portuguese Africa, except by starting a war or engaging in bald colonial
expansionism.[5]

At Port Louis, Mauritius, an immigration officer directed the landing
of the refugees from the *Dryad*, the boats working to and from shore
throughout the afternoon. Colomb was interested in seeing what became
of them, seeking to compare their experience to that of the Africans set
down at Aden amongst stone and airless heat. So he went and observed
where they were accommodated, finding clean, airy houses, separate ones
for men and women. Suits of bright cotton clothes distributed and good

food provided, the Mauritius government did its work with generosity and diligence, to his mind.

But then came the question of the refugees' fate after a brief period of recuperation. Mauritius, Colomb knew, was one great sugar factory. Sugar was all, and when market and nature were benign, all prospered. If a cyclone struck or the market was glutted, all suffered. The Africans he left there would find work on the sugar plantations usually contracted to a planter who would provide food, housing and clothing in exchange for labour obligations for five years. The planters could provide for them only as well as sugar provided for the planters. All shared the risk. And when the period of work obligation was up, what then? Compete in the labour market against the far more numerous Indian labourers on the island? And what hope for education was there? What exactly was this freedom that he, to Colomb's mind, was *thrusting upon* the people he was leaving there?[6]

CHAPTER 17

'FALSE AS WATER'

Dark days for Meara and Sulivan at Zanzibar, while Colomb wins a joyless victory in Madagascar

HMS *Nymphe*, Zanzibar harbour, September 1869

Edward Meara's *Nymphe* lay at anchor in Zanzibar harbour, the hands cleaning, the carpenter making a new mast for one of the boats, and the sailmaker and his crew busy. The main task of the day was to set up new running gear – to rig and adjust new permanent rope. The tropical sun incessantly assaulted the working manila rope of the ship, and it was time to replace it.

For good news, Edward Meara found in Zanzibar a letter from his commanding officer reporting promotions for his men. Sub-Lieutenant Norman Clarke, who had worked long and hard in the feverish creeks of this coast and at Madagascar hunting slavers, was made lieutenant in recognition of his cutting-out of a slave dhow in this very harbour when he had received a spearhead through the leg. So too was Sub-Lieutenant Tom Hodgson promoted. His arm was wounded, hand nearly exploded, that tumultuous night and he was recovering in England.

For bad news, Meara learned that the British consul on this island, part of whose role it was to judge the legality of the squadron's captures, had ruled against him in a recent case involving a ship condemned to fire by Lieutenant Clarke in Keonga Bay that spring. Though it had four enslaved crewmembers, the other men on board had insisted they were merely fishing. The captain's brother had drawn a knife and refused to leave the burning dhow. Clarke had declared it a slaver on the basis of the enslaved crew, cooking materials consistent with feeding a large number, and the fact it carried a slaving licence that was out of date. Everything hinged on the licence – now lost – being out of date since these were the sultan of Zanzibar's waters and the alleged slaver could have pled that he was shipping slaves from the mainland to Zanzibar perfectly legally. Put simply, if the licence had been in order, the crew of the *Nymphe* had no case. When Dr Kirk investigated, he interviewed the interpreter of the *Nymphe* and judged that the man was only semi-literate: he could not have read the date on the slaving licence. The seizure was unlawful – never mind the four enslaved people on board.

For Kirk, this represented a model case for the principle that the Royal Navy should tow suspected slavers into a port like Zanzibar in order to get his judgment on a case before burning the ship. (Clarke and his crew of boarders were forty miles from the *Nymphe* at the time and judged they could not sail her to their mother ship.) It served, too, to discourage the Royal Navy from seizing ships 'merely' because they carried enslaved people. And it was, as he reported to the Foreign Office, an opportunity to 'convince the Arabs of British justice'.

The burning of the ship not upheld by Dr Kirk, Edward Meara was by law personally responsible for the ship owner's losses – both of his ship and of his cargo, which had been sold at Zanzibar. Meara had known he was liable in such cases. And Meara had read a directive from his commodore reminding his captains to tow ships into port whenever possible. Knowing the risks, had Clarke and Meara scorned them for the sake of bounty money, were Clarke and Meara betrayed by an illiterate or piratical interpreter, or was it an illegal act of renegade justice against people holding four kidnapped men? There is no direct evidence to confirm any of these, though Edward Meara certainly showed a pattern of pushing up to, and perhaps past the limits of his orders for the sake of what he thought justice. And he was soon to do so again.

Heath had been outraged to hear of Kirk's decision weeks earlier, and suggested to Meara that he challenge the ruling in England, but Meara wanted the matter put behind him. So one morning, bearing a bank draft, Edward Meara and several of his senior officers made the quick crossing from the *Nymphe* to shore and alighted. The British Residency was on the beach barely above the waves at their highest tide, white-walled and many-windowed, with a low wall surrounding a small garden in front. An outbuilding beside it held a small but precious store of naval supplies and one room a small cache of coal. Dr Kirk had private quarters in the rear of the place. Edward Meara and his men were led in to a large room set aside in the Residency for proceedings of the Vice-Admiralty court with high ceilings, dark beams crossing them, and iron posts supporting these.

There was Dr John Kirk, who welcomed them with conciliatory talk — he had to work with the Royal Navy as well as his political overseers, after all — telling the captain that though he had ordered restitution, he believed that Meara and his men had acted under their instructions as they understood them. He had instructions from the Bombay governor's office to stop condemning ships on the grounds that they were merely transporting slaves. The Royal Navy needed to prove that Africans were transported for the express purpose of sale. Kirk reminded Meara that he was acting on orders from above.

Hamed bin Sahel, owner of the dhow burnt by Meara's lieutenant, entered as did the representative of the sultan of Zanzibar, vizier Sheik Suliman bin Ali. His fine house stood immediately next to the British Residency. Dr Kirk laid out papers: a document clearing Meara and his officers from further indemnity and a receipt. Edward Meara produced the draft on a bank in the sum of 709 silver Maria Theresa dollars.

Papers exchanged, papers signed, and with that Edward Meara had paid a slaveholder, a man he believed was a slave-trader, at the command of the British government. And on top of that, Meara was directed by Dr Kirk to return the man's slaves to him as well.[1]

·   ·   ·

Dr Kirk wanted Captain Meara to return Hamed bin Sahel's 'property' to the slaveholder in the name of 'British justice', yet at the same time Kirk wanted a captive held by the sultan returned to him. In the same days of September 1869, the consul was scandalised to hear that a white boy had recently been given to the sultan of Zanzibar as a gift. One of the sultan's cousins bought the boy, a twelve-year-old from Ottoman Trebizon on the Black Sea, at Mecca for the extraordinary price of 1,000 silver dollars. Managing to speak to the boy to confirm the rumours, Dr Kirk demanded that the sultan release him in the most forceful language he had used with him. He wrote, 'this traffic in Europeans and Asiatic slaves is to us much more revolting than the negro slave trade'. The boy was soon seen in the palace covered with gold lace and Kirk had no doubt about 'the vilest of purposes' for which he was intended.

The sultan refused to surrender his captive and the outraged Kirk had no recourse short of a violent international incident. Of course the Zanzibar slave market was full of East African girls intended for such purposes, but there was no outward sign that this raised the ire of the Doctor.[2]

HMS *Daphne*, Zanzibar harbour, September 1869

To visit that slave market and to visit the widow of his former interpreter Jumah, George Sulivan arrived the next day for what might be his last visit to Zanzibar. He was leaving Africa because recently on the Mozambique coast a passing Royal Navy ship had given him the news for which every midshipman yearned and lieutenant strained: he was promoted to captain. Even as a commander he had been called 'captain', as was anyone who led a Royal Navy ship; but, blessed was he among men, he was made post-captain. Through seniority, the mystery of luck, perhaps his successes against the slave trade the previous year, he had been picked from among the crowded list. He was a rare and glorious being, the envy of all lesser sea officers.

Soon after hearing the news, Sulivan's thoughts turned to the journey to England promised by promotion to receive his outward marks of
naval glory, the new star on his epaulette and another ring on his sleeve.
Promotion meant England, and though he knew it might not have been
the most heroic thought, he welcomed the break from the enervation,
frustration and long stretches of monotony between desperate encounters
that as often brought tragedy as triumph.

But first he had a debt to repay to his old shipmate Jumah. So the
Daphne steamed slowly into Zanzibar harbour to form a mirror image
to her black-hulled twin sister *Nymphe* moored there. And after learning
of Meara's chastisement in the British Residency, he left the ship with
Abdallah, Jumah's assistant, while the crew set to work with perennial
cleaning and coaling. They worked their way through the narrow streets
of the close-packed town until they came to the right house where they
were met at the door by some men, kin of Jumah's widow.

She was above, in mourning in her bed, they said. No, it would not be
correct for the strangers to wait upon her, they said. Sulivan replied that
unless he saw Mrs Jumah before departing this place, which he would do
very soon, it would be far more difficult to make arrangements for her
to receive his pay and prize money. Discussion, then, among the men as
Abdallah translated bits for Sulivan. They argued about the appropriate-
ness of such a visit.

Finally the men ushered the captain and Abdallah into the shade of the
house, up stone steps, and to her room. Entering, Sulivan saw a long couch
to the right, women seated there, an older lady among them apparently
Jumah's mother. They lifted their hands and spoke, distraught, Sulivan
catching Jumah's name repeated. A voice from the other side of the room
took up the lament, too, coming from a bed with curtains drawn. One of
the menfolk offered him a seat in a chair close to the head of the bed and
Sulivan sat beside the curtain.

When the lament ceased, the captain introduced himself, Abdallah
repeating. A woman's voice greeted him with grateful words and asked

about Jumah and the circumstances of her husband's death. Sulivan told her that in time the Consul John Kirk would supply her with the funds owed to Jumah and explained how to receive them. She seemed to know a bit of English, but did not attempt to speak it. At one point she drew the curtain back a bit to see this man who took Jumah to his fate on a black ship.

Leaving the house, George Sulivan decided to have what might be his last look at the slave market of Zanzibar, for he was bound for Bombay to hand over the *Daphne* to her new commander and he might never serve again in these waters. He wound his way through shady narrow streets, open shops lining them. These were usually tended by turbaned Indians, sitting cross-legged. There were shops selling weapons, Birmingham and Sheffield tin goods, sometimes slave food – rank shark meat, rotting vegetables. There was a constant exchange for ivory, Zanzibar and Pemba cloves, and copal to be turned into varnish. Here piles of tusks, numbered and separated by size and quality; there, Indians cleaning and sorting copal.

Captain Sulivan found the narrow lane that led to the place, then followed to where it opened on a square. In one corner East Africans were lined in a semi-circle, most standing, some sitting, some seeming too weak to stand. Within the semi-circle stood perhaps half a dozen men examining the East Africans, speaking, scrutinising some more. *Like farmers valuing cattle at an English fair*, thought Sulivan; and, indeed, sometimes the slave dealers herded the slaves with shepherds' crooks.

In another corner were children who sat until it was time to be inspected. Some appeared to be around five, but they looked much older already. Sulivan had seen children of the East African coast in their homes; there they played like all children with any simple toy that came to hand, chattering and sprightly, but here it was as if these children had passed from one world into another. Their parents and friends were gone, and now they saw only what was new and strange and cruel. The saw only slaves and masters. Now they sat silent and appeared unseeing and unfeeling. But unlike Colomb, Sulivan knew that this was not their natural state.

In another portion of the market were the young women and girls
in different lots; one group intended for work, another for sex. Some
appeared about twelve years old, with faces painted and some cloth around
the hips.

It had been years since he had first seen the market, but he remembered the crashing sensations that he had felt then. He had experienced
almost more sorrow and empathy than he could stand, then sickness,
then rage, then hate that he felt was not right in a Christian like himself.
But he could not deny that he failed this test of loving his enemy. He
wanted to beat the man with a shepherd's crook, then hang the dealers
and buyers.

He still fought the urge to violence now, even after years of visits to
the place. But he admitted to himself that after all this time, after all his
experiences, the feeling of desperate pity was callousing, while rage still
burned as hotly as ever. It was as if it were easier to feel anger than gutting
empathy.[3]

HMS *Nymphe*, Zanzibar harbour, October 1869

It was October now, and it would soon be time for *Nymphe* to point towards
Bombay for the squadron's late season rendezvous. But before going to
Bombay, her captain had to decide whether to obey the order of Consul
Dr Kirk to return Hamid bin Sahel's slaves to him.

The former slaves were in the Seychelles, and before Meara could visit
there he had work to do. Just before leaving Zanzibar, Dr Kirk sent Meara
some intelligence: there were rumours of a large gathering of slavers at
the coastal island of Lamu at the northern edge of the sultan of Zanzibar's
dominions, the edge of the zone in which the slave trade was legal according
to the treaty with Britain. Perhaps they were preparing a joint run north
against the blockade. *It being well known that our cruisers are well to the
south,* Dr Kirk wrote in his alert, *I have no doubt that the slavers will make a*

rush from the Somali ports at the earliest possible time. It was a kind of peace offering to Meara, perhaps, or a token that he was still an opponent of the slave trade, whatever the appearances.

So the *Nymphe* parted from the *Daphne* and Zanzibar to hurry to the north and set a trap for the rumoured slaver flotilla. There she waited. One pre-dawn morning, as the ship lurked under coastal cliffs, a lookout saw a lateen sail on the horizon. As he had so often before, Lieutenant Clarke climbed down to the cutter with his boarding party. As he had so often before he found an innocent trader. And so routine continued. The heat of the day mounted as the riflemen took target practice and sailmakers Ed Fretter and George Hill made repairs to a mainsail, while Mason and Staunton, carpenters, worked on a new rack for rope. The days repeated themselves with the monotonous pattern varying only in the details.

Either Kirk's slavers had eluded him or the whispers he had heard were false or misleading. The cutter crews boarded only eight ships over as many days, while he met many French-flagged dhows, untouchable unless there was indisputable evidence that they were engaged in slave trading. The season for running slaves up the East African coast was over, and Heath's squadron would regroup in Bombay. Meara would soon be out of time to point towards the Seychelles.

One morning, breakfast completed, the night's haze cleared from the surface and the men saw creatures rolling out of the sea. It was a large pod of whales, breathing as they arched up to roll over the sea. Later three whalers appeared in chase, hunting them down.

No, Edward Meara would not go to the Seychelles and hunt down former slaves to deliver them to Dr Kirk and the aggrieved dhow-owner. It was simple enough to his mind: those people had said that they had been enslaved and they had wished to get away to the Seychelles. The question ended there for Meara. He would not deliver them and he would refuse to pay for them as well, though he paid for the goods sold out of the dhow.

When he wrote to explain himself to the Admiralty, Meara explained that he answered to the higher spirit of his orders, which he believed then and believed now he was following. *And my orders,* he thought, *were in the cause of humanity.* The next day he ordered a course set for Bombay.[4]

HMS *Dryad*, central eastern coast of Madagascar, October 1869

At about the same time as John Kirk was handing Edward Meara a defeat in favour of a slaveholder in autumn 1869, Philip Colomb was trying to relieve some of the political pressure on Meara for his confrontation with the Malagasy at Majunga that March – undiplomatic at best, threatening at worst. Colomb tried to prove that the Malagasy were indeed deeply implicated in the slave trade – and poor liars besides.

First, the thorough Colomb wanted to be get official sanction for taking the five men who'd swum aboard at Majunga to Mauritius. So the *Dryad* arched over the top of the island of Madagascar to its east side and the village of Tamatave where the British consul was stationed. With about 5,000 inhabitants, it crowded on a point with the sea at both shoulders, with blue mountains rising toward the interior beyond.

The ship moored and in drizzling rain with squalls running past, Philip Colomb and the five African men were pulled from the *Dryad* to the shore. The group made its way to the consul's house, a small place with a veranda. They entered, and Colomb and the men came before Consul Conolly Pakenham. A large deputation from the court of the Queen and Tamatave officials were there too. After the five East Africans swore an oath to speak the truth, it did not take much interviewing to establish the backgrounds of four of them, named Morjakibo, Sabouri, Semaquail and Majan. They were clearly Mozambicans, and had been in Madagascar no longer than a few months before they ran for *Dryad*. But the fifth man, it became clear in time, was born in Madagascar, and the British could not legally remove him from the place. He was enslaved, but slavery was perfectly legal in Madagascar and Britain's treaty with Madagascar certainly did not give them the power to carry him off. As Dr Kirk did to Meara, Consul Pakenham ordered Colomb to return the enslaved man to these Malagasy officials; Colomb would comply.

The next day the four Mozambican men were escorted to an English merchant barque, *Perseverance*, in the harbour, which would take them to Mauritius. The fifth man was already back in the hands of the Malagasy.

Armed with the ruling from the Vice-Admiralty court, and certain that the certified testimony of the four Mozambicans proved that the Malagasy authorities had lied to him about the origins of the East Africans recently landed there, Philip Colomb set a course back to Majunga. He had several aims in mind: first, he knew that the Majunga authorities had made complaints about Edward Meara's conduct that spring, calling him rageful and intimidating, so Colomb wanted to catch the Majunga authorities in the wrong, and give Commodore Heath ammunition to defend Meara and the *Nymphe*. Colomb also wanted to rattle the nerves of his hosts there. Thinking again about the operations of the market, he wanted to shake it up, wanted a scene to be spoken of for years to come. Yes, he wanted to free illegally held slaves there too, but he never felt much hope of that.

A week later *Dryad* anchored at Majunga on the opposite side of the great island and Colomb, Saleh bin Moosa, and a group of officers made the usual parade of palanquins up to the fort, ending in pomp and courtesies. In the great hall Philip Colomb presented Governor Ramasy with a bottle of quinine, cologne and boots purchased at Mauritius, in honour of his 'helpfulness' in the affair of the 140 illegally landed Mozambicans. Then, breaking the customary flow of diplomatic banter, Colomb suddenly declared his intention to speak with the governor alone. It was as if he had thrown a wine glass in the middle of a chamber concert, the music of polite chitchat quickly wandering into discordant strains and breaking altogether. The company unsure, Governor Ramasy visibly flustered, the captain was secretly delighted. He had spent hard months under a blasting equatorial

sun hunting down this trade, always reacting, reacting – often too late;
but now he was not the one waiting. Rather he had all the knowledge he
needed, and could lead his victim into a trap by his nose.

When the governor collected himself, he and his secretary and translator
led Colomb, Lieutenant Henry Walker and Saleh bin Moosa into a dusty
side-chamber. Colomb reported the release of the four former slaves at
Tamatave. Now he asked whether the governor understood why they had
been released.

'No, not at all,' said the Malagasy translator.

'They were released because they had not been two months in
Madagascar.'

'Governor say he know nothing about it,' said the translator.

'Does not the governor remember that his officers saw and spoke to
every one of these men on board the *Dryad,* and that when he says he
knows nothing of it he says that which is not true?'

The governor fell silent. Colomb thought it had been a misstep on
the part of the governor and his officers to inspect the runaways, for now
they could not deny knowing the truth. He moved on, politely suggesting
that the entire town was full of people illegally enslaved from across the
Mozambique Channel, and that that there was no way that the governor
did not know this.

Governor Ramasy, animated, denied it. Why should the captain believe
him now?

'Well … it might be,' fumbled the governor's translator, '… possible
that there were newly imported Mozambiques in the town, but the matter
was not before him officially … so to speak.'

Leading him further into the trap, Columb asked, 'Was it not his duty,
this being the case, to afford the illegally held slaves an opportunity for
escape?'

'Well, yes. It was the Queen's orders that no slaves were to be landed.
If any were landed he did not know, but of course they had no business
in the country.'

Columb closed the trap: 'Then no obstacles would be put in their way to escape to our boats?'

The governor hesitated before finally he agreed that there should be no one on the island brought there as slaves since the treaty of 1865, and there could be no cause to stop them leaving.

'If, then, on a certain morning our boats were to lie off the shore,' said Columb, his entire manoeuvre revealed, they 'would not prevent such slaves from escaping to them if they could?'

Now the governor and his secretary spoke at length, agitated. At length they stated that they would not.

'But illegally held slaves could not know what the boats were near the shore for, unless it were announced. The governor must therefore, at a given hour next morning, send round the town and proclaim liberty for the illegally held slaves, who might thereupon be off to the boats before their masters could stop them.'

The governor and his secretary again spoke agitatedly until the secretary translated that the governor would make the proclamation at the appointed hour, would make sure no slave was held back, and would guide the captain around the town afterwards to assure him that all were delivered.

And, Colomb said, until the appointed hour – eight o'clock the next morning – everyone in the room would keep the plan perfectly secret. The Malagasy men agreed.

After that, the five men returned to the others. Diplomatic decorum resumed until the officers took their leave of their hosts. The captain and the others made their way back down the road to the shore and boat, but not all of the party returned to the *Daphne*; Philip Colomb told Saleh bin Moosa to find a place in town to watch events overnight.

The next morning at eight o'clock there were no East Africans on the shore, nor were there any visible in the town. Soldiers from the fort appeared, though, apparently in case any Africans did emerge from the shadows to make a run for the boats. Still, Philip Colomb sent boats near the beach. At one point there was some agitation when it seemed that some Mozambicans had tried to run for the boats, but they were caught by the Malagasy guards.

Soon Bin Moosa appeared and, returned on board, made his way to the captain and reported that around midnight commotion had spread through town. It seemed that word had come from the fort that any illegal slaves found tomorrow – any Africans landed in the town since 1865 – must be given up. For the townspeople, the answer was simply not to allow their illegal slaves to be found. Bustle and hurry spread through the town and the roads soon jammed with slaves being driven into the bush. By daylight the town seemed empty.

It was what Philip Colomb had expected. He had forced the governor to promise justice and faithfulness and the man could provide neither. Colomb chalked it up partly to an inherent deficiency in the Malagasy race; but also to the fact that, whatever the lofty words of the Madagascar government, there were formidable interests there invested in the slave trade and its great profits.

But in a way Colomb was satisfied, having further undermined the security of the market in slaves. *The slaveholders of Majunga,* he reflected, *now look on their property as very insecure.* He could, with what he considered proof, report to his commodore and home government that the Malagasy on this coast were directly complicit in the overseas slave trade. And he had thereby lent a hand to his old shipmate and brother spider, Meara.[5]

PART III

'Sold to slavery, of my redemption thence'

CHAPTER 18

'THE DESPERATE TEMPEST'

The political storm breaks over the squadron

IF COLOMB'S was a moral victory for the squadron and a warning to the slavers at Majunga, it was the last such success it would enjoy; the storm that had so long loomed broke over the squadron in late autumn 1869.

HMS *Daphne*, Bombay harbour, October 1869

The *Daphne* arrived from Zanzibar at midday, a hot breeze blowing from the north and east off the mainland of India. The crew busied themselves with the work of coming into port, cleaning, watering, coaling, with a season of refitting to come. George Sulivan busied himself with the work of leaving his ship and post, the most responsible command of his career, the most powerful ship, a ship he had brought to this ocean from England. He had to make way for *Daphne*'s new captain. Ants, he discovered, had devoured his ornithological specimen, the eagle-skin he collected off the Mozambican coast; only the long, sharp talons remained.

At the squadron's station a captain always had reports to write and correspondence to read; but here Sulivan found more: copies of dispatches and reports that had passed between Bombay and London. They made dire reading. Some suggested that the squadron's interpreters were ignorant or corrupt; others that the squadron's captains flouted their lawful limits and were over-zealous. In one letter, the governor of Bombay argued that a dhow captured carrying slaves on the open sea should have been left alone. His argument was that the ship had been seized outside any waters governed by a treaty between Britain and any local sovereign, but it was owned by an Omani – and Britain had a treaty with Oman that acknowledged the institution of slavery in those lands. Further, the dhow had carried only six slaves, not scores, so the squadron should assume they were not borne for sale, that they were, in the words of government officials, simply 'domestic slaves'. (This category itself – 'domestic slaves' – was offensive to George Sulivan. It was not of the officials' invention, but he felt that they used it to obscure the reality of the slaves' situation. It was a term meant to suggest that the Africans would not, in official opinion, be sold as convenient at the next port.) And, Bombay pointed out, the dhow had been carrying a great deal of cargo.

The dhow had been carrying considerable cargo – what did that have to do with the fact that its captain had made chattel of people, thought Sulivan? Had it not supported the market in slaves? And was there not blood, fire and war at the root of it all on the East African mainland? The enslaved men had been only six, had not been chained, could not be proved to be being carried to market; yet experience showed captains, and sometimes their passengers, made personal speculations in a handful of captives. And years of observations showed that the markets of the Indian Ocean were as often supplied this way as with ships with crammed slave decks.

By custom, captains on the East Indies station received invitations to some of the fine houses on Malabar Hill when they were in port at Bombay. Bankers, successful assurance brokers, railway builders and the upper stratum of the civil service often gathered there at extravagant feasts, since their relative wealth in India was so great. On one occasion, George Sulivan made his way there for supper, passing through streets usually crowded with bullock carts and often countless bales of cotton. He found himself seated near an official familiar with the Vice-Admiralty courts that judged the legitimacy of the Royal Navy's condemnations. They spoke, and Sulivan learned that the man knew of the attention recently drawn to the squadron's captures.

'If we go on condemning these vessels for having only a few slaves on board,' he said, 'we shall be having our supplies cut off again from the interior.' Ivory, always ivory on the mind of Bombay; and in 1868 the supply from the East African interior had been short.

One of George Sulivan's last duties aboard the *Daphne* was to write a final report to Commodore Heath. *I have been led to conclude by many circumstances,* he wrote, *that the suppression of the Slave Trade and the interests of the Indian Government do not coincide. And there is a tendency to sacrifice the slave to the political advantage gained in relation to the chiefs and others of the slave holding tribe.*

They were significant threats, these opinions of Bombay, but George Sulivan hoped they would not be supported by London. *For that would be a step backwards,* Sulivan thought, that would result in undermining hard years of effort on this coast: the commodore's organised efforts and his own work – as a midshipman in *Castor*, as commander in *Pantaloon*, as captain in *Daphne*.

It was a false hope.[1]

Westminster, London, November 1869

On a chilly, cloudy late autumn day, representatives of ministries that most directly oversaw the work of slave trade suppression – the Foreign Office, Admiralty and Treasury – gathered at the Foreign Office. Summoned by Lord Clarendon, the Foreign Secretary, they were to respond to the raft of complaints levelled at Leopold Heath's squadron that had been arriving from the east for months. They would write new instructions for Commodore Heath's squadron, a squadron that – without any directive from London – had overhauled the approach and increased the intensity of anti-slave trade operations in the Indian Ocean.

A series of figures began arriving at Whitehall. There was William Wylde, the man in charge of slave-trade matters at the Foreign Office; there was the Foreign Secretary's first lieutenant, Arthur Otway, with a silvering mane of hair; there was a Royal Navy captain, Henry Fairfax, formerly lieutenant of the *Ariel* with experience hunting slavers from the Cape station. Henry Churchill, consul of Zanzibar, was absent because he had to travelled to Germany to take a cure. There was the stylish young gentleman, Hussey Vivian, senior staff in the Foreign Office and protégé of the Foreign Secretary. In contrast with him, there was the older Henry Rothery, a member of an obscure sect of lawyers practising an ancient body of ecclesiastical and maritime law. Charles Dickens called their society, the Doctors Commons, desperately old-fashioned, a group which 'in the natural course of things would have terminated about two hundred years ago'. The treasury employed Rothery to advise them on slave-trade matters.

The men made their way to Lord Clarendon's rooms, where the smell of tobacco smoke was never far off – in a prior posting to Spain, the Foreign Secretary had acquired the habit of smoking a kind of miniature cigar – and so the meeting began. William Wylde and Henry Rothery took the lead in the proceedings, producing a list of episodes in which the squadron had condemned dhows on evidence that the two ministries agreed was insufficient: there had only been slave fittings on the ships, or, while there had been slaves on board, the Royal Navy commanders could not absolutely prove they were being shipped for sale. And far too often the squadron's ships were claiming that they had no choice but to burn condemned slave ships on the spot. True, various diplomatic staff in the region acting as Vice-Admiralty judges had reviewed and confirmed the condemnations, but they had acted in error. Stricter rules should prevent this.

The committee agreed, of course, that it would like to see the end of the slave trade at some future date once an alternative economy developed. But the primary concern of most of the men in the room was promoting the trust and goodwill of the Zanzibar sultan and his merchant princes.

Otherwise, prestige loss and commerce dampened, the sultan and other rulers might turn to the French.

So the men drew up a list of new procedures for the Foreign Secretary to hand to the Admiralty which, in an inferior position to the other ministries, would have to accept and pass along to Heath. Hussey Vivian volunteered to write a draft to give to Lord Clarendon, though he warned that the hunting season would slow his work.

A few weeks later, with winter descending on London, Lord Clarendon was preparing to send on the committee's report and new naval instructions to India. The Foreign Secretary was approaching seventy and his side-whiskers and most of the sparse hair on his head were mostly white. In this post he had served under three governments and seen revolution in Europe, the Russian War at the Crimea and Baltic, and the Civil War in America. For many years he had worked under just a few guiding principles: maintain the friendship of France while watching her ambitions, expand free trade, and at all costs do not be dragged into war by the hot-headed. For over a year, a Royal Navy squadron on the east coast of Africa had been violating two, perhaps three, of these principles. It was interrupting the free flow of trade directly and, by stirring up trouble, threatened it indirectly. It was both interfering with French business and encouraging Indian Ocean kingdoms to look to the French as chief protectors. If not checked it might lead Britain unwillingly down a blind path to unwanted fighting.

Lord Clarendon was now taking action on this squadron, Commodore Heath's. His committee had duly declared that the squadron was burning ships without sufficient cause, antagonising the rulers of the Indian Ocean, and stated that its official view was that the slave trade would have to be stopped slowly, piecemeal. To put down the trade and institution of slavery, these very Indian Ocean and Arabian Sea rulers would some day have to be called upon to cooperate. These rulers would have to enjoy support from their domestic merchant elite who now felt threatened by the squadron, and whose ships and cargoes had been seized because they carried a handful of slaves. The focus, the committee stated, should be on supervising the legal trade and preparing the economies of the region for eventual abolition, not making all-out war on the institution. This personal war of the squadron was based on a false over-reading of their instructions. No, Britain must not be hasty in pushing towards the abolition of slavery on Zanzibar or a ban on the import of slaves from the coast. *It would deprive the inhabitants of Zanzibar of that labour on which they have hitherto relied for the cultivation of their fields and estates,* the committee stated, *and would most certainly ruin many useful branches of industry which are now springing up on the island.*

The new rules practically forbade seizing a ship on the grounds that slaves were aboard; it must appear to be a significant slaver. The ship then must be taken to a Vice-Admiralty court immediately, even at the cost of ending a mission, unless it could be absolutely proved that it was a physical impossibility for the cruiser to bring it to port.

All satisfactory for the Foreign Secretary. Of course, could he eliminate slavery and the trade with a stroke of his pen from this office he would. But in the real world *the object*, he told himself, *could be purchased at too high a price.* Lord Clarendon had periodically had to cool the abolitionist zeal of diplomatic personnel around the world who had threatened carefully laid arrangements. But he had never had to intervene with a commodore before now. The committee report and new instructions sent off east, the squadron should now be brought to heel.[2]

Along with the report and new instructions, Lord Clarendon ordered another letter to be sent to the Admiralty and Commodore Heath. Two captains of the squadron had, it seemed, taken to freeing slaves. Commanders Colomb and Meara had been accepting escapees from slavery on their ships. Clarendon dictated that the runaways who had made it onto the Royal Navy's decks should have been forcibly returned to their masters. The British ships had each been in the territorial waters of a friendly power. The captains had, he judged, 'deprived the subjects of that power of their lawful property'.

.   .   .

The Somerset ruling of 1772 in a way paralleled the cases of Colomb, Meara and Sulivan refusing to allow escapees to their ships to be returned to their captors. James Somerset, enslaved by a Boston customs agent, was brought to England in 1769 and there fled from his master. Captured again, his owner locked him on a ship bound for Jamaica to be sold as a plantation labourer. Seeing an opportunity to test whether slavery was legal in England, abolitionists took the ship's captain to court for false imprisonment. It was during this trial that barrister Bull Davy famously argued that 'the air (of England) is too pure for a slave to breathe in'. Once in Britain, no one could be a slave, for beside the common idea that Britain was somehow an inherently 'free' place, in contrast to places imagined unfree such as Catholic France or Czarist Russia, there was no legal basis for slavery in England, it having died with the last medieval serf. The defence, meanwhile, argued as Lord Clarendon did in 1869 that slaveholders had the right to have their 'property' restored. Lord Mansfield ruled in favour of James Somerset, and abolitionists used the ruling to wage their war against the trade and institution in the coming decades.

Part of Lord Mansfield's ruling pointed out that 'a foreigner cannot be imprisoned here on the authority of any law existing in his own country', and it was in this sense that Colomb, Meara and Sulivan seemed to feel that they had no obligation to return fugitives to Portuguese or Malagasy authorities. Unless the *Amazons*' decks transmuted into Portuguese Mozambique or Madagascar, the captains would not recognise slavery on their ships. From the commodore down, the squadron's officers understood that British law was in effect on British ships, whether or not those ships were in the territorial waters of a country with legal slavery. Even the aggressive Meara would not allow a runaway who had hidden in his gig drawn up on the beach to be carried to the *Nymphe*; but when the man swam to the *Nymphe* afloat in the harbour, Meara judged it altogether different.

The Foreign Office was concerned with maintaining good relations with slaveholding countries and worried about letting this issue drag Britain into unexpected or deeper commitments. It was not difficult to imagine a situation in which Royal Navy or ships or steamers flying the Union Jack were swamped with runaways. To its official mind, sheltering runaways was like sheltering another country's lawbreakers. There were those, too, whose racial conceptions made them think domestic slavery was an acceptable state for the supposedly less-advanced African. And, as always, the question of where to take refugees was a serious one.

Not long after his return to England, George Sulivan received a letter from the Foreign Office bearing an official rebuke. The Foreign Secretary was displeased over the incident that took place in the harbour of Mozambique Town when Sulivan protected escaped slaves who had fled to the *Daphne*, one of them with a bar fused to his leg. Captain Sulivan, the letter stated, should have handed them back to the man who had come on board to demand their return.[3]

HMS *Dryad*, at sea bound for Bombay, December 1869

As the squadron's new instructions were en route to India, HMS *Dryad* started for the squadron's winter rendezvous at Bombay. A hot wind descended from India to seep over the Indian Ocean. Jib sails at her head and staysail at her mizzenmast, *Dryad* sailed very close hauled to the wind, her screw, meanwhile, boiling the sea.

Philip Colomb was sitting at his round table in the great cabin in the early afternoon, dinner time at sea, when he noticed that his new assistant steward was missing. The work of departing Zanzibar and wrapping up the patrol had kept him too busy to think about the East African boy until now. Colomb questioned one of the stewards.

'Sabourri is sea-sick, Sir. He's been werry sick ever since we come to sea.'

'Oh, is that it? He'll soon get over that. However, I will see him after dinner.'

Sabourri was fourteen years old, a refugee from slavery taken out of a slave ship some years back. An English resident of Zanzibar had adopted him and taught him English and the Bible. Not a week before, the man had approached Colomb at Zanzibar, asking him to employ Sabourri on board the *Dryad* for a spell. He suspected that the boy was inclined to stealing and needed to learn discipline as only a man-of-war could teach. Though he had a pedantic inclination, Philip Colomb did not want to be a schoolmaster; yet he liked the man and really had very little excuse not to take the boy on as the ship was full of them, even from such exotic places as America, and surely had far harder cases than this. Colomb agreed to take the boy on board.

At his first interview with him, the captain took a liking. Colomb chastised himself for being sentimental, but the boy was handsome and soft-spoken. The captain always assessed the intelligence of Africans with whom he dealt – his constant triangulation, like racial reckoning – and he plotted the boy as an intelligent, perceptive sort.

Sabourri did not appear after dinner was cleared away, so the captain made a search himself, leaving his cabin, passing the marine, passing the wheel, and down the steep companionway on the quarterdeck. Colomb was amid the various stores now, and he soon found the boy lying in his steward's storeroom, clearly exhausted from sickness, barely able to look at Colomb. It appeared a debilitating case of sea-sickness such as very often overcame landsmen new to the sea.

When the boy did not recover by supper, Colomb had Dr O'Connor look at him. He did not like Sabourri's appearance. Not seasickness – something else, perhaps a reaction to food. The doctor recommended a hammock in the open air, and one was slung for Sabourri under the forecastle close to the sailor's water closets. The sick berth attendant, John Shilston, stayed with him. Shilston was a thirty-year-old Devonshire man, a capable man; not only capable, Philip Colomb observed when he looked in on them: tender. *Caring as only seen in blue-jackets and women*, thought the captain.

The next evening Colomb hosted the doctor and senior officers for dinner. Daniel O'Connor was good company. A particularly small man, he shared an Irish background with Colomb, though the doctor was of south-western stock and Colomb's people were Dublin patricians. They also shared the experience of war and hardship in Chinese waters. At one point in the supper the doctor was called away by a message from the forecastle; word was that the child was worsening.

The doctor departed and Philip Colomb began to fear the worst, the worst for the child and the worst for the entire crew: a plague on board that might cut scores of them down, a killer that might decimate them before they could reach Bombay, and no hope for them there either. By the time O'Connor returned, the table had been cleared and the captain was alone. John Shilston, the doctor said, had collapsed and now struggled to live. He had gathered from Shilston's messmates that he had been weak and, yes, had diarrhoea – common enough complaints of the sailor in the tropics; but now the doctor and captain knew the truth, the plague that Colomb had feared – it was cholera.

Sabourri was quarantined in his place under the forecastle. A new nurse took John Shilston's place, one of the Kroomen, which could only have swelled their reputation for fearlessness. Colomb and O'Connor made plans for what they would do should a third case of cholera appear, though there was little hope if that came to pass.

The next morning, John Shilston's heart stopped beating. The wind died almost completely away, and Philip Colomb had the drummer beat to quarters. Colomb read prayers, and the body of good John Shilston was committed to the deep. That morning, too, men cleaning the gunner's storeroom discovered a nest of termites. There was an infection in the body of the *Dryad*, and they worked to root it out. In the coming days Philip Colomb and the doctor visited Sabourri frequently. The boy seemed to collapse on himself. He tried to speak but could not, managing once to take the captain's hand.

But Sabourri lived. And cholera did not cut down the crew; there were no more cases. In a little over a fortnight, the lookout raised the lights marking Bombay harbour in the dark before dawn. Dawn itself revealed sisters *Nymphe* and *Daphne* moored in the harbour. All was busy-ness and hurry in the days to come. The *Dryad* docked for extensive refitting and her crew left her to sling their hammocks in a hulk for the time being. Sabourri was housed with a kindly merchant in the port.

At some point, though, the boy left the house and plunged into the living current of the great city. A search was made by the bosun and some hands, but it appeared the Sabourri did not want to be found. And so the boy, having escaped slavery, cholera, and the bosun of the *Dryad*, charted his own course.[4]

HMS *Forte*, Suez, Red Sea, November 1869

In November 1869 Leopold Heath attended the opening of the Suez Canal at Ismailia, Egypt. The opening of the canal, creating a more direct sea route between Britain and India, was of massive importance to the British empire. Maintaining the integrity of this route would be a major responsibility for the Royal Navy's Bombay station, and that meant maintaining peace and security in the Red Sea, Persian Gulf and Arabian Sea. War, piracy and lawlessness were a threat to the flow of trade.

At the ceremony Heath shared a shaded pavilion with some of those who made the world turn: earls, lords, baronets, ladies. The British ambassador to Egypt was there, and the powerful commander-in-chief of the Mediterranean, Sir Alexander Milne (though his deep-draft iron-clad flagship was not, since it, like *Forte*, did not dare enter the canal). Famous British engineers Hawksley and Bateman were there to honour the French engineer de Lesseps. Leaders of the Chambers of Commerce of England and Scotland's industrial and trading capitals stood by. Through this new route would flow their raw cotton from India, tea and silk from China, ivory and cloves from Zanzibar. On a grander pavilion nearby sat a sparkling covey of kings and queens and princes.

After all of the goings-on of speeches, imperial visits and flotillas, Leopold Heath turned his attention to his squadron, and to the storm that had now fully broken over it. He had watched the barometer fall since late spring, since he and his captains had burned more slavers than the station ever had before. Now, he realised that he had been sailing in the eye of a typhoon for a long time without knowing it. London had joined Bombay in scrutinising their actions, and London was not pleased. The Foreign Secretary accused the spiders of burning ships on mere suspicion alone – and repeatedly. Among others, he cited the case of a capture made by Colomb and the *Dryad* that spring, a case in which Philip Colomb had found only one captive on board, a boy of about ten. The child had been an obvious abductee from Zanzibar, speaking no Arabic though the dhow's captain had claimed he was a crewmember, and was most likely a side-spec-ulation of the captain, intended for sale in the Persian Gulf. But the opinion of the Foreign Office was that the word of an African child should not be taken over the dhow captain. The dhow should have been towed to a port to appear before a Vice-Admiralty judge, the ship's captain appearing in order to defend himself, if there was any reasonable doubt about the case.

Heath received a copy of a report from one of the Treasury's lawyers, Henry Rothery, counselling the government that the squadron was running away with its zealotry. Among others, this lawyer cited Edward Meara and the *Nymphe*'s capture of a dhow at Kiswara on the coast in April. There had been six enslaved Africans on board who had told the *Nymphe*'s interpreter that they were to be sold at a port down the coast. But the lawyer wrote that Meara's condemnation of the dhow was a sham. These slaves were the personal slaves of the crew or passengers on the ship, and while they might have reported that they were to be sold on the east coast, this was nonsense: that was like sailing coals to Newcastle, Rothery argued. Slaves sailed east and north from the coast, not south. The slaves were lying, he wrote, to get out of their situation.

Forte sailed down the long Red Sea and across the Arabian Sea to Ceylon, where it picked up supplies at the small dockyard there, then back west to Bombay for the squadron's winter rendezvous. At dawn on New Year's Day she passed past the white Colaba lighthouse with its large Union

Jack flying above and eased to her mooring place in Bombay harbour. She found the sisters *Daphne, Dryad* and *Nymphe* already there.

There Heath found a stack of correspondence from London: letters from multiple ministries, the report by the Foreign Office committee that met to rein in the squadron, a new set of slave trade suppression instructions written by politicians and clerks. New prohibitions, that is, and Heath had the task of telling his captains that they were hamstrung, at best – their campaign against the slave trade, he feared, might be dead.

Two years before he had left Bombay for Abyssinia at the head of an invasion. There he did what he did best: he moved ships and men rationally; followed the most direct route between order and execution; understood his orders and knew to whom he was responsible; had the ships needed to complete his work. As he had waited for the soldiers, marines and sailors to finish their work in the hills of Abyssinia, he had started planning his next campaign, analysing the possibilities of a coherent, consistent anti-slave trade strategy. He thought that he understood his straightforward orders: to fight slavers. He thought he had time to see the fruit of his new strategy, two or three years, perhaps, two or three slaving seasons. But it turned out that he and his captains – dedicated men, energetic men, he believed – had had just one year.

The soft-handed men of officialdom wrote that Heath's squadron was 'inspiring alarm and mistrust' in East Africa and Arabia, wringing their hands. *Good*, thought Heath, let the alarm sound that if you carry slaves on these coasts you risk having your ship burned to the waterline by the Royal Navy. Let slavers look at the horizon with mistrust, fearing that the masts of a British cruiser lay just under it, with your ship boarded, wares taken out and sold, the profits going to reward your foe. He and his men had burned or condemned scores of ships, 10,000 tons of shipping, in a year. They had lifted over a thousand men, women and children from the decks or stinking holds of slavers in 1869 alone. And he was proud.

Leopold Heath knew that the new rules from London would cast a chill on the squadron. More than that, they served notice that its civilian overseers considered the squadron half-lawless, its officers in danger of having their captures and condemnations of cargo overturned, with their personal money on the line. They were in danger of having reprimands placed in the margins of their service records, their careers jeopardised. The new rules, to Heath's mind, were a threat to any officer who showed too much zeal.

And in the days to come the commodore was proved right. Captain Sulivan made his thoughts clear before he left for England. The squadron was being thrust in the pillory, a sign over them, *Thus to any who interfere with the financial interests of India.* While Philip Colomb thought the recriminations from political quarters unseemly and exasperating, especially when the work was as demanding and dangerous as wartime service, the captains on the station agreed that the new rules meant any of them taking slaves out of a ship carrying less than a crammed deck was risking himself and his senior officers. Perhaps they were doing the Africans less than no good, either, given that a Vice-Admiralty judge like Dr Kirk might seek to have freed Africans restored to their abductors.

There were some consolations. Edward Meara could report the success of the *Nymphe* and *Daphne* at Bahrain, with peace restored and a prince amenable to British persuasion installed. This was, perhaps, a good development in their fight against the trade bound for the Persian Gulf. And Heath could give Captain Colomb the news that one of his Kroomen, Jim George, had received a medal from the Royal Humane Society for his rescue of dozens from a beach in May.

Leopold Heath kept his secretary busy, writing back to London, defending his captains against charges of near-renegadism. He warned his superiors what their new guidelines would mean for his efforts against the slave trade, telling them to expect far fewer captures in the future.[5]

CHAPTER 19

'AFTER EVERY TEMPEST COME SUCH CALMS'

News of their work precedes the captains to Britain, to good effect

THEIR TIME on the station up, Meara departed for England in early spring 1870, Colomb late spring, and Heath in the summer, having been successfully checked by the government. Meara and the *Nymphe* had released over 400 people and discovered the illegal captivity of over 200 at Majunga, Madagascar; Colomb had released over 360; Heath released 80, and Sulivan took over 1,000 people out of slave ships in his longer period in the squadron.

Heath was right about what the new rules would mean for the fight against the slave trade. From 1870 the number of the squadron's captures plummeted; while over 1,000 people were removed from slave ships in 1869, only 302 were in 1870, with most of those freed from a single slave ship. In the next two years numerous alleged slavers were absolved and recompensed by Dr Kirk and other judges because captains could not prove the captive Africans on board were being taken for sale. In several instances restitution required delivering people back into a state of slavery.

But what Heath and his squadron did not seem to know was that, while it was being checked, the squadron's campaign made the news back in Britain. The newspapers retold stories of rescues, desperate fights and scenes of misery, often lightly re-working Leopold Heath's official reports to the

Admiralty to look like timely correspondents' dispatches. And making the newspapers was key: from the 1850s the number of cheap newspapers in Britain increased dramatically; the majority of the middle class could read, and the illiterate often had opportunities to hear the newspaper read. Beginning after Sulivan and *Daphne*'s first successful experiment with laying traps at chokepoints in 1868, the squadron made headlines, with stories multiplying greatly after the successes of the full spider's web in spring 1869.

The stories made good copy, with their *Boy's Own* action – sailors clambering over the sides of slave ships to battle villains. And in a period when newspapers began to compete with each other to offer the most provocative images, the stories provided exciting material. In their depictions of *Daphne*'s men boarding a slaver at sea or the crew of the *Nymphe* cutting out a ship in Zanzibar harbour, illustrators let their imaginations run wild so that boardings looked like battles. Stories of the squadron's work included descriptions of the brutalised and starving African kidnapees too: both lurid and genuinely heartrending. The steady stream of stories, often reproduced across many smaller provincial newspapers at the same time and totalling around sixty over three years, seemed to appeal to national pride in both originating the abolition movement and distinguishing what readers thought of as 'the British race' against 'those barbarous and backwards races' that engaged in the slave trade.

Readers' eyes opened to a trade that thrived after the public thought West African trade was crushed, and to the way the British and Indians were either complicit or officially uncaring. This provided an opportunity for critics of the hands-off Gladstone government. Meanwhile, the Anti-Slavery Society spread the word in its publications, reporting on the hobbling of the squadron and on the censuring of his captains for protecting escapees. 'REBUKE TO CAPTAIN SULIVAN', it announced, describing how the Foreign Office reproved the *Daphne*'s captain for rescuing Mozambican runaways. Each story painfully exposed Britain's moral liability in tolerating the legal trade between Zanzibar and the coast opposite.

The force of these reports and criticisms was multiplied by the unexpected discovery that David Livingstone was alive in 1869 and the mission sent to find him in 1871. Livingstone served as a sort of prick to the conscience of the nation, with the *Pall Mall Gazette* writing that he might be disappointed to find that his country had not acted against the trade in his absence but had, in fact, officially looked the other way.[1]

Penny Illustrated Paper, November 1868

The horrible traffic has not yet ceased. It is an exciting chase of a slaver that forms the subject of one of our illustrations. The zealous activity of our jack tars on such an occasion is well depicted. Gratifying it is to think that their zeal has not been thrown away, but that they have succeeded in rescuing a goodly number of slaves from the hands of their barbarous gaolers.

Penny Illustrated Paper, November 1868

SUPPRESSION OF THE SLAVE TRADE ON THE EAST COAST OF AFRICA.

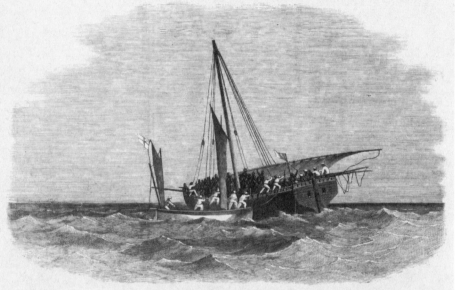

THE CUTTER OF H.M.S. DAPHNE CAPTURING A SLAVE-DHOW OFF BRORA.

ONE of our Engravings represents the running on shore of an Arab slave-dhow, in order to escape capture by H.M.S. Daphne, whose life-boat is seen landing through a heavy surf, in the endeavour to rescue the slaves. The Arabs engaged in the slave trade, when they find escape impossible, prefer risking the lives of the slaves and wrecking their vessel to being captured by a British ship, and many lives are frequently lost in the attempt to run ashore. From the information which our officers have received from liberated Africans, it appears that the Arabs impress upon their wretched slaves the necessity of using their utmost endeavours to prevent themselves falling into the hands of the white men, who, they tell them, are little better than cannibals. On the present occasion only seven little children were rescued, who, when the main body, consisting of about 180 men, women, and children, fled inland, were unable to keep up with them. Our Illustration of this scene shows H.M.S. Daphne in the offing, with two dhows in tow, captured the previous day. A second Engraving represents the capture of one of these by the ship's cutter.

THE FARM.

The *Mark Lane Express* returns of the yield of the white crops for last season show that the average weight and quality of wheat was from 2 lb. to 3 lb. per bushel greater than usual. Out of 528 returns only thirteen are under an average, and 381 are over it. The barley returns are unfavourable, and the bulk of the crop is too thin to be fit for malting, owing chiefly to hasty ripening, especially on the light soils. The oat crop is very bad; and 387 returns out of 490 are under the average. Of these 135 range from one fourth to entire failure. As regards the bean crop, only seventy-three out of 411 returns are an average or over it; and it is noteworthy that the winter beans are all good, while the spring-sown are bad, at least, in those cases where the returns make a distinction. Peas have done better than beans; and 174 returns speak to an average and over, while 229 are under one. Some of the crops were worm-eaten; but, generally speaking, the quality seems to be good. These valuable annual returns, which say a great deal for news-paper enterprise, contrast very favourably with the curious specu-lative tables as to stock and cultivation recently put forth by the Board of Trade.

Mr. W. E. Forster has explained to the House of Commons that the present effect of the Order in Council (which is in force) is that unless sheep arrive in the same vessel as foreign cattle they may be landed at any of the usual ports; and if on examination they are found to be healthy they may be re-moved and sold without restriction. Since Sept. 1 there has been a falling off of 77,494 in the number of sheep imported, as com-pared with the previous corresponding period. The Govern-ment do not intend to accept Lord Robert Montagu's bill; but, from a conviction that legislation is needed, and that it should affect animals suffering under other contagious orders as well as rinderpest, they intend to bring forward a bill of their own.

A memorial is in course of signature among the Shropshire breeders requesting the council of the R.A.S.E. to abolish the inspectors of wool and shearing, in consequence of the dissatis-faction which they are alleged to have given at Leicester. Mr. Horton, on behalf of the breeders of "Shrops;" Mr. Robert Game, for the Cotswold breeders; Mr. Brown, for the Norfolk; and Mr. John Tredwell, for the Oxford Down, are taking a leading part in the movement. The memorial begs the council to invest the judges with full power to decide upon the eligibility of the animals for competition, and asserts that "the practice of inspecting the wool and disqualifying sheep by private parties, whose names are not published as inspectors, is most objectionable, as being at variance with the rules of the society, subversive of the privileges and power that should alone be exercised by the judges, and a system which fails fairly to prevent the evil it is intended to remedy, by its having been known to permit the competition of animals

Illustrated London News, February 1869

THE CUTTER OF HMS DAPHNE CAPTURING A SLAVE-DHOW OFF BRORA

Reading Mercury, September 1869

Letters received from Zanzibar speak of the activity of the slave trade upon the east coast of Africa, and likewise mention the strenuous efforts of her Majesty's cruisers to suppress it. The Arabs have lost a thousand slaves in the last three months ...

Christian Observer, October 1869

So far as the West Coast of Africa is concerned ... the African Slave Trade is a thing of the past. But while this happy result is chronicled concerning the old Atlantic Slave Trade, the annual reports of our Consul at Zanzibar, and the despatches of the naval officers in command of the few vessels which form the East African Squadron, tell a very different story. ... From these reports ... we learn some particulars of the ... evils and misery inflicted on that hapless land.

Morning Post, October 1869

Convictions as to the safety of Dr Livingstone have now been confirmed by the intelligence received only a few days since from Bombay.

... The motives which chiefly induced him ... consisting in the ardent desire cherished by the great traveller to continue his crusades against the slave trade still extensively carried on in the south-eastern districts and to follow up the important discoveries made by the late captain Speke and his comrade Major Grant.

Penny Illustrated Newspaper, December 1869

A BLOW FOR FREEDOM

Our Jack Tars are happily engaged in no war with the enemies of their native land, but they have this year struck more than one good blow against the inhuman slavers who still carry on their infamous trade on the east coast of Africa. The crew of her majesty's ship *Nymph*, Captain Meara, have in particular distinguished themselves.

Mission Life, January 1870

One thousand slaves have been liberated during the last three months, and the dhows containing them have been destroyed. ... In the meantime, we trust that some of the entanglements at present surrounding the question (and also our efforts) may be swept away, and that the attention which our Government has centred on the abominable slave trade, as it exists in the Sultan of Zanzibar's dominion, will not prove abortive.

Western Times, May 1870

ABORIGINES PROTECTION SOCIETY – The thirty-fourth annual meeting of this society was held on Wednesday evening at the London Tavern. Sir Charles W. Dilkie, Bart., M.P. presided. Mr. F.W. Chesson, the secretary, read the annual report. ... Sir T.F. Buxton, Bart., in moving the adoption of the report urged that vigorous measures should be adopted for the suppression of the Zanzibar slave trade, for which purpose it was our right and duty to interfere.

Pall Mall Gazette, May 1871

We shall rejoice to welcome Dr. Livingstone back to England; but we fear that the traveller's own joy will be somewhat impaired on learning that during his lengthened absence little of nothing has been done in the matter he has most at heart. The slave trade on the east coast of Africa flourishes in spite of the numerous despatches that have passed between the English Government and its representative at Zanzibar. It is true that we have a treaty with the sultan, but by one of its articles we have bound ourselves not to interfere with domestic slavery.

Anti-Slavery Reporter, July 1871

BRITAIN A PARTICIPANT IN THE SLAVE-TRADE

Is this to be the lamentable result of our long and arduous agitation on behalf of outraged humanity – that Great Britain shall, in this era of civilisation, be stigmatised before the nations as a co-partner with Zanzibar in this infernal work of making merchandise of our fellow-men?

Anti-Slavery Reporter, July 1871

Restricted in powers, and discouraged in their work, some of our best officials in those slave-holding and slave-trading regions seem to have lost some patience and almost all hope of witnessing the extinction of the accursed system.

We hope, however, that the Committee of the House of Commons on the East African Slave-trade may prove the commencement of a new and effective system of British legislative action. We are persuaded that the national sentiment and will on this point are unchanged; and publicity will materially aid in forming and calling forth such an unequivocal expression of this that willing statesmen will be encouraged, and reluctant statesmen be compelled, to take decisive action in the matter.[2]

The presiding government of the day, William Gladstone's, was of the school that looked to commerce, Christianity and civilisation to eventually starve the slave trade. Besides, even Leopold Heath and other supporters of strong measures admitted that at their best the Royal Navy only diverted a fraction of those carried to sale from slavery. So why, multiple Liberal ministers asked, spend so much money on the blockade and the Zanzibar consulate? In its advice to Gladstone, the Treasury cited the expense of the Royal Navy presence, but also cautioned what success would require. Was Britain prepared to be a solo police force on that coast since, as it appeared, the USA and Europe were unwilling to join the effort? And if the sultan of Zanzibar and other regional rulers absolutely refused to shut down their slave markets, asked the Treasury, was Gladstone's 'government prepared to reduce their territories to the condition of the protected states of India, or to go even further, and absolutely annex them'? Would justice be purchased through the expansion of the British empire?

Yet in 1871 abolitionists in Britain managed to secure parliamentary hearings on the East African slave trade. Between news of the spider squadron's success and overriding, Livingstone's rediscovery, and the ways that the abolitionists used both, the Gladstone government felt it risked public agitation getting out of control. Best to reduce pressure on itself and make the abolitionists in parliament take responsibility for what the government considered an expensive and complicated predicament. So, with its abolitionist chairman and a number of sympathetic members on it, the committee began collecting testimony in summer 1871.[3]

Westminster, London, July 1871

Since the end of his assignment in the East Indies, Leopold Heath had been given a new task, joining a group of officers considering the possibilities of torpedoes for port defence. Now he entered the Palace of Westminster, stepping in from the cloudy day, almost cool. MPs were preparing to go home for the summer, but both chambers would be busy later today. He found the committee room and took a seat within; twelve MPs were already there.

There was the Quaker reformer Charles Gilpin behind a great brown beard, a driving political force in securing the Select Committee. The bald, stout Arthur Kinnaird, Scottish evangelical clergyman and long-time abolitionist. George Shaw-Lefevre, shrewd-looking, recently made Secretary to the Admiralty, and the Prime Minister's protégé Lord Cavendish. Sir John Hay, a fellow veteran of the Russian War at the Crimea, a handsome man under his angular brown beard. Chairing the hearing, Russell Gurney, judge and MP for Southampton, possessing the aquiline nose correct for a judge, in his late sixties, but his dark wavy hair and side-burns only beginning to grey.

At one o'clock the hearing began. First summoned was Major-General Rigby, a former Zanzibar consul who had spent most of his life in India and Aden and spoke eight languages. He had worked against the slave trade diligently during his time in Zanzibar, but had limited means. He had reported to the East India Company, whose efforts against the trade were paltry. He had no squadron backing him and little support politically. He had successfully – at least for a time – stopped slaveholding among the British Indian merchants in Zanzibar and on the coast, and freed several thousands from the state of slavery. Leopold Heath could not hear everything that was said, but General Rigby predictably argued for the total and immediate halting of the trade by whatever means necessary.

In the middle of the afternoon Heath was called forward. The chairman spoke. Russell Gurney had a quiet air, but his dark eyes showed intelligence. 'You had the command of the squadron on the East African coast?' So the interview began. Questions followed about the suitability of the ships on the station. Heath told them that the *Amazons* had done their job well. Then questions about his tactics. Heath told them about his spider's web. Questions about their rate of success.

'No matter how many ships you have,' said Heath, 'there will of course always be some vessels which escape being boarded. It is quite possible that though we boarded 400 dhows during the season I have spoken of, there may have been 400 others that passed outside us.'

More questions about numbers of slavers that must evade capture.

'You regard that as an unsatisfactory result of all our national efforts for the suppression of the slave trade?'

'Very unsatisfactory.'

Now questions turned to potential solutions to the trade from the East African coast. If even the most diligent squadron could not stop perhaps half of all slavers, what then?

Lord Cavendish spoke. His features were as soft as Russell Gurney's were honed. 'You said you were for some time on the west coast of Africa?'

'We obtained possession of the port of Lagos, did we not?' asked Lord Cavendish.

'Yes, I was there at that time.' Some weeks after Heath's nightmare raid on the town, the navy made a second, more organised assault. While this time not a rash attack, it still cost fourteen lives, with over sixty hurt – maimed men and boys, from midshipmen to marines to Kroomen to commanders.

'Had that a great effect?'

'I think that it has had a very great effect indeed. It has been a great encouragement to legitimate trade, and I should anticipate the same sort of result from taking possession of the government of Zanzibar.'

'You think no efforts of our cruisers are likely to be productive of great success till the transport of domestic slaves is prohibited?'

'That is my opinion.' The legal trade hid the illegal while the civilian overseers further hampered their efforts.

Finally, Lord Cavendish asked, 'Do you think the sultan would consent to the entire prohibition of all movement of slaves between the coast and the island of Zanzibar?'

'He certainly would not do so willingly.'

'You think pressure might be applied to him that might oblige him to consent?'

'I think you have only to say what you want and you will have it done,' replied Heath.

More questions followed, but it was growing late and the Commons was sitting that evening. The committee asked Leopold Heath to return for another sitting.

At the next, there were more questions about tactics, then about relations between the sultan of Zanzibar and the Persian Gulf sultans. Their approach was academic, never hounding. They seemed to sympathise with the challenge the commodore had faced with limited resources. Still, they asked about the criticism his captains had received from political authorities around the Indian Ocean and in London. Heath rose to the defence of his officers, but managed to control his temper, a temper that sometimes revealed itself in his letters to the Admiralty.[4]

None stoked that temper like Henry Rothery, the Treasury's legal advisor on the slave trade. Leopold Heath thought him stupid at best, and quite possibly a perjurer in his condemnations of the squadron. In his letters to the Admiralty, Heath wrote that Rothery had a personal basis for his critiques of the squadron's tactics; Rothery, in turn, called Heath 'insolent and arrogant' in his memos. Heath called Rothery's findings 'arbitrary' and 'irregular' in his letters. Rothery was one of the men behind the committee that issued the new instructions for the squadron at the end of 1869, helping to stop the squadron's work by essentially halting any captures except those of very heavily laden slavers, requiring that most slavers be towed to one of a few ports for adjudication or be at dire risk of being overturned.

Henry Rothery sat in this room at this very moment. Leopold Heath's second interview over, Rothery was called forward.

'You are legal adviser to the Treasury in all matters relating to the slave trade?'

The committee asked him about the functioning of the Admiralty courts around the Indian Ocean, about where he thought Africans taken from slavery should be settled, about prize money and bounties, and about the abuses that Rothery alleged.

'The Admiralty instructions issued in 1870 were drawn up in consequence of reports made by you?'

'Yes.' Rothery explained how the squadron had overstepped its bounds and how it was necessary to keep a closer eye on it; he hinted that the captains on the station indulged in wilful ignorance of the rules for the purpose of playing pirate.

'We had no idea that the officer commanding could have so misapprehended his instructions. The instructions are entitled, "Instructions for the Suppression of the Slave Trade," and not of "slavery,"' Rothery said. Perhaps, he suggested, it was because of some kind of fanaticism.

'I may mention another instance which led to the issue of those instructions,' he said. 'One of our officers captured a vessel, and brought the slaves – the slaves being domestic slaves – to Zanzibar; Dr Kirk or Mr Churchill said that the vessel was undoubtedly a legitimate trader, but that officer, notwithstanding that the vessel was restored, carried off the slaves to the Seychelles.'

'In your opinion is it exceedingly important that every protection should be given to honest trade there?'

'I think it should be encouraged in every possible way,' said Rothery.

'I presume it is to the increase of legitimate trade that we may look, more than anything else, for the suppression of the slave trade?'

'I should have thought entirely.'[5]

The next day Commander Colomb took his seat.

'You were employed for some considerable time on the east coast of Africa in the suppression of the slave trade?'

'Yes.'

Sir John Hay, the retired captain, asked him practical questions about the right ships for the duty, about how long officers should work on the station, about their preparation.

'Did you find great difficulty owing to the fact that the home trade in slaves at Zanzibar being legal, the foreign slave trade to the Persian Gulf was able, under the cover of that, to evade the action of the cruisers?'

'I think that made the greatest difficulty. I think that threw a great barrier in the way of dealing with the trade about Zanzibar. I think the whole state of things would be altered if all slave trade to and from Zanzibar were made illegal.'

'Do you think it possible to stop it altogether by naval operations so long as that mode of evading it is open to the Arab dhows?'

'No, but I should say that I doubt whether it would be possible to stop it altogether by any forcible measures. I think the stoppage of it altogether must be done by dealing with the authorities at the ports of debarkation by means of treaties.'

'Would you anticipate any great advantage from treaties?'

'Yes, because I think when armed with a treaty the naval force can act more efficiently. The treaty does not act so much directly as indirectly by keeping the people in fear. I would not trust altogether to the moral force of treaties in those cases, but treaties give the naval officers a great deal more power than they otherwise would have.'

More questions: about the fate of captives on the overseas trip; about where best to post patrols; about allegations that the squadron precipitously burned dhows.

The Scottish evangelical Kinnaird asked, 'Was there any commendation for, or special notice taken of, activity on the part of any of the officers commanding the cruisers?'

'My own experience is that it was a little the other way.'

'You thought that no encouragement was given you?'

'I speak, of course, of what happened to myself. I had one or two letters from the Foreign Office which were not commendatory, but the reverse.'

'So that there was rather discouragement than encouragement, in putting down the slave trade?'

'So far as my experience goes.'

Questions followed about the hard future ahead of people taken out of slave ships, then about whether slavers might evade a stronger naval force by going overland to the north.

'Is there anything further which you wish to state to the committee?' asked Sir John Hay.

'I should like to mention that there is a trade to Madagascar which is still in a more or less flourishing state.'

Colomb had noticed that the committee members focused all their questions on the trade permitted by treaty between the mainland and Zanzibar, and the smuggling trade to the north. They had kept their hands off the matter of the trade between Mozambique and Madagascar – where both the Portuguese and Malagasy were supposed to have made it illegal.

The committee indulged Colomb in letting him describe this trade for a few minutes, but no more. It seemed as if they didn't want to touch it. Perhaps the politicians found the matter too fraught – a tangle of international relations. The traffic across the Mozambique Channel was closely tied up with the French and the Portuguese and their trade in *engagés* from Portuguese colonial lands or Madagascar. The French, too, were openly covetous of Madagascar, their sugar islands surrounding the great island; aggravating the Malagasy might drive them into the welcoming arms of the French. The traffic in the enslaved to the north involved Zanzibaris, Omanis, Persian Gulf adventurers and Swahili blockade-runners. It was a situation in which the 'enemy' was easily distinguished by race and religion and neatly set in opposition to the side of 'good'. For whatever reason, the Select Committee turned Colomb from the subject, then dismissed him.[6]

CHAPTER 20

'MAY THE WINDS BLOW TILL THEY HAVE WAKEN'D DEATH!'

The last effort to compel Zanzibar

Cheltenham, England, July 1871

AS HIS FORMER COMMODORE AND shipmate appeared before members of parliament in July 1871, Edward Meara became a father for the first time. He married less than a month after arriving back in England, and his wife had now given birth to a daughter here in his new home, Clarence House, Imperial Square, Cheltenham, an elegant villa with a broad garden square in front of it and a staff of servants.

At forty years old, Edward Meara set aside one life and began another, with trips to Bath and seaside resorts, patronising charities and attending balls. He was on half-pay, but wealthy from his father's estate and his wife's. He had been schooled at Cheltenham College in his early teenage years, so coming to Cheltenham was something of a return, and it all meant something of a return to being a gentleman's son.

And it was something of a turning away from his past twenty years in the Royal Navy, where he had spent long days and nights in West African creeks clouded with mosquitos, where he had seen terror and death – towns in flame and icy wrecks and William Mitchell's life's blood leaving him on board *Nymphe* in Zanzibar harbour.

He was still occasionally badgered by the Admiralty and Treasury, directed to refund prize money because a capture was judged not to be a slaver, and to explain himself for refusing Dr Kirk's order to re-enslave several Africans.

He had recently been called upon to explain his refusal to Consul Kirk so, sitting in Clarence House one day, Edward Meara took up pen and paper and wrote. *With reference to that part of Dr. Kirk's letter stating that I refused to give up the slaves after the decision of the court,* he stated, *I beg to state that I certainly did.* Then, not reaching far for a justification, he wrote, *For in the evidence of the slaves, they were slaves.* It was the response of one who did not feel he had to explain himself because he believed in the fundamental justice of his actions. And because he was about to retire.[1]

Flushing, Cornwall, summer 1871

Meanwhile, George Sulivan was at his mother's home in Flushing, Cornwall, a village that looked across the harbour to the busy quays of Falmouth. It was a modest house on narrow St Peter's Road, which rose gently round the peninsula. The view was all water, shipping, sky.

In the house with him was his much older sister, two young maids and his mother, Henrietta, now eighty years old. Her health was failing, but her eyes were still clear. His mother had carefully tended his morality as he grew up in the form of an elementary code of conscience and justice, paired with the plainest Christian observance and aversion to sectarianism. She had spent long years worrying over him and his brother, a decorated veteran of the Russian War, a long-time shipmate of Mr Charles Darwin, whose book had made such a stir. She worried for their safety and for their integrity and conduct, but was not a worrier. A forceful character, she had been the daughter of a man rich with Spanish prize money, then she had been the daughter of a bankrupt man; she did not complain, just adjusted. She was wise enough to worry about her sons' tact as religious nonconformists in the political arena of the Royal Navy, and wise enough to counsel a young Midshipman Sulivan that though their family carefully

observed the Sabbath, he did not profane it by following orders and performing his duties on that day.

For now, she had both of her remaining sons on dry land, safe: one
made post-captain and one retired with a knighthood. Though some of
her children already lay in the family vault, the sailors in her family had
been lucky. Her father, a companion of Nelson and Cockburn, had died
retired on land at seventy-six, having very happily spent his hoard of prize
money. Her husband had battled the French, Spaniards and Americans in
the same wars, and he had died at home, in Flushing, at seventy-seven,
without the slightest whiff of gunpowder in the air, without shot at his feet
in the cold ocean.

George Sulivan was made a post-captain, but on shore with half pay. He
had ascended to that place so long coveted, but now was fit for even fewer
postings, fit only for the heavyweights of the Royal Navy. The Sulivan
name evoked respect and kindness in that corner of Cornwall, but of all
the spiders, Sulivan had the least wealth and fewest connections. He had
prize money from his captures, modest bounties, but no one ever became
really wealthy from slave bounties. Colomb, Meara and Heath had family
fortunes, incomes, rents, office. Sulivan was connected, but only to naval
forefathers, siblings, cousins, nephews. So he waited. He could not know
whether a posting would come tomorrow, or whether he had seen his last
command.[2]

Westminster, London, May 1872

The next spring, Philip Colomb was speaking at a Pall Mall club for officers
of Britain's various military services, an elegant building with an Athenian
façade, columns and a suitably martial frieze.

'At least one-third of the cost of the candles for those ships may be
saved, while the ships themselves will be much better lighted,' said Philip
Colomb to the assembled men. 'But if not better lighted, we can give

them one-third more light than is now allowed them, without calling upon Government for more money.'

He was presenting a paper on more efficient lanterns for Royal Navy ships with greater lighting power, cleaner burning, and safer.

As he had for years, Colomb was studying new technologies and techniques; not shying from the general conservatism of the Royal Navy; free with his critiques. And he had the spreading success of his signal system on which to stand. Lighting ships was not Philip Colomb's primary study, though; the Admiralty had him working on a set of plans for coordinated fleet manoeuvres. Now that all ships-of-the-line were fitted with steam propulsion, they were capable of precise movement in almost any weather – if they could keep their boilers fed; so Colomb was tasked with creating a common guide for these, with patterns for attack and defence under varying conditions. It was the natural outgrowth, too, of the increasing adoption of his plan for flashing-light codes which allowed greater coordination at night.

But along with all this, Philip Colomb's mind was still on the slave trade. After putting in his hours on his appointed task for the Admiralty, he worked on a book. He had scribbled in a journal when time allowed since the start of his commission in the *Dryad* and now he was assembling these snippets, elaborating and adding. George Sulivan shared some of the photographs that he had taken aboard *Daphne* with him, and the sprightly Lieutenant Henn shared some of his drawings.

The time was ripe. The public was now well aware of the trade on the east coast. Not quite a year ago, he and his commodore had appeared before the House of Commons committee. There followed a constant calendar of abolitionist meetings on the subject and Colomb wanted to contribute to the work of keeping the matter in the public eye. He wrote, always careful to present his story coolly, dispassionately; careful not to look like a hot-headed abolitionist, but engaging in an exercise in dispassion.[3]

Surrey, England, March 1873

Anstie Grange, a grand house of red brick and mellow stone on a hilltop above the Weald in Surrey: Leopold Heath had built the house ten years before when he was employed studying gun developments at the Royal Arsenal. His father was a lawyer, printer, ultimately a judge, and wealthy in land; so Leopold Heath was wealthy by inheritance. He had hardly built Anstie Grange on a mere captain's pay.

But Heath was no longer a captain, he was now an admiral. With the retirement of another since Heath returned from the Indian Ocean, Leopold Heath had received his flag, the blue flag of a rear admiral. He was then fifty-four years old. That was two years ago, and he still did not have a commission – the head of a foreign station, a great ship of the line, perhaps a port.

He moved constantly between Anstie Grange and London to the northeast, attending to financial business, going to shareholder meetings and royal affairs in gold epaulettes. The government approached him, introducing the idea of joining the Board of Admiralty. That would require a parliamentary contest and a descent into party politics – an unwelcome thought. He declined.

After years in the Indian Ocean he had rediscovered his family, and he found that he liked to spend time with them: his wife with whom he liked to take long walks and go up to London to see art, and his seven children. When he had left for Bombay his eldest boy Artie was just thirteen, now he was over sixteen and Heath began to take his adulthood seriously, speaking to the boy at length about his future, explaining the operations of the estate to him, speaking with patience and describing things carefully. He played chess with him and the younger children, competing hard with the older boys and losing only rarely.

Teenage Arthur even attempted a serious philosophical discussion with his father, guided, apparently, by the writings of Herbert Spencer. Heath admitted to his son that he had not read him. Arthur argued something out of Spencer's book about how men's striving for selfish advantage was the great mover of society. Leopold Heath tried to dissuade his son of the idea, and hoped he succeeded.

Recently, Queen Victoria herself had made known her support for a complete halt of the slave trade by sea on the east coast – a sign that Gladstone's government was becoming serious about the matter. And Leopold Heath publicly supported the abolition of the trade, too. But would it have to do so by force? Perhaps the way that a young Commander Heath had tried under a terrorising fire at Lagos, his shipmates killed right beside him?

Finally came the decision. The months had turned to years, and still no commission. If one came now it meant more years away from his family and his expanding interests in the business world in the City. No, it was unlikely now that Heath could advance in rank on the active list, and he shared the sense of most fellow Royal Navy officers that treading water was unseemly. It was time.

One morning he came downstairs and found his family at breakfast – all there, healthy, cared for. Only a few years ago he and the hands of the *Forte* had lifted stiff, skeletal bodies out of a slave ship, the bosun rigging a cradle for a motherless infant and trying to find a way to feed her. Leopold Heath came downstairs to tell his family of his retirement. He would stay with them.[4]

The 1871 Select Committee before which Heath and Colomb appeared issued a report strongly favouring ending the trade. The committee concluded that the trade between Zanzibar and the coast opposite – a trade left legal by Britain's treaty with the sultan – made it too difficult to police the trade to distant ports. It provided cover for slavers to operate and too often captives first taken to Zanzibar were ultimately carried off across the sea – a point Heath and Colomb had argued. Because of that fact, the seaborne trade must be completely stopped – now, not after many years of the gradual workings of the invisible hand.

The question was how to accomplish this. In 1870, Mejid bin Said died and his brother Barghash assumed the throne. His health recovered, Consul Henry Churchill had returned to Zanzibar to convince the new sultan there to halt the trade. He had been rebuffed, the sultan pleading that if he halted the trade the rich men who relied on it would see him killed or overthrown. It would take work to get the sultan to close his market and halt the trade in his waters. Money, some other bargain, perhaps even direct force. That remained to be seen.

The wheels of parliament moved slowly and there was no immediate plan. And public pressure lessened right after the Select Committee reported in favour of action because the slave trade was thrown from the headlines by a new sensation – a story having to do with the CSS *Alabama*, the ship the *Amazons* were designed to defeat. The United States had taken the United Kingdom to court since the *Alabama* was built in a British shipyard before proceeding to sink over fifty American ships. At stake was the relationship between the countries which had been badly strained during the American crisis and questions about British sovereignty.

But savvy abolitionist politicians took up the matter of the East African slave trade and, armed with the Select Committee's endorsement for action, they set off on a tour of public meetings to agitate for government action.

As he waited for a commission, George Sulivan decided, like Philip Colomb, to write a book about his experiences fighting the slave trade. Other veterans of the squadron, too, were writing letters to the editor, articles, pamphlets, and publishing drawings in the newspapers. George Sulivan had seen them, and knew the power that the rediscovery of Livingstone had contributed, knew the good work his commodore and Captain Colomb had done at Westminster. He had read about the growth of a movement to take action against the trade on the east coast, a series of public meetings led by prominent abolitionist politicians. So he would prod, too: show the fire and murder at the base of the trade, the obliteration of families, the cruelty of the slave carriers, the hypocrisy and inhumanity of governments all around the Indian Ocean. He had the photographs he had taken of starving children lifted out of slave ships. He had a drawing of a dhow collapsing in the surf on the beach, bodies tumbling out of it.[5]

Hawarden Castle, northern Wales, November 1872

Prime Minister William Gladstone was at his estate in northern Wales, a great pale-stoned manor house surrounded by a park, brook and wood. He was composing a note to his Foreign Secretary in Westminster. It had to do with the East African slave trade matter.

Gladstone had been dragged into the thing. It really was not his preoc-cupation, but the passion of those somewhat distasteful radicals his Foreign Secretary called 'the Anti Slave Trade People', those like Arthur Kinnaird, who had compelled a parliamentary committee on the matter; Kinnaird, whom Gladstone's Foreign Secretary considered rather self-important. He and many others had shepherded an outcry among the people so that finally Gladstone's government had been obliged to promise action in the Queen's Speech last year. It was his Foreign Secretary's opinion that the matter had become a potential weapon for the opposition in parliament.

The Prime Minister was certain that he was no less sorry for the plight of the slaves than the next man, though he was sure he was not one of those, as he called them, 'negrophilists' who would sacrifice the lives of white men to save black. After all, those blacks were, to his mind, a less developed race and of lower capacity. Besides, maintaining squadrons to fight slavers cost money, tax money, and taxes were the bane of commerce; and commerce was the surest way to put down slavery, commerce must eventually insinuate itself into the depths of Africa creating alternatives to the trade in slaves.

But today, pushed by public opinion and the opposition he and his cabi-net were experiencing, he wrote to the Foreign Office. He was working out the details of whom to send to Zanzibar to deal with the sultan, the powers to give that representative, the terms they should lay before the sultan. It seemed that they had landed on a man to send, Sir Henry Bartle Frere, who had great experience in those parts and was a favourite of the abolitionists.

Frere began his career as an agent of the East India Company and rose to become the governor of Bombay and the new British government of India. Exceptionally, he was a longstanding opponent of the slave trade in the Indian Ocean. He retired from his governorship in 1867 but was still closely involved in Indian Ocean matters, especially active in publicising the ongoing slave trade in those waters. He even mounted a speaking tour after the 1871 Committee hearings at which Heath and Colomb testified did not result in immediate action by the government.

Sending Frere would appease the stirred-up 'Anti Slave Trade People', but Gladstone wrote that he was quite uneasy about using force to end the trade. And he wrote about his concern that forbidding the traffic in *any* Africans between the coast and Zanzibar might be rather too harsh. Wouldn't this, he worried, interfere with what were called 'bona fide' needs for slave labour not destined for a slave market?[6]

Just before the Gladstone government sent its envoys to Zanzibar to negotiate the closure of the slave trade, Sulivan's and Colomb's books were published. They were widely reviewed in newspapers and periodicals, praised from the *Athenaeum* to the *Pall Mall Gazette* to the *Westminster Review*. Reviewers compared them to *Uncle Tom's Cabin*, called them powerful without being over-wrought. The specifically abolitionist press celebrated both books for how they were maintaining the public's interest in the matter. They were frequently both commended for their use of woodblock transcriptions of photographs which, reviewers wrote, did more than mere words to drive home the brutality of the trade. Indeed, one of the images from Sulivan's book, that of a skeletal little boy, accompanied advertisements for abolitionist rallies.

Then the British mission headed by Sir Henry Bartle Frere was off, its movements and progress related in the newspapers. A few weeks before, they reported that the party had arrived in Aden, then Zanzibar and a grand reception by the sultan. But recently there had been more discouraging news: that the sultan had said that he was powerless to stop the trade, that those who profited from it would see him killed before he agreed to halt it; reports that the merchants of Zanzibar had pled with the mission that halting the slave traffic would ruin the Zanzibar economy.

The new sultan, Barghash, needed to be forced if he was to keep his throne. Frere, acting largely of his own accord, agreed to force him, tearing up the old treaty allowing the transport of captives between the coast and the island. The Royal Navy presence on the coast, including the now-veteran *Daphne*, blockaded Zanzibar and the sultan's coastal ports. It stopped the island's merchant shipping, embargoing everything but American and European merchants, and the Royal Navy unleashed pent-up frustration over being hamstrung by the fine points of the legal vs. illegal trade.

It was the kind of unilateral strong-arm action and commitment that William Gladstone had wanted to avoid – especially for the sake of 'mere' Africans. But the blockade worked. The newspapers at home published the news with pride: facing such power and blockade, the sultan capitulated. The slave market on Zanzibar was closed, the importation of Africans to Zanzibar banned, the trade by sea in the waters of the sultan illegal. The sultan of Muscat at the mouth of the Persian Gulf agreed too, and banned the trade in his waters. Consul Henry Churchill's effort to keep Indian Zanzibaris from holding slaves – once halted by the Bombay government – was now enforced. The Frere mission and Royal Navy promised the total ruin of the rich men of Zanzibar far more directly than the elimination of the slave trade, and it had worked.[7]

CHAPTER 21

'HERE IS MY JOURNEY'S END'

A return that marks the beginning of the end

Falmouth, Cornwall, June 1873

Before leaving Zanzibar, the Bartle Frere mission had interviewed Royal Navy officers on the spot asking how a ban on the slave trade might be enforced. They had told them that a base of operations would be needed at Zanzibar, a large ship equipped with many boats, some steam-powered, and a great store of supplies, good medical accommodations, a large crew and an experienced leader.

And so, in early summer 1873, the commission came. George Sulivan had a ship, a posting like none other in the world, and the fulfilment of a mission that had occupied him since he was a midshipman.

He was to prepare to meet the mammoth HMS *London* in Plymouth. She was a 72-gun second rate with two ranks of gun ports, two rows of stern windows, a wide poop deck and forecastle, over two hundred feet long and with 260 sailors and marines. *London* was almost as old as he was, a veteran of Sebastopol in the Russian War. In truth she was a giant of a bygone era, though she had been refitted with steam engines. But she was no cruiser: her role was to be the centre of operations, a stationary headquarters in Zanzibar harbour and a carrier for large and capable boats. And so George Sulivan, who had begun his work on the east coast of Africa over twenty-three years before in cramped midshipman's berths, would return in a ship only slightly smaller than HMS *Victory*. His great cabin would be roomier than his mother's house.

His mother Henrietta learned the news of the success at Zanzibar and of her son's commission to return to his work there, but now she could rest assured that her son would not be the one running up malarial rivers after dug-in slavers. While her youngest boy's mighty command was fitting out alongside a jetty at Plymouth, she departed this life.

HMS *London*, Zanzibar harbour, November 1874

London sailed from Plymouth via Madeira, Rio de Janeiro and the Cape to her new station. It was late equatorial November when George Sulivan and his great ship approached her new home, the wide harbour of Zanzibar, sounding and sounding again on the approach. The wind picked up quickly and she shortened sail. Finally, finding herself in 60 feet, she dropped anchor. The sleek new gunboat HMS *Rifleman* was there to greet her, and

HMS *London* in Zanzibar Harbour, 1881

the light two-gun *Nassau*, whose shallow draft would allow her to patrol the bays of the coast. Sulivan's *Daphne* had been busy over the summer and autumn stalking the seas around Zanzibar to enforce the treaty. She, too, would appear in the harbour in the coming months.

Soon Sulivan ordered the 21-gun salute to the new sultan, Barghash, and paid his respects in the chequered hall. Then the captain settled down to work; he had to rig a hospital and machine shop on board and set up a forge. He was going to need more men, ideally Kroomen, and more senior officers for leading boat patrols. He needed to write to the Admiralty as soon as possible. The new treaty and the arrival of the *London* would not end the slave trade on this coast. To bring about that end he needed to keep *London* focused on Zanzibar.

In November 1874 a great ship sailed into Zanzibar harbour. Its captain had been mocked in this very place by slavers eight years before as he stood helpless on the much smaller deck of HMS *Pantaloon*. But no longer; there were no slavers here anymore.

There were no slavers to be seen under the sun, at least. And the captain of the great *London* was here to keep it that way and follow them into the shadows. The trade was no longer legal, but it was not ended. The captain was there to end the beginning and begin the end. Many years of work lay ahead for Sulivan and his successors working at Zanzibar, but that beginning would not have been made without the focus and commitment of Leopold Heath, the efforts and blood sacrifice of the squadron, and the abolitionists at home who used their stories to force action in the face of those who wanted to wait for the slow workings of free trade.[1]

HMS *Castor*'s pinnace, Mozambique Channel, November 1849

A small sailed boat detached from the 36-gun HMS *Castor* was patrolling for slavers off the coast of Africa in the Mozambique Channel. It was deep night with no moon, though stars dimly lit the sea, quiet. The narrow boat was moving slowly up the coast on its way to the next river, the next village to hunt. Only the young man – boy, really – at the stern, Sulivan, the midshipman, was awake. The others curled in corners or on the hard planks, sleeping. Nothing but an occasional flutter of the sail or ripple of water from the cat's-paw breeze broke the silence.

Now something drew his attention to the coast, about two miles away across the dark. The heavens above it lit up, again and again. Soon lightning poured over the entire coast in a cascade, illuminating that world over the water almost without ceasing. It was like nothing that he had ever seen before. Delirious light – supernatural, rapturous light – over Africa. And yet all silent: no rumble of thunder, no rain, reached him.

He watched for hours, never tiring of it, though after watching so long his eyes were dazzled. He thought of God. And in the awe, the elation, he felt God. It was a show of raw Godly power over Africa. *This* was where to look for God – not in stained glass or priestly prattle. And he remembered then how it was said that the Creator, with all the elemental power of nature, still could speak with 'a still small voice'. *The Lord passed by, and a great and strong wind rent the mountains, … and after the wind an earthquake; but the Lord was not in the earthquake: And after the earthquake a fire; but the Lord was not in the fire: and after the fire a still small voice.*[2]

*

The closure of Zanzibar's slave market and the arrival of the great HMS *London* to enforce the end of the slave trade in Zanzibar waters was the beginning of the end of the East African slave trade. It was not the end, but it was a victory in a battle without which the war could not have ultimately been won. Slavery remained legal on Zanzibar and in the sultan's dominions, while the local trade in the sultan's terra firma territory continued.

But on the seas the immediate consequences of the new campaign were drastic. George Sulivan and the station commodore had five to seven ships well-suited to direct against the slave trade on the coast: *Briton, Columbine,*

Daphne, Nassau, Rifleman, Shearwater and *Thetis*. With the *London* as a kind of miniature dockyard and receiving centre for released Africans, the ships engaged in the hunt rarely had to leave their work. The coast was divided into rational hunting zones, with suitable ships appointed to each on the sound basis of Sulivan's and others' experience (in later years one captain carried Colomb's book as his main source of guidance), and all the while *London* loomed like a mother spider at the heart of the new web. There were more years of hard effort by the Royal Navy, political work bringing pressure to bear on Indian Ocean princes, and more blood sacrifice by sailors. But in the coming decade the slavers risked running the Royal Navy's gauntlet much more rarely.

Far more often they tried to march their victims overland. The Royal Navy did send boats up rivers to try to thwart this, and investigators too. It is very hard to arrive at the numbers of East Africans marched northward during the *London* era, but probably some few thousands annually. Sultan Barghash declared the overland trade illegal in his dominions in 1876, which at least made his governors subject to punishment if they failed to enforce it. Meanwhile, to the south, the trade in so-called *engagés* continued under the French flag. This hypocrisy is reminiscent of today's ongoing traffic in forced labour.

Of course, there was never going to be a happy solution for the disposition of kidnapped East Africans. Either their homelands were flung into chaos and hunger, or they had no homes at all to which to return. But, as George Sulivan himself had long hoped, the Church Missionary Society established a town of freed slaves on the African mainland near Mombasa in 1875. Others were released on Zanzibar in the hopes of providing an alternative to slave labour, which the sultans allowed to persist for years.

After a decade of the tropical sun's assault, HMS *London* had to be broken up in 1884. Thereafter slavers immediately reappeared on the coast in force, and there followed a few slaving seasons reminiscent of the pre-Heath era, with poor attention paid by the British and poor results. But then the Royal Navy returned to the scene with a new round of fury in the late 1880s. In 1890 the British declared a protectorate over Zanzibar, and soon, at the price of greater colonial intrusion, the institution of slavery itself was abolished in 1897 by Britain's client Sultan Hamoud. With some exceptions, the slave trade by sea from the region was over.[3]

NOTE ON SOURCES AND METHODS

This is a true story. No detail has been invented. If I write what a certain individual saw, for example, or what a person thought, it is because he wrote as much in a letter or memoir. The book is written with the aim of suggesting that details are invented and lightly flung off the pen, but in fact so many were each won at the price of long hours in the archives. This book contains roughly the same number of endnotes as my first, a traditional scholarly monograph, but my goal was for it to read like a book without endnotes.

Finding just the right detail to add was an enjoyable exercise in ingenuity. And it was enjoyable because, while most historians relish the fascinating detail, the way we make scholarly arguments often precludes their inclusion. An anonymous peer reviewer might accuse us of a lack of focus or professional correctitude, an editor cut and slash in order to get to the argument more quickly.

My sources were very many, as the following pages of endnotes demonstrate, but I will describe a key handful here. First were the ships' logs themselves, preserved in the United Kingdom's National Archives, an institution that is a credit to the entire nation. These describe the daily activities on board in a terse, summary manner; but with care much can be extracted from them. They inform their reader about the officers and activities of the watch, sail sightings, weather conditions, exceptional events like a broken spar, a visitor to the ship, a death. Occasionally there are extended marginal notes describing an action, and these, of course, were like gold. How did I know that weed had grown on the belly of this or that ship, how do I know how the sails were set at a given moment? Because the log recorded it. Additionally, the commodore's station journal was like a log centred on the flagship and offered even more detail about ship visiting, signals sent and received, and so on. This is how I can write that George Sulivan was signalled to dinner aboard the *Octavia*, for instance. The 'muster' or 'establishment' books for each ship, which reveal details about the crew – including Kroomen – are also in the National Archives.

Key, too, were letters from many individuals which were abundant and also preserved in the National Archives. Commodore Heath's correspondence with the Admiralty provided invaluable insight into the state of his thinking before and during the campaign. These were long and forthright. Heath's captains' letters to him were crucial in reckoning their thinking and activities. This was perhaps the main way I had access to Edward Meara, who has largely been absent from history until now. We know about Meara's thinking thanks precisely to the correspondence generated by the politicians who were so disturbed by it.

George Sulivan's descendants, the Hodson family, have carefully preserved an excellent collection of his letters, photos and other documents. I am extraordinarily grateful to the Hodsons for granting me the use of these items as well as for their warm hospitality.

The India Office Records at the British Library – another credit to the nation – provided the records that allowed me to portray the thinking of Dr John Kirk, Henry Rothery and other officials from around the Indian Ocean.

Fortunately, the plans of the *Amazons* are preserved by the National Maritime Museum, and I was kindly welcomed to the ship plan archive in Woolwich by that generous institution. This allowed me to describe the various corners of the ship, to move the actors across and through it, and so on. Other sources in the archives in Greenwich allowed me to write, for example, that Heath and Maxwell explored on horseback to the echoes of jackals.

Geographical descriptions come from letters, memoirs and reports, but also from sailor's atlases from the period. In that way, I relate the general appearance of the place. If I write that one of the actors saw something particular, I have from some source a direct indication thereof.

Colomb and Sulivan's memoirs of this campaign of course provided me with the greatest wealth of fine detail on their activities, feelings and perceptions. If I write that Philip Colomb imagined his wife crying at the moment of his departure for the Indian Ocean, if I describe the sound of stokers' shovels biting into coal, it is because he wrote so in his book. Like any professional historian, I still handle these with a critical eye, thinking about the various contexts in which they are situated, the motives and prejudices of the writers. Often, I was able to compare these literary and polemical items against other sources, like their more official dispatches to their commodore. These memoirs are widely available and I encourage everyone to read them. They are written, though, in the particular prose-aesthetic and mindset of their time that can make reading a windward labour. Other accounts include an essay by Lieutenant John Challice, Dr John Noble's medical log now in York Minster archives, and drawings by Lieutenant Henn.

And while my aim was to hide the archival work behind this book, so too have I left unspoken my engagement with a number of historical debates on this subject. The last best book on the topic of the navy and the trade on this coast in particular was by Dr Raymond Howell in 1987, and I honour Dr Howell and his *Royal Navy and the Slave Trade*. He offered a scholarly sweep of a history of the entire period of British engagement with the slave trade on the east coast; as it was a survey, he was unable to delve into the details of activities and personalities there which my approach allows me. Nor did he have a chance to highlight the manner in which abolitionists in the United Kingdom latched on to the case of the squadron and its suppression in their promotional activities and in parliament. I hope he enjoys what I've done. Dr Lindsay Doulton was able to examine the Heath's squadron's effect on the public discourse in Britain to some extent in her recent DPhil thesis, for which I am grateful.

I hope I am adding to the fine work Dr Richard Huzzey did with his *Freedom Burning: Anti-Slavery and Empire in Victorian Britain* (2012). Readers might compare the ways Heath and his captains struggled with the correct exercise of power and justice with the metropolitan politics of slave trade suppression so well described in Dr Huzzey's book. And as I fill in and work around the histories of Howell and Huzzey, I write in polite disagreement with Mr Alastair Hazell, author of *The Last Slave Market* (2011), with whose characterisation of Dr Kirk I cannot agree. I am grateful to Professor Matthew Hopper for his fine *Slaves of One Master*; his material on the Persian Gulf and the date trade, especially, is fantastic. The origins and flows of capital in this broad phenomenon are critically important to understanding.

Finally, I write in the face of a deeply noxious vein of writing, which I will not dignify by citing, that highlights above all else the connection between this slave trade and the religion of the sultans who profited from it, some of those who financed it, and the dhow-men who bore it over the sea. While it is true that these individuals were Muslims, their religion was no more, no less pertinent to their actions than the Christianity of those who carried on the westward trade or the Hinduism of the merchants and most of the lenders who facilitated it. And it should be abundantly clear that many of the consumers in the east coast market – French, Malagasy, Portuguese, even British – were Christian. The nominally Christian British empire, meanwhile – indeed the devoutly Christian William Gladstone at its helm – fretted over whether to dispossess slaveholders of their 'lawful property'. It should be clear, too, that complicity to varying degrees spread far and wide.

ACKNOWLEDGEMENTS

I was able to share this story because – while working on an unrelated project – my hand fell on a copy of George Sulivan's memoir on the shelves of the Cecil H. Green Library at Stanford University. It was a serendipitous discovery possible because Stanford maintained a true research library, full of real books among which one might make discoveries, curated by expert librarians. I am grateful to Stanford's librarians, all those who support Stanford's libraries, and dedicated librarians everywhere, especially those who defend that piece of technology – still the best – the book.

I am grateful to the National Maritime Museum archive and their ship model library staff at Chatham, who shared with me and a student a model of the *Nymphe* as well as many other treasures. The same thanks go to the Museum's ship plan staff at the Brass Foundry, Woolwich, including the patient and helpful Andrew Choong.

Thanks to the staff of the Yorkminster Archives, the Scottish National Archives, the British Library and their India Office Records library. And thanks to the ILL and other staff at Case Western Reserve's Kelvin Smith Library.

I am particularly indebted to the staff of the UK National Archives at Kew (still called the Public Record Office when I began researching this book), and grateful that the people of Britain support that exceptional institution so historians and others can try to unravel how things came to be both in Britain and throughout the world.

I am extraordinarily grateful to the Hodson family for granting me the use of George Sulivan's papers and photos as well as for their warm hospitality. And thanks to Mr J.J. Heath-Caldwell who transcribed a number of unique documents related to his ancestor, Sir Leopold Heath.

Many thanks to the excellent history work of Drs Caroline Shaw, Richard Huzzey, Matthew Hopper, Erik Gilbert, Raymond Howell, and many more scholars, too numerous to mention here in full, but to whom I am nevertheless deeply grateful.

Thanks to my department colleagues and students, including under-graduate Mr Evan Cerne-Iannone and graduate student Mr Sandy Clark.

I am grateful for research funding from the Baker Nord Humanities Center, which has been a generous supporter over the years.

Thank you to John Silbersack, Peter Mayer, Gesche Ipsen, Deborah Blake, and all those with a hand in producing this book.

Thank you to those who have dedicated their work and resources to battling human trafficking.

I am most grateful to my wife and son to whom this book is dedicated.

NOTES

Part and chapter titles are drawn from Othello, *whose protagonist was a kind of Venetian navy captain and who was enslaved for a time. For his memoir, Philip Colomb used a quote from* Othello *for an epigraph: 'I pray you, in your letters,/When you shall these unlucky deeds relate,/Speak of me as I am: nothing extenuate,/Nor set down aught in malice.'"*

The epigraph is a hadith of the Prophet Muhammad, quoted in William G. Clarence-Smith, 'Slavery and the Slave Trades in the Indian Ocean and Arab Worlds: Global Connections and Disconnections', Proceedings of the 10th Annual Gilder Lehrman Center International Conference, *Yale University, 24; and his 'Islam and Abolition in the Indian Ocean', in Gwyn Campbell, ed.,* Abolition and its Aftermath, *Studies in Slave and Post-Slave Societies and Cultures (Oxford: Routledge, 2013), 160.*

Introduction

1 The details about the captives under the slave deck of the small dhow come from interviews made aboard HMS *Forte* in May 1869. The shallow hold would have been quite warm given the eighty human bodies, the air temperature of 86, and sea temperature between 86 and 88 per *Forte*'s log. These rare instances of 'slave narratives' are recorded in Slave Trade Records of the East India Station, National Archives ADM 127/40. This large volume contains no pagination; these narratives appear at the very end of the volume. The details about the ship's capture by HMS *Forte* come from Percy Scott, *Fifty Years in the Royal Navy* (New York: George Doran, 1919), 28; and *Forte*'s log for May 1869, National Archives ADM 53/9931. This scene is revisited later in this history and reveals that *Forte* fired multiple warning shots, finally heard by the slaver crew.

2   It took ten years for the 1833 Slavery Abolition Act to be extended to territories governed by the East India Company. For a highly readable account of the struggles of the West African 'Preventative Squadron' turn to Siân Rees, *Sweet Water and Bitter: The Ships that Stopped the Slave Trade* (London: Chatto & Windus, 2009); see her ch. 18 for the eventual slow-down in the trade, notwithstanding American smugglers tempted to run the blockade by high prices fetched in the US market. For the current state-of-the-art overview of Victorian anti-slavery, see Richard Huzzey's excellent *Freedom Burning: Anti-Slavery and Empire in Victorian Britain* (Ithaca, NY: Cornell University Press, 2012).

3   The assertion that the West African Slave Trade Suppression campaign was the most expensive humanitarian operations in history and the 2% of national income average come from Robert Pape and Chaim Kaufman cited in Christopher Leslie Brown, 'Abolition of the Atlantic Slave Trade', in Heuman and Burnard, eds., *Routledge History of Slavery* (New York: Routledge, 2011), 281–97. Richard Huzzey's calculations provide my figure of around 0.3 to 1.3% of national expenditure; see his *Freedom Burning*, ch. 3 and especially fig. 5. For details of the ships and manpower involved, see David Eltis, *Economic Growth and the Ending of the Transatlantic Slave Trade* (Oxford: Oxford University Press, 1987), 90–2 and elsewhere. See also Keith Hamilton, *Slavery, Diplomacy and Empire: Britain and the Suppression of the Slave Trade, 1807–1975* (Eastbourne: Sussex Academic Press, 2009).

4   For just a couple of many sources of information on Kroomen's strength, see Richard Burton, *Wanderings in West Africa from Liverpool to Fernando Po*, vol. 2 (London: Tinsley Bros., 1863), 26–7; and Charles W. Thomas, *Adventures and Observations on the West Coast of Africa and its Islands* (New York: Derby and Jackson, 1860), 108. The Kroomen's strength was a matter of practicality. Head Kroomen selected their men on the basis of their ability to load ships with heavy casks, coal bags, etc. Thomas reported that it was said that a common standard was whether a man could carry a beef cask of 200 pounds above his head into deep surf. More on the Kroomen comes from Philip Colomb, *Slave-catching in the Indian Ocean: A Record of Naval Experiences* (London: Longmans, 1873, 249–50, and Diane Frost, 'Diasporan West African Communities: The Kru in Freetown and Liverpool', *Review of African Political Economy* 29 (June 2002), 285–300. For one of many sources of information on the Krooman tattoo, see House of Commons Parliamentary Papers, *Reports from Commodore Sir George Collier Concerning the Settlements on the Gold and Windward Coasts of*

Africa, vol. XII [90], 15. For the old Krooman saying, see MacGregor Laird and R.A.K. Oldfield, *Narrative of an Expedition into the Interior of Africa by the River Niger*, vol. 1 (London: Richard Bentley, 1837), 33. On the Head Krooman taking responsibility for the discipline of Kroomen, see Colomb, *Slave-catching*, 249. More details come from William Allen and T.R.H. Thomson, *Narrative of the Expedition Sent by Her Majesty's Government to the River Niger* (London: Richard Bentley, 1848), 122–3. For Krooman pay and much else see Robert Burroughs, '"[T]he True Sailors of Western Africa": Kru Seafaring Identity in British Travellers' Accounts of the 1830s and 1840s', *Journal of Maritime Research* 11 (Sept. 2009), 61 and elsewhere.

1. 'On the brow o' the sea'

1   On evictions, palm-greasing and alleged bribery, see entry for County Waterford in D.R. Fisher, ed., *The History of Parliament: The House of Commons 1820–1832*, vol. 3: *Constituencies*, pt. 2 (Cambridge: Cambridge University Press, 2009); also Royal Commission on the State of the Law and Practice in respect to the Occupation of Land in Ireland, 1845, *State of the law and practice in respect to the occupation of land in Ireland: evidence taken before Her Majesty's Commissioners*, part II (CMD 616), appendix B, 23; for contract-shredding, see *Freeman's Journal*, 11 Sept. 1837, 2. On May Park, including its 'pretty' situation, see Samuel Lewis, *A Topographical Dictionary of Ireland*, vol. 1 (London: S. Lewis, 1837), 158; for fox-hunting, see *Waterford News*, 26 Jan. 1849, 3; on the matter of butter, see William Blacker, *An Essay on the Improvement to be Made in the Cultivation of Small Farms* (Dublin: William Curry, 1837), 87; on gardener Mr Hessian's strawberries, see Martin Doyle and Edmund Murphy, *Irish Farmer's and Gardener's Magazine and Register of Rural Affairs*, vol. 1 (Dublin: William Curry, 1834), 50. Meara's siblings were George E.J., William H.P. and Theodosia C.S. Meara. Arabella was born after Edward. Mother Sarah Catherine (Ward) Meara died the same year, though it remains unknown whether this was due to complications of childbirth. George Meara had more children with his second wife, Elizabeth. Data about May Park estate come from historic maps available on the excellent Ordnance Survey, Ireland website, www.osi.ie. For Meara's appointment to the *Heroine*, see *United Service Magazine, 1849*, pt. 2 (London: H. Hurst, 1849), 310. For George E.J. Meara's grooming in society, see *Freeman's Journal* (Dublin), 7 Jan. 1845, 2; 6 Jan. 1851, 3.

2   For some details of *Heroine* and her class see Hansard Parliamentary Debates, 29 Apr. 1847, vol. 92, col. 162, and David Lyon and Rif Winfield, *The Sail and Steam Navy List* (London: Chatham, 2004), 127. On the sorts of slavers the British encountered on the west coast during these years, see 'Proceedings during the year 1845 in the British and Brazilian Court of Mixed Commission, Sierra Leone', in House of Commons Parliamentary Papers, 1847, vol. 67, *Slave Trade*, 77–81. Today, the Gallinas is called Moa. For the background to British efforts near the mouth of the Gallinas and the particular trouble with the Zaro, see Commander Dunlop to Commodore Fanshawe 13 Oct. 1849 in Foreign Office Librarian, *British and Foreign State Papers, 1849–1850*, vol. 38 (London: Harrison and Sons, 1862), 384–6. Details of the fight with the Zaro come from Commander Marsh to Commodore Fanshawe 10 Jan. 1850, House of Commons Parliamentary Papers, 1851, vol. 26, pt. 1, *Piracy; Slave Trade*, 229–30. Further details come from HMS *Heroine*'s log, National Archives ADM 53/3580. Meara's commendation is noted on his service record, National Archives ADM/196/70.

3   Details about HMS *Niger* come from the invaluable Lyon and Winfield, *The Sail and Steam Navy List*, 212. Reporting Commander Heath's appointment to her, the *London Standard*, 15 July 1850, 4, noted Heath's luck in getting the command and notes that it was a powerful vessel to be classed a sloop – a commander's command. For a general account of the Preventative squadron during this period, see Rees, *Sweet Water and Bitter*, especially ch. 16. The fear of British subjects in the hinterland of Lagos and violence at Badagry is reported in a series of letters between Heath, his superiors, the British missionaries and merchants at Badagry, and the second-in-command to Akitoye, the uncle of Kosoko, in June and July 1851: House of Commons Accounts and Papers, *Consuls; Slave Trade* (47, part 1), vol. 103 (Nov. 1852-Aug. 1853), 249–58, 281. Consul Beecroft is depicted in a portrait by an unknown artist held in the Whitby Museum, Yorkshire, item number WHITM:PEF277. His feeling that African chiefs were all the same and would bow before a show of force is a near-quote of his report that appears on pp. 306–7 of the Parliamentary Papers cited above. For the debacle of an attack on Lagos, see especially Heath's report of 17 Dec. 1851 to the Sec. of the Admiralty reprinted on p. 188. For this see too the report of Commander Forbes, *Philomel*, to Commodore Bruce, 26 Nov. 1851, 295–6. This collection of letters and a story in *Royal Cornwall Gazette*, 19 Sept. 1851, 6, relates the capsizing of the *Niger*'s boat and loss of John Milne Duffus. He is described in *Aberdeen Journal*, 8 Oct. 1851, 4. Commodore Bruce comments on the particularly impassable surf here in the Parliamentary Papers cited above. On the military preparedness of Lagos, see *The Destruction of Lagos* (London: James Ridgway, 1852), 19; this book was written anonymously. Further details about the desperate raid on Lagos come from *Nautical Magazine* 21 (Feb. 1852), 109–10. For the men dying under Lagos by Heath's side, see Leopold Heath, 'A Sketch of the Life of Admiral Sir Leopold George Heath' (1885), reproduced in George Heath, *Records of the Heath Family* (privately published); this item was transcribed by J.J. Heath-Caldwell at http://web.archive.org/web/20160824184244/http://www.jjhc.info/heathleopold1907.htm. For Commodore Bruce's indignation at the event, see multiple letters and reports in the Parliamentary Papers cited above, 283–4, 292, 294–5, especially 302, 306.

4   Estimates of the number of Africans who were annually kidnapped and carried overseas to slave markets are very difficult to calculate, but the scholars who roughly draw this conclusion are Moses D. E. Nwulia, *Britain and Slavery in East Africa* (Washington: Three Continents Press, 1975), 24, 67, and Matthew S. Hopper, *Slaves of One Master* (New Haven: Yale University Press, 2015), 36–9.

5   Details about George Sulivan and others in the family come from Henry Norton Sulivan, *Life and Letters of the Late Admiral Sir Bartholomew James Sulivan, K. C. B.* (London: John Murrary, 1896), vii–viii, 394, 416, and elsewhere. Details about George's religious upbringing come from his mother's serial letter to George Sulivan, Sulivan papers held by the Hodson family, 28 Nov. 1849. And the Bartholomew James book cited above makes his strict Sabbath observance clear too: p. xxxi. Data on Thomas Ball Sulivan come from the *Dictionary of National Biography* 55 (London: Smith, Elder, and Co., 1898), 157. The detail about the Sulivan name being a ticket to respect and kindness in Cornwall comes from Henrietta Sulivan to George Sulivan, 10 August (no year given), in the Sulivan papers held by the Hodson family. George Sulivan's descendants, the Hodson family, have carefully preserved an excellent collection of his letters, photos and other documents. I am extraordinarily grateful to the Hodsons for granting me the use of these items as well as for their warm hospitality. Details about George Sulivan's great naval family come from Bartholomew James, *Journal of Rear-Admiral Bartholomew James, 1752–1828*, Publications of the Navy Records Society VI (London: Navy Records Society, 1896), ix. For an introduction to the naval Sulivan family, see Peter Collister, *The Sulivans and the Slave Trade* (London: Rex Collins, 1980), 1–19. For the details of the attack, G.L. Sulivan, *Dhow Chasing in Zanzibar Waters and on the Eastern Coast of Africa* (London: Samson Low, 1973), 17, 25. See also M.D.D. Newitt, 'Angoche, the Slave Trade and the Portuguese c. 1844–1910', *Journal of African History*

13 (1972), 659–72. From the Sulivan papers preserved by the Hodson family comes the letter of Henrietta Sulivan to George Sulivan, Sulivan papers, 28 Nov. 1849.

6   Details from this section come from Colomb's service record, National Archives ADM 196/36; *Phoenix* Muster Book, National Archives ADM 38/8724, and *Phoenix*'s log for Feb.-Oct. 1854, National Archives ADM 53/4630. Details about *Phoenix*'s mission come from M.J. Ross, *Polar Pioneers* (Montreal: McGill-Queen's University Press, 1994), 348. Impressions of Inglefield come from E.A. Inglefield, *Words of Advice to Young Naval Officers* (Liverpool: Webb & Hunt, 1864). On Inglefield's artistry, E.A. Inglefield, *A Summer Search for Sir John Franklin* (London: Thomas Harrison, 1853), 24; National Maritime Museum, photograph collection G4264, G4269, G4270, and others. Colomb's verdict on arctic landscapes comes from P.H. Colomb, 'The Evolution of the Blue Jacket', *North American Review* 161 (1895), 268.

7   On details of Colomb's machine, his struggles with his superiors and his dangerous straying towards impertinence, see Caird Library, National Maritime Museum, HMS *Mercury* MER/102, Letter of Lieut. PH Colomb to Rear Admiral Smart, 24 Feb.1863; for his superiors suggesting Colomb was a 'fool', see 'The Evolution of Modern Signalling: The Late Admiral Colomb and Night Signalling', *United Service Magazine* 32 (1905), 181; for more details and Heath's endorsement, see pamphlet, *Colomb's Patent Flashing Night Signals* (Devonport: Colman and Son, 1862), 7; on the sense of Colomb's signal computer as a 'hurdy-gurdy', see 'Discussion: The Telephotos: A New Means of Electric Signalling', *Journal of the Royal United Service Institution* 38 (Feb. 1894), 111. A portrait of Colomb is in *The Engineer* (20 Oct. 1899), 403.

2. 'The valiant of this warlike isle'

1   For Livingstone, see David and Charles Livingstone, *Narrative of an Expedition to the Zambesi, 1858–1864* (New York: Harper, 1866), 620–5. Richard Huzzey's work on slave trade suppression politics and political culture is the state of the art. I draw here from his 'The Politics of Slave-trade Suppression', in Huzzey and Robert M. Burroughs, *The Suppression of the Atlantic Slave trade: British Policies, Practices and Representations of Naval Coercion* (Manchester: Manchester University Press, 2015), 34–7 and elsewhere. For the dominant theory of the laziness of the poor and the need to inculcate them – white and black – into 'habits of work' see Thomas C. Holt, *The Problem of Freedom:*

Race, Labor, and Politics in Jamaica and Britain (Baltimore: Johns Hopkins, 1992), 35 and elsewhere. On Sulivan writing in terms similar to Wilberforce's or Stowe's, see *Dhow Chasing*, 141, 231, and elsewhere. For Dickens and Africans, in this case Zulus, see 'The Noble Savage', *Household Words* VII (1853), 141–8; the line 'free of course he must be' comes from a Dickens letter quoted in Susan Zlotnick, 'Contextualizing David Levy's *How the Dismal Science Got its Name*', in David Colander, Robert E. Prasch, Falguni A. Sheth, eds., *Race, Liberalism, and Economics* (Ann Arbor: University of Michigan Press, 2004), 87. For Trollope see *The West Indies and the Spanish Main* (Leipzig: Bernhard Tauchnitz, 1860), 50, 179; I would not have found Trollope's comments without Richard Huzzey's reference in *Freedom Burning*, ch. 1. 'Human-equality fanatics' and 'abolition mania' come from 'A Poor Peacemaker', *The Slavery Quarrel, with Plans and Prospects of Reconciliation* (London: Hardwicke, 1863), 50. And for those who argued against the expense of suppressing the slave trade in 1850 at the behest of the romantic abolitionists, see one response in 'A Barrister', *Analysis of the Evidence Given Before the Select Committee upon the Slave Trade* (London: Partridge and Oakey, 1850), 5–6 and elsewhere. Robert M. Burroughs' is a useful summary of arguments for or against slave trade suppression in the middle of the nineteenth century in the public discourse: 'Slave-trade Suppression and the Culture of Anti-Slavery in Nineteenth-century Britain', in Burroughs and Huzzey, eds., *The Suppression of the Atlantic Slave Trade*, 125–45. For the proposal the Britain not invest so much in suppressing the east coast slave trade because slavery there was 'merely' domestic, see MP Colonel W.H. Sykes in *Hansard Parliamentary Debates*, House of Commons, 4 June 1868, 3rd series, vol. 192, col. 1131. For abandoning the role of 'knight-errant', see MP Matthew Marsh, *Hansard Parliamentary Debates*, House of Commons, 1 Mar. 1864, 3rd series, vol. 173, col. 1347.

2 Napier is pictured in Frederic A. Sharf, *Abyssinia, 1867–1868: Artists on Campaign* (Chestnut Hill, Mass.: Boston College Museum of Art, 2003), 32. A portrait of Heath is in the possession of descendant Michael D. Heath-Caldwell and published at http://www.heathcaldwell.com. The details of what was visible from the deck of *Octavia* come from Trevenen J. Holland and Henry M. Hozier, *Record of the Expedition to Abyssinia*, vol. 2 (London: W. Clowes and Sons, 1870), 344. Details about Heath's massive responsibility at Abyssinia come from Holland and Hozier, *Record of the Expedition*, 175, 207–9, 360. Further details come from Commodore Heath's East Indies Station Journal, National Archives ADM 50/293. Northwestern University has a photo album of the

flotilla at Annesley Bay and other aspects of the landing; http://web.archive.
org/web/20160706190426/http://winterton.library.northwestern.edu/browse.
html?id=inu-wint-3. On the Sevastopol landing, details come from Heath's own
Letters from the Black Sea (London: Richard Bentley and Son, 1897), 26–8, 53–6,
and elsewhere. On Heath's reputation as clever and capable, see Scott, *Fifty Years
in the Royal Navy*, 27. On Heath's belief that organisation had precluded Russian
resistance, see Heath, *Letters*, 54–5.

3   Details in this section regarding the Abyssinian campaign come from
Commodore Heath's East Indies Station Journal, National Archives ADM
50/293; Also Tozier, *Record of the Expedition*, 344. 'Undoubted duty of England'
comes from Heath to Sir S. Fitzgerald, Bombay, 19 Jan. 1869. Other evidence
of Heath's thinking on the slave trade in this section come from Heath to Henry
Churchill, 25 Aug. 1868, British Library, India Office Records, India Political
Despatches, L/PS/6/560 1/11 Coll 1/11. More on Heath's turning his attention
to the next mission, fighting the slave trade even before leaving Abyssinia and
collecting such documents, see Heath to the Secretary of the Admiralty, 7 Apr.
1868, http://web.archive.org/web/20160707202227/http://www.jjhc.info/
HeathLeopold1907admiraltyletterbook1868.htm. For his time spent with William
Maxwell as well as the detail about jackals in the hinterland around Annesley
Bay see National Maritime Museum, William Henry Maxwell Journals, MAX/1,
Section 1868.

4   For the Foreign Office and Admiralty's discussions on the quality of ships
on the station and awareness of the poor state of the station's ships as well as
the relative lack of attention to the slave trade on the east coast compared to
west, see Admiralty Memo of 20 July 1866, National Archives FO 84/1268
and accompanying notes regarding discussion with Foreign Minister Lord
Stanley. Sulivan's contemporary Devonport, Plymouth, with plumes of coal
smoke is pictured in an 1870 watercolour by Henry Thomas Dawson, Jr.;
http://www.devonportonline.co.uk. Other details about Devonport come
from a W.H. Maddock lithographic map, 1877; http://web.archive.org/
web/20160708184440/http://www.cyber-heritage.co.uk/maps/olflft.jpg.
Thanks to the generosity and patience of the staff of the National Maritime
Museum ship model archive at the Chatham Dockyard Museum I was also able
to examine an enormously detailed contemporary model of the Devonport
dockyard. Details of *Daphne*'s master (a position becoming known as 'navigating
lieutenant') and first lieutenant come from their service records, National
Archives ADM 196/22 and 196/15 respectively. Details about the *Amazon*

class come from Lyon and Winfield, *The Sail and Steam Navy List*, and G.A. Ballard, 'British Sloops of 1875, the Wooden Ram-Bowed Type', *Mariner's Mirror* 24 (1938), 302–17. For the *Amazons* being an answer to the *Alabama*, see Admiralty Surveyor, '*Amazon* Class, Particulars of New Design', 3 Dec. 1867, National Archives ADM 1/6020. There was some question about whether the ram was really a ram or just an added pocket of buoyancy. At least some Royal Navy captains thought the ram-bow was for ramming and attributed the idea for the ram to George Sulivan's brother Bartholomew James Sulivan; see *Journal of the Royal United Services Institution* 16 (1873), 16. Richard Hill writes about the craze for rams in these years in *War at Sea in the Ironclad Age* (New York: Collins, 2006), 35. Sulivan's June 1867 commission is in the Sulivan papers preserved by the Hodson family. Details on the crew, work done on the *Daphne* in this period, and more come from the log, National Archives ADM 53/9582. Note that *Daphne*'s log for this period is in two volumes with the same catalogue number. See also Collister, *The Sulivans*, 90–1. *Canopus* was one of the receiving ships that supplied *Daphne* with men. Details about the royal marines who first joined *Daphne* come in part from research done on Royal Marine Light Infantryman Aaron Tall located at http://www.worldnavalships.com/forums/archive/index.php/t-11719.html. Additional information about Dick Osborne comes from *Daphne*'s Establishment Book, National Archives ADM 115/245. Before she left England, *Daphne*, still manned by many green men, participated in a Naval review before Queen Victoria and the Ottoman sultan. *Nymphe* also participated and the two were sometimes paired in a kind of contra-dance at sea during the review. For the naval review see 'Rehearsal of the Fleet Preparatory to the Grand Naval Review', *Isle of Wight Observer*, 13 July 1867.

5 Weather and sailing details around *Daphne*'s time in West African waters come from *Daphne*'s log, National Archives ADM 53/9582, including 19–20 Oct. 1867. Further details come from Sulivan, *Dhow Chasing*, 132–4. For John Bull, formerly of *Pantaloon*, see *Pantaloon*'s Establishment Book, National Archives ADM 115/724. More than one Krooman was given the name 'John Bull' in those days, but *Daphne*'s Establishment Book confirms that these were one and the same, National Archives ADM 115/245. For the old Krooman saying, see Laird and Oldfield, *Narrative of an Expedition into the Interior of Africa by the River Niger*, vol. 1, 33. On the Head Krooman taking responsibility for the discipline of Kroomen, see Colomb, *Slave-catching*, 249. More details come from Allen and Thomson, *Narrative of the Expedition Sent by Her Majesty's Government to the River Niger*, 122–3. See *Daphne*'s Establishment Book, ADM 115/245; *Nymphe*'s

Establishment Book, ADM 115/691 for the Kroomen entered on the ship's books. Regarding Sulivan's experiences saving crewmates near drowning, see a letter from Captain J.A. Paynter, 6 Oct. 1860, in the Sulivan papers preserved by the Hodson family. This letter describes two rescues. Sulivan was recognised by the Royal Humane Society for one of his rescues. Richard Francis Orton's service record is at the National Archives ADM 196/15. He enrolled as a naval cadet in 1860. The Registrar General's index shows him to have been born in 1846 in Cambridgeshire.

6   For *Daphne*'s duties during the Abyssinian campaign, see Heath's station journal, National Archives ADM 50/293 from this time period. Weather and other details form this time come from *Daphne*'s log, National Archives ADM 53/9582. Details of *Daphne*'s activities at Mahé come from *Daphne's* log, National Archives ADM 53/9582; Sulivan's impressions of Mahé, Seychelles, *Dhow Chasing*, 135–7; other details in this scene come from Heath's East Indies Station Journal, National Archives ADM 50/293.

3. 'His bark is stoutly timber'd'

1   Abdul Sheriff's remains the authoritative work on nineteenth-century Zanzibar: Abdul Sheriff, *Slaves, Spices, and Ivory on Zanzibar* (Athens, OH: Ohio University Press, 1987), 49, 54, 65, 135, 226, 229, appendices, and elsewhere. With it, read Erik Gilbert, *Dhows and Colonial Economy in Zanzibar: 1860–1970* (Athens, OH: Ohio University Press, 2005). Some details about Zanzibar's economy come from Nwulia, *Britain and Slavery*, 97 and elsewhere. Details about the ship and the setting in the harbour of Zanzibar in this section come from *Pantaloon*'s log, National Archives ADM 53/8772. This includes a reported complement of 130 which varies from other sources. The layout of *Pantaloon* is preserved by the National Maritime Museum, ship plans NPB8563–5. Other details comprising the scene come from Sulivan, *Dhow Chasing*, 112, 331. See, for the Indian Hindu or 'Banyan' merchants participating in or financing and profiting from the slave trade on Zanzibar itself, Caird Library, National Maritime Museum, Admiral Sir Arthur Mostyn Field papers, FIE/43100, 99. For this, too, see *The Examiner*, 1 Feb. 1873, 9. A rare, perhaps unique, photo of HMS *Pantaloon* is among the Sulivan papers preserved by the Hodson family. Frederick Cooper wrote the foundational book about East African plantation slavery, especially on Zanzibar and neighbouring Pemba, with *Plantation Slavery on the East Coast of Africa* (New Haven: Yale University Press, 1977). More recently, Elisabeth

McMahon has closely studied slave society on the east coast, especially on Pemba, in *Slavery and Emancipation in Islamic East Africa: From Honor to Respectability* (Cambridge: Cambridge University Press, 2013). Information about clove harvesting comes from Cynthia Brantley, *The Giriama and Colonial Resistance in Kenya, 1800–1920* (Berkeley: University of California Press, 1981), 17.

2   These treaties against the overseas slave trade were the Moresby and Hammerton Treaties which limited the trade to the coast and coastal islands from Lamu (in what is today Kenya) in the north and Kilwa (in what is today Tanzania) in the south. For details on the Zanzibar-centred trade see Sheriff, *Slaves, Spices, and Ivory*. For a history of British perfunctory attempts to enforce the Moresby and Hammerton Treaties, see Raymond C. Howell, *The Royal Navy and the Slave Trade* (New York: St. Martin's, 1987), ch. 1, especially 35–6. For the sad state of the ships on the station, especially when slave trade suppression duties were largely moved from the Cape station to East Indies station at Bombay, National Archives FO 84/1268, Admiralty Memo 20 July 1866, 2; for this see also Howell, *Royal Navy*, 36, 44. For a description of Zanzibar and neighbourhood, see Richard Burton, *Zanzibar: City, Island, and Coast*, vol. 1 (London: Tinsley Bros., 1872), 256–7; Christiane Bird, *The Sultan's Shadow: One Family's Rule at the Crossroads of East and West* (New York: Random House, 2010), 107–8. Details of Heath's arrival and visit to the sultan come in part from Commodore Heath's East Indies Station Journal, National Archives ADM 50/293. The phrase 'the time has come' appears in multiple letters from this period, e.g. Leopold Heath to Henry Churchill, 25 Aug. 1868, British Library India Office Records, India Political Despatches, L/PS/6/560 1/11 Coll 1/11. For another instance, Leopold Heath to Secretary of the Admiralty, 2 Sept. 1868, British Library, India Office Records L/P&S/18/ B85, 2. The sultan is pictured in the British Library, 1867 photograph of Sultan Majid bin Said, BL Photo 1000/42 (4344); see also Baird, *Sultan's Shadow*, 181. On Churchill's presence, see Confidential Letter from Leopold Heath to the Secretary to the Secretary to the Admiralty, 2 Sept. 1868, British Library, IOR L/P&S/18/B85, 2. Details about Heath's conversation with the sultan and other details come from Leopold Heath to Henry Churchill, 25 Aug. 1868, India Office Records, India Political Despatches, L/PS/6/560 1/11 Coll 1/11, 2, 3, and Leopold Heath to Secretary of the Admiralty, 2 Sept. 1868, British Library, India Office Records L/P&S/18/ B85. It is uncertain whether Heath knew it, though it would be a surprise if Consul Churchill had not told him, but Sultan Majid did take active steps to fight the smuggling of captives to the north. Earlier in 1868 he had sent 150 men to battle the Omani slavers on the eve of their sailing with kidnap victims. That raid seems to have largely failed, though. In another instance, the sultan's vizier permitted the consulate's marines to police suspected haunts of Omani smugglers while the fleet was preoccupied with the Abyssinian War. See British Library India Office Records, India Political Despatches, L/PS/6/560, Coll 1/11, Letters of Consul Churchill to Secretary of State, Government of Bombay, 9 Apr. 1868, L/PS/6/560, Coll 1/11. On Heath thinking he left an impression of his earnestness, and his feeling that he was taking on the duty with more energy than anyone had done previously, see Heath to Sec. Admiralty, 1 Mar. 1869 in *British Sessional Papers*, House of Commons: Correspondence Relating to the Slave Trade on the East African Coast, LXI, 67.

3 Philip Colomb's service record has a number of marginal notes documenting commanding officers' praise of his intelligence: National Archives ADM 196/36. Most details from this section come from Colomb, *Slave-catching*, 2, 7, 21–3, 110.

4 As always, the ship's log provides detailed information about temperature and wind conditions as well as the activities occurring on board during this period including repairs and occurrences around the ship, such as the discovery of a body, and so on; *Nymphe*'s log for Nov. 1868, National Archives ADM 53/9548. For Meara's past experiences see his service records, National Archives ADM 196/70 and ADM 196/13; and *Cork Examiner*, 2 Jan. 1866, 1. Details of the crew come from National Archives ADM/115/691, Record and Establishment Book of the *Nymphe* to 1871. For the massive heat of the lower deck see data from the trial of the *Daphne*, *The Times*, 5 July 1867, 5. The impression of constant infernal heat also comes from an anonymous slaver-hunter centred on Zanzibar, who wrote in 1870, 'Living on board a gun-boat, therefore is rather hot work, what with the sun above and the engine-fires below – for the chase is an everyday occurrence', *Chambers's Journal*, 12 Feb. 1870, 110. Details of the architecture and layout of the *Amazon*-class gunboats comes from National Maritime Museum NPB7942 and NPB7944; further details come out by comparing these with *Daphne*'s upper and lower deck plans. Meara's experience on the *Magnet* comes from his service record. *Magnet* was tender to the 'blockship' – a converted steam guard ship – *Pembroke Times*, 21 Mar. 1859, 12.

4. 'The imminent deadly breach'

1 Details about Madagascar and Pakenham come from Sulivan, *Dhow Chasing*, 138–9; Gwyn Campbell, 'Madagascar and the Slave Trade', *Journal of African*

History 22 (1981), 216–17 and elsewhere; and Gill Shepherd, 'The Comorians and the East African Slave Trade', in James Watson, ed., *Asian and African Systems of Slavery* (Berkeley: University of California Press, 1980), 79 and elsewhere. The description of Queen Ranavalona II comes from Alfred Chiswell, 'A visit to the Queen, Madagascar', *Newbury House Magazine* 9 (1893), 465. Churchill's evidence before the 1871 House of Commons select committee on the East African slave trade describes cynical French 'liberating' African slaves for the price of five years of indenture service: House of Commons Parliamentary Papers, 1871 (420), *Report from the Select Committee on Slave Trade (East Coast of Africa)*; together with the proceedings of the committee, minutes of evidence, appendix and index, 24. For Sulivan's revelations about the relationship between Pakenham and the Malagasy, see Sulivan, *Dhow Chasing*, 138–9; some of the text in this passage is a verbatim quote of Sulivan relating Pakenham's briefing. For Sulivan's personal impression of Pakenham, as for example energetic, see Sulivan, *Dhow Chasing*, 138. Heading, wind and sail conditions come, as always, from *Daphne*'s log, National Archives ADM 53/9582. On Sunley, see Henry Hutton to Acting Colonial Secretary, Cape Town, 25 May 1861, in House of Commons Parliamentary Papers 61 (6 Feb.-7 Aug. 1862), 65–6, and *Anti-Slavery Reporter*, May 1883, 129–31. Other details about *Daphne*'s time in the Comoros come from Sulivan, *Dhow Chasing*, 140. Details of *Daphne*'s approach to the Kiswara, weather, etc. come from *Daphne*'s log, National Archives ADM 53/9582. Details about Doctor Mortimer come from Edward T. Mortimer service record, National Archives ADM 196/78. Details of the doctor and captain's exploration and encounter with the small village come from Sulivan, *Dhow Chasing*, 148–50.

2 Material from Livingstone in this section comes from David Livingstone [Horace Waller, ed.], *The Last Journals of David Livingstone, in Central Africa. From Eighteen Hundred and Sixty-five to his Death* (New York: Harper & Bros., 1875), 64, 182. On Livingstone's dependence on Tippu Tip see Bird, *The Sultan's Shadow*, 277–8. On Tippu Tip generally, Heinrich Brode, *Tippoo Tib. The Story of his Career in Central Africa: Narrated from His Own Accounts* (London: Arnold, 1907); Robert Ross et al., *The Objects of Life in Central Africa: The History of Consumption and Social Change, 1840–1980* (Leiden: Brill, 2013), 31–3; Prem Poddar et al., eds., *A Historical Companion to Postcolonial Literatures: Continental Europe and its Empires* (Edinburgh: Edinburgh University Press, 2011), 55. Estimations of prices paid for kidnapees come from Colomb who gathers his information from explorers Speke and Burton and Consuls Pelly and Disbrow, *Slave-catching*, 55–8; this is reinforced by a *Times of India* article of 7 June 1867.

SQUADRON

The exchange rate of roughly five Maria Theresa silver dollars to one British pound sterling in the late 1860s comes from Robert Geran Landen, *Oman Since 1856* (Princeton: Princeton University Press, 2015), 129.

3   For the fascinating hybrid character of the *Amazons*, see Ballard, 'British Sloops of 1875, the Wooden Ram-Bowed Type', 302–17. For other details in this section, including the former strategy of policing close to Zanzibar, see Howell, *Royal Navy*, 21–3, 44, 53. For the feast that the sultan offered the officers of the *Octavia* and his secretary of state serving them, see *Letters of Bishop Tozer and His Sister, Together with Some Other Records of the Universities' Mission from 1863–1873* (Glasgow: Universities' Mission, 1902), 170. Heath's letter to the Admiralty announcing his new efforts and recommending political and diplomatic changes is Heath to Admiralty, 2 Sept. 1868 transcribed at http://web.archive.org/web/20160707202227/http://www.jjhc.info/HeathLeopold1907admiraltyletterbook1868.htm. Details in this section on *Daphne* and Sulivan at Zanzibar come from National Archives, *Daphne*'s log, ADM 53/9582, and Sulivan, *Dhow Chasing*, 153–4 and elsewhere. Sulivan used the term 'run the gauntlet': Sulivan, *Dhow Chasing*, 153. For Sulivan's belief that the Indian traders were testing him, Sulivan, *Dhow Chasing*, 154. On Sulivan's deceptive manoeuvring see National Archives, *Daphne*'s log, ADM 53/9582, and Sulivan, *Dhow Chasing*, 156. The details of the episode of the dhow run aground, including Sulivan's thoughts, come from Sulivan, *Dhow Chasing*, 158–63. On the types of activities carried on by the *Daphne* in this period, including firing warning shots, see *Daphne*'s log, ADM 53/9582. Details from the interviews of Zangora and others come from Sulivan, *Dhow Chasing*, 185–7. Lt. Henn had already served on over half a dozen ships by this time. His details are at National Archives ADM 196/17. Henn was an artist and his role in the squadron's efforts after their assignment on the station will become apparent. The details of the large slave dhow with 156 captives and the murdered infant come from *Daphne*'s log, ADM 53/9582, and Sulivan, *Dhow Chasing*, 168–9. On the calculations a slaver made regarding running aground, see Sulivan, *Dhow Chasing*, 115, 169. For the story of Marlborough, *Daphne*'s log, ADM 53/9582, and Sullivan, *Dhow Chasing*, 179. On Sulivan's observations of the refugees grouping themselves, his favourable and unfavourable reactions, and Billy and Thomas Balmer, see *Daphne*'s Establishment Book, ADM 115/245; Sulivan, *Dhow Chasing*, 173–7. Two men died within hours on 6 Nov. 1868 and the woman died on the 7th. The burial of another man on the 10th records the 64-pound ball for bearing down the body; *Daphne*'s log, ADM 53/9582.

5. 'In her prophetic fury sew'd the work'

1   Abdul Sheriff believes that perhaps 3,000 abductees were moved north of Zanzibar waters annually by sea in the 1860s, though does not venture an estimate of those bound from Zanzibar or more likely Kilwa to Madagascar and other eastern destinations. He supposes, then, that the Mozambican coast supplied the vast majority of these. For this and other details in this section see Sheriff, *Slaves, Spices, and Ivory*, 49–53, 65, 106–7, 204–7, 231. Many details in this section, including Heath's thoughts from around this time on the relative statuses of slave and free come from Leopold Heath to Sec. of the Admiralty, 1 Mar. 1869 in *British Sessional Papers*, House of Commons: Correspondence Relating to the Slave Trade on the East African Coast, LXI, 67–8. Also Leopold Heath to Seymour Fitzgerald (governor of Bombay), 19 Jan. 1869 National Archives ADM 127–40, 1–3; Leopold Heath to the Secretary to the Admiralty, 2 Sept. 1868, British Library IOR L/P&S/18/B85, 3. Details of this rendezvous come from Commodore Heath's East Indies Station Journal, National Archives ADM 50/293. On the commander of *Octavia* who revelled in ordering the lash, see Scott, *Fifty Years in the Royal Navy*, 27–8. Heath credits the manoeuvre of staying away from Zanzibar and pouncing down from the north to officers with whom he spoke at Annesley Bay in a letter to the Admiralty, 1 Mar. 1869, British Library IOR L/P&S/18/B84, 2. On Colomb calling Heath's strategy a spider's web and the squadron spiders, *Slave-catching*, 185.

2   The report that Sir Seymour found Heath's interview with the sultan of Zanzibar 'very objectionable' comes from a note of Charles Gonne, Secretary to the Government of Bombay to the Secretary of the Foreign Department, Government of India, Calcutta; British Library IOR L/PS/6/560 1/11 Coll 1/11, 1. A likeness of Sir Seymour Vesey Fitzgerald is at the National Portrait Gallery, item NPG Ax17766. For the concerns that occupied Sir Seymour, with the slave trade conspicuously absent, see among many other potential sources, Peter Harnetty, *Imperialism and Free Trade: Lancashire and India in the Mid-Nineteenth Century* (Vancouver: University of British Columbia Press, 1972), 89, 109 and elsewhere; *Popular Science* (October 1882), 859; and *Allen's Indian Mail and Register of Intelligence for British and Foreign India* 29 (1871), 47, 55, 119, 467. Sir Charles Aitchison's photo is at the British Library, Dunlop Smith Collection, Photo 355/3/(17) and at the Library of Congress, item number 2013646213. For Aitchison, including his millenarianism, George Smith, *Twelve Indian Statesmen* (London: John Murray, 1897), 287–307; and his reputation for masterful inactivity, *Dictionary of National Biography* 64 (London: Smith, Elder, and Co., 1901), 26. Aitchison's notes are within the same file as Sir Seymour's, British Library IOR L/PS/6/560 1/11 Coll 1/11.

3 For information on Edward Lechmere Russell, see C.E. Buckland, *Dictionary of Indian Biography* (London: Swan Sonnenschein, 1906), 308. For Russell's opinion of letting go ships with small numbers of enslaved Africans, see British Library, India Office Records L/P&S/18/ B85, 8–9. Moses D.E. Nwulia nicely described this in his *Britain and Slavery*, 86–7. For Russell's idea that Africans might be better off enslaved than liberated, as 'unfortunate' as he found slavery, see British Library, India Office Records L/P&S/18/ B85, 6. The argument that economic principle determined that enslaved people were not usually mistreated made a reappearance in a 2014 review in the *Economist* of Edward Baptist, *The Half Has Never Been Told: Slavery and the Making of American Capitalism* (New York: Basic Books, 2014). Russell's letter to the Bombay government of 29 Jan. 1869 in British Library, India Office Records L/P&S/18/ B85, 9.

4 For the suggestion that Heath couldn't have grasped the scale of the forces he was prodding, and for the connections between India and East Africa in this period, see ch. 6 of Thomas R. Metcalfe's excellent *Imperial Connections: India in the Indian Ocean Arena, 1860–1920* (Berkeley: University of California Press, 2008). For the economics of the slave and other trades, the Indian merchant/ finance community of Zanzibar and Bombay, Sewji and his customs farming, and the idea that the sultan relied on Sewji's capital and Sewji's capital on the Pax Britannica, Sheriff, *Slaves, Spices, and Ivory*, 104–9, 147. For Zanzibar's Indian trade community and its mortgage lending and human collateral on loans, Frederick Cooper, *Plantation Slavery on the East Coast of Africa* (New Haven: Yale University Press, 1977), 142–6. For the particular desirability of the ivory re-sold at Zanizbar, Edward A. Alpers, *Ivory and Slaves: Changing Pattern of International Trade in East Central Africa in the Later Nineteenth Century* (Berkeley: University of California Press, 1975), 87.

5 For Henry Churchill's warning against Indian slaveholders and traders see his January 1869 notice reprinted in National Archives FO 881/1742, 37. On the Kutchee's rejection of Churchill's authority to the point of laughing, see H.A. Churchill to Secretary of the Government of Bombay, 26 Feb. 1869, in *Memo, Slave-dealing and slave-holding by Kutchees in Zanzibar*, 1870, British Library, India Office Records L/PS/18/B90, 1–2. For Churchill's preference for immediate abolition, see Churchill to Acting Secretary, Government of Bombay, 1 Mar. 1869 in National Archives FO 881/1742, 1; on Churchill's fear of violence during these days, see H.A. Churchill to E. Meara, 3 Feb. 1869, British Library, India Office Records, IOR L/PS/9/48, Secret Letters Received from areas outside India, 2. For the sultan's warnings about Churchill stirring unrest, *Memo, Slave-dealing and slave-holding by Kutchees in Zanzibar,* 39.

6. 'With all his might'

1 For the story of Meara boarding the 'French' dhow, see Commander Meara to Sir L. Heath, 5 June 1869 in British Library, India Office Records L/P&S/18/ B85, 12; see also the passes issued at Nosy Be reprinted in British Library, India Office Records L/P&S/18/B85, 9–10. On the custom of considering the deck of a naval ship British soil, see Royal Commission on Fugitive Slaves, *Minutes of Evidence and Appendix* (London: Eyre and Spottiswoode, 1876), xx. Details of the episode of Meara at Majunga come from *Nymphe*'s log, National Archives ADM 53/9548; letter of Meara to Heath 29 Oct. 1869, and letter of Madagascar Secretary of State to T.C. Pakenham 4 Apr. 1869, reprinted in Foreign Office, *British and Foreign State Papers, 1869–1870,* vol. 60 (London: William Ridgeway, 1876), 529–32, 543, 546–7; Royal Commission on Fugitive Slaves, *Minutes of Evidence and Appendix* (London: Eyre and Spottiswoode, 1876), 180. On the understanding between Heath's officers that a captain sending men ashore to raid for captives could not expect the backing of the rest in case of mishap, see Colomb, *Slave-catching,* 208. The appearance of the approach to the fort comes from Colomb, who visited only months after Meara: *Slave-catching,* 327–28. For the timing of *Nymphe*'s arrival in this tense atmosphere see her log from this period, National Archives ADM 53/9548.

7. 'If it prove lawful prize'

1 See Philip Colomb on the pervasiveness of drunkenness in this period in 'The Evolution of the Blue Jacket', 269, 274 and elsewhere. Details from this period of refitting at Bombay, including the carpenters' and gunner's drunkenness, come from *Daphne*'s log, National Archives ADM 53/9582. Log entries from earlier months show the first lieutenant's struggles with alcohol. Log entries also record a constant stream of accidents involving the men running the ship. 1869's deaths and illnesses were recorded in House of Commons Parliamentary Papers 45, *Health of the Navy* (9 Feb.-21 Aug. 1871), 261–2. On the *Daphne*'s engine crushing one of the men's legs and the attempt to amputate and save the man, see *Allen's Indian Mail*, 3 Mar. 1869, 198. Other details from this section come from entries during this period in Commodore Heath's East Indies Station Journal, National Archives ADM 50/293. The story of *Daphne's* early days on her station in the spider's web, including the freeing of the father and son and Sulivan's personal inclination to see slavers hanged, come from Sulivan, *Dhow Chasing*, 141, 201–2 and *Daphne*'s log from mid-March 1869, National Archives ADM 53/9582.

2   For the slave and tonnage bounties, see House of Commons Parliamentary Papers, *Slave trade (tonnage bounties, &c.). Return of vessels, 1864–1869*, 1870 (411), 8–10; also Howell, *Royal Navy*, 47 n. 13; and Colomb, *Slave-catching*, 81. Also see Colomb, *Slave-catching*, 81–3, for a description of how bounty claims proceeded and how the shares were divvied up. See those pages in Colomb as well as Nwulia, *Britain and Slavery*, 83, for the sense that bounty inducements still did not make the slave suppression duty attractive for monetary reasons. A worker in an iron workshop who was trained in as an apprentice would get 30 shillings per week in 1867 according to Thomas Wright, *Some Habits and Customs of the Working Classes* (London: Tinsley, 1867), 99. A footman working in a wealthy household might make 10 shillings per week, but have room and board. A worker in a textile or drapery factory might make 10 shillings per week (25 pounds per year) but get room at the factory: *Tempted London* (New York: A.C. Armstrong, 1889), ch. 2. Other wages are printed in a series of letters by Henry Mayhew in the *Morning Chronicle* in 1849. For the Treasury habitually deducting 10% of tonnage and seaman adding 10%, Howell, *Royal Navy*, 164–5.

3   Details from the story of the *Nymphe* coasting northward, Lieutenant Clarke at Keonga, and the *Nymphe* at Kiswara or Kiswere come from *Nymphe*'s log for 26 Mar. to early Apr., National Archives ADM 53/9548, also Clarke to Edward Meara, 5 Jan. 1870, and Meara to Leopold Heath, 24 May 1869 and 5 Jan. 1870, in Slave Trade Records of the East Indian Station, National Archives ADM 127/40. Great detail about the Keonga encounter comes from the records of Dr Kirk's examination of both *Nymphe* and dhow crews preserved in National Archives FO 84/1307 pp. 314–24. Landscape details about Kiswara or Kiswere Bay come from US Navy, *Africa Pilot*, vol. II (Washington, DC: Government Printing Office, 1916), 334–5. The details about the experience of boat work in the squadron come from G. Keith Gordon who was a young officer on the station in 1872. He also offers excellent details of captures, of the suspected role of Zanzibari Indians in the trade, sailing a captured dhow, and more; for details of boat work, see G. Keith Gordon, *Seventeen Years in the Royal Navy:*

1865–1881 (Bandera, Texas: Frontier Times, 1942), 38–40, 45. Further details about the Kiswere/Kiswara incident come from H.C. Rothery, *Report [to Lords Commissioners, Treasury] respecting Dhows lately captured by Her Majesty's ships* Peterel *and* Nymphe, 21 Aug. 1869, British Library IOR, L/P&S/18/B84, 19–25. In this memo Rothery writes, on p. 22, 'Commander Meara has confused two things which are essentially different, namely, slavery and the Slave trade.'

8. 'Of moving accidents by flood and field'

1   For this early period of *Dryad*'s hunting, including the hunter's eagerness of the crew, the concern to see dhow before dhows saw *Dryad*, Colomb's use of the 'spider's web' metaphor, and more, see Colomb, *Slave-catching*, 193–4, 196, 198, 200 and elsewhere. See also *Dryad*'s log for mid- to late Apr. 1869, National Archives ADM 53/9913.

2   Details of the activities of Colomb and his crew off Ras Madraka in Apr. 1869 come from *Dryad*'s log for mid- to late Apr. 1869, National Archives ADM 53/9913, and Colomb, *Slave-catching*, 200–7. In his memoir of these experiences, Philip Colomb changed the names of the fellow sailors that he describes. He calls his coxswain 'Fletcher' in his book. Throughout this book, I call the actors by their real names instead of using Colomb's pseudonyms.

3   Philip Colomb tells the story of Saleh bin Moosa's background and his conversations with him in *Slave-catching*, 108–10.

4   The story of Bin Moosa and John Pitcher's encounter with Omani villagers come from *Slave-catching*, 209–10.

5   For *Daphne*'s exploits off Mukalla and Aden, the crossing to the Seychelles, and visits to former refugees, see Sulivan, *Dhow Chasing*, 195, 204–6; and *Daphne*'s log for Apr. to June 1869, National Archives ADM 53/9582. Details of Mukalla come from James Horsburgh, *The India Directory, or, Directions for Sailing to and From the East Indies*, vol. 1 (London: W.H. Allen, 1852), 364.

9. 'Destiny unshunnable, like death'

1   For the story of *Dryad* and her boats taking seven dhows in tow, examinations of the captains and some crew, release of one captive boy, and Colomb's thoughts on these occasions, see Colomb, *Slave-catching*, 210–25, and *Dryad*'s log for late Apr. 1869, National Archives ADM 53/9913. For Colomb's racist opinion that Africans did not sufficiently resist slavery because they did not have the 'white man's sense of injustice' or freedom, see Colomb, *Slave-catching*, 30–1. He repeats these racist sentiments at pp. 266–8 of the same source. The intelligence and ability of the Kroomen, whom he very greatly admired and credited as being 'almost as intelligent as white men', did not seem to overturn his racist conclusions.

2   Details of the *Nymphe*'s deadly encounter with a slaver in Zanzibar harbour come from British Library IOR L/PS/9/48, Secret Letters Received from areas outside India, Letter of John Kirk to G. Gonne Sec. to Government of Bombay, Political Dept., 12 Apr. 1869, 1–2; for more details see Meara to Leopold Heath, 5 May 1869 in House of Commons Parliamentary Papers, 1870 [C.141] Class B, *East coast of Africa. Correspondence respecting the slave trade and other matters*, 82; and, in the same source, Clark to Meara, 16 Apr. 1869, 82–3; for details about Clark, see Bernard Burke, *A Genealogical and Heraldic Dictionary of the Landed Gentry of Great Britain and Ireland*, pt. 1, 4th ed. (London: Harrison, 1862), 248; for Clark going inland following the tracks of enslaved Africans, see Meara to Leopold Heath, 5 June 1869 in the same source, 81; see also 'The Slave Trade on the East Coast of Africa', *Nautical Magazine and Naval Chronicle* (London: Simpkin, Marshall, and Co., 1869), 699; on the breech-loaded M1866 Snider-Enfield Mark I, see 'The Snider Breech-Loader Rifle', *The Engineer*, 9 Nov. 1866, 362. The reasons for Meara earning a reputation as a semi-pirate among the Zanzibaris will become clear but see, for two examples, John Kirk to Secretary of the Government of Bombay, 10 Apr. 1869 in House of Commons Parliamentary Papers, 1870 [C.141] Class B, *East coast of Africa. Correspondence respecting the slave trade and other matters*, 49. See also Consul H.A. Churchill's embarrassment caused by the squadron sometimes putting articles taken out of slave ships up for sale even before the dhows had been officially condemned in *Memorandum by Mr. Churchill respecting Slave trade on the East Coast of Africa*, no date, BL IOR, L/P&S/18/B84, 49. For more details about the shootout in Zanzibar harbour and the burial of William Mitchell, see *Nymphe*'s log for Apr. 1869, National Archives ADM 53/9548.

10. 'Most disastrous chances'

1   Details about the *Forte* come from National Maritime Museum, Ship Plans NPB2269 and NPB2270. The National Maritime Museum also holds a painting of *Forte* before her slight lengthening and conversion to steam: item BHC3737. Some details about the *Forte*'s capture come from Scott, *Fifty Years in the Royal*

Navy, 28. The identity of the bosun comes from *Forte*'s Establishment Book, National Archives ADM 115/410. For more details about *Forte's* capture of a full slaver, see *Forte*'s log for May 1869, National Archives ADM 53/9931.

2   The story of the dhow that ran on the beach and the effort to land and preserve as many captives as possible is told by Colomb, *Slave-catching*, 235–53. This section includes his sort of confession that he was not usually motivated by a sense of humanity or philanthropy, but also the sense that, upon watching the desperation of the victims of the swamped dhow, he was watching the suffering of his fellow human beings. For details about the cutter see pp.273–4 in the same source. Further details about the incident come from Colomb to Secretary of the Admiralty, 12 May 1869, House of Commons Parliamentary Papers, 1870 [C.141] Class B, *East coast of Africa. Correspondence respecting the slave trade and other matters*, 79, and in the same source, Colomb to Leopold Heath, 10 May 1869, 80–1; see also Acting Lieutenant William Henn's report to Philip Colomb, 6 May 1869, in National Archives, East India Slave Trade Records, 1869, ADM 127/40; and in the same source, Colomb to Leopold Heath, 10 May 1869, and Gunner William Wilkie to Philip Colomb, 7 May 1869. See also *Dryad*'s log for early May, National Archives ADM 53/9913, and *Dryad*'s Establishment Book, National Archives ADM 115/290.

3   For *Nymphe's* time at Seychelles, including the anchorage, appearance of the island, and disposition of refugees from slavery, see the depiction by William Cope Devereux, assistant paymaster on HMS *Gorgon* which cruised the East African coast for slavers in 1861, in his *A Cruise in the Gorgon* (London: Bell and Daldy, 1869), 142–4. For more on *Nymphe*'s time at the Seychelles, including the landing of the invalided Hodgson, ship's leave, deserters, and the influx of syphilis, see *Nymphe*'s log for mid- and late April 1869, ADM 53/9548, *Nymphe*'s Establishment Book, ADM 115/691, House of Commons Parliamentary Papers 45, *Health of the Navy* (9 Feb.-21 Aug. 1871), 246, and the day book of John Noble, surgeon on *Nymphe*, York Minster Archives Add MS 130. For the Seychelles merchants' dependence on the squadron's business, see Mahé merchants' petition of 24 Nov. 1869 to Leopold Heath in National Archives, East India Slave Trade Records, 1869, ADM 127/40. For prostitution at Mahé, Seychelles, see House of Commons Parliamentary Papers 45, *Health of the Navy*, as cited above. For the rescues of 266 and 153 captives see *Nymphe*'s log for mid-to late May, ADM 53/9548; see also Meara to Leopold Heath, 27 May 1869, in National Archives, East India Slave Trade Records, 1869, ADM 127/40; for Charles Hemus Hopkins, see his service record at National Archives ADM 196/73. For the appearance of the former slave depot in Aden harbour, see Colomb, *Slave-catching*, 262. See pp. 260–1 in the same source for the total slavers taken that spring, p. 260 for Meara's joke that the slavers seemed to intend to discharge their captives on *Nymphe*, and p. 263 for the happiness at receiving their awards of tonnage and slave bounties. On the trading of charts, etc. see Meara to Leopold Heath, 27 May 1869, as cited above. On the fate of former slaves landed at Aden, see Charles Vivian, House of Commons Parliamentary Papers, 1871 (420) *Report from the Select Committee on Slave Trade (East Coast of Africa)* together with the proceedings of the committee, minutes of evidence, appendix and index, 5. See this source, too, for the numbers of victims 'legally' imported to Zanzibar, v; as well as National Archive FO 84/1292, 101–6. And for total captures in the 1860s, see Howell, *Royal Navy*, 45.

11. 'Too true an evil'

1   On Viceroy John Lawrence and Zanzibar, as well as the way that Zanzibar fell in a sphere shared by Calcutta and London, and Calcutta as an imperial centre, as well as Fitzgerald's hearty rejection of schemes for renegotiating India's relationship with Muscat for the sake of fighting the slave trade, see Robert J. Blythe, *The Empire of the Raj: India, Eastern Africa and the Middle East, 1858–1947* (Basingstoke: Palgrave Macmillan, 2003), 43–7 and elsewhere. For the importance of the Persian Gulf to India, including how that relationship involved slave trade suppression, see Hopper, *Slaves of One Master*, ch. 3 and elsewhere. For Zanzibar's importance to Bombay and India in general as a market and source of luxuries and cash, see Sheriff, *Slaves, Spices, and Ivory*, 136 and throughout. For the Earl of Mayo's reputation for thinking the slave trade question a 'troublesome irrelevancy which diverted attention from what he considered to be the main point', R.J. Gavin, 'The Bartle Frere Mission to Zanzibar, 1873', *Historical Journal* 5 (1962), 132. For the persistence of slavery in India, Howard Temperley, 'The Delegalization of Slavery in British India', in *After Slavery: Emancipation and its Discontents*, ed. Howard Temperley (London: Frank Cass, 2000), 169–87. For the fact that an Oman-area trader could buy twenty captives in Zanzibar for ten baskets of dates bought on credit then sell them for 1,000 Maria Theresa dollars, see letter of Ibrahim bin Sultan to Majid bin Said, sultan of Zanzibar, 7 Jan. 1869, British Library, India Office Records, L/PS/9/48, 2. Sir Edward Russell's warnings to Bombay are at Russell to G. Gonne Sec. to Government of Bombay, Political Dept., 29 Jan. 1869, in British

Library, IOR L/P&S/18/B85, 9. On the Bombay government approaching Heath still in port, see, in the same source, Heath to Sir Seymour Fitzgerald, 16 Feb. 1869, 9; see also Heath to Secretary of the Admiralty, 9 Apr. 1869, 7, which includes the Advocate General of Bombay arguing that domestic slaves ought not be grounds for condemnation and Heath's response. This response also included extracts from captured letters that proved that sometimes a dhow carrying only a few captives – ostensibly 'mere' domestic slaves – could be in fact bound for sale. For the sense that Heath believed it inconceivable that the squadron limit its seizures to dhows with large numbers of slaves because it would practically legalise the trade, see, again, Heath to Sir S. Fitzgerald, 16 Feb. 1869, as cited above (this includes Heath's comment on Sir Russell's 'heartburnings'). The Admiralty instructions are at Secretary to the Admiralty to Leopold Heath, 12 Mar. 1869, National Archives, East India Slave Trade Records, 1869, ADM 127/40. Notes on the back of this correspondence show that Heath circulated these instructions among his captains while still in Aden in early June 1869. Enclosed with these were the letter from the sultan of Zanzibar to Consul Henry Churchill, Dec. 1868 (no day given), and Churchill's response, 10 Dec. 1868, and the letter of Arthur Otway to Secretary of the Admiralty, 10 Mar. 1869.

12. 'The wind hath spoke aloud at land'

1   On Portuguese as slave carriers and the Mozambique area as the source of roughly 8% of the Atlantic trade, Hugh Thomas, *The Slave Trade* (New York: Simon and Schuster, 1997), 804. The American barque *Minnetonka*, curiously named after a lake in Minnesota, was slaving in this region as late as 1857: House of Commons Parliamentary Papers LXI (Dec. 1857-Aug. 1858) 29, *Slave Trade*, 222. On early modern Mozambique Island, Malyn Newitt, 'Mozambique Island: The Rise and Decline of a Colonial Port City', in Liam Matthew Brockey, ed., *Portuguese Colonial Cities in the Early Modern World* (Farnham: Ashgate, 2008), ch. 4 and 117–19, especially. For general information on the Portuguese in Mozambique in the 1800s, including details on Matekenya (Paul Marianno Vas dos Anjos I and II and III) and Bonga, see M.D.D. Newitt, *Portuguese Settlement on the Zambezi: Exploration, Land Tenure, and Colonial Rule in East Africa* (New York: Africana, 1973), 275–81 and elsewhere. For impressions of the first Paul Marianno, see Thomas Boteler, *Narrative of a Voyage of Discovery to Africa and Arabia, 1821–1826*, I (London: Richard Bentley, 1835), 270. For Kirk witnessing

the handiwork of Matekenya's war-making and famine, see John McCracken, *A History of Malawi, 1859–1966* (Woodbridge, Suffolk: Boydell and Brewer, 2012), 34. For Bishop Tozer hearing songs of Matekenya, see Edward Steere, *Swahili Tales as Told by Natives of Zanzibar* (London: Bell and Daldy, 1870), viii. For songs about Marianno's line, see Leroy Vail and Landeg White, 'Plantation Protest: The History of Mozambican Song', *Journal of Southern African Studies* 5 (Oct. 1978), 21; also, for Matekenya's wife, Kathleen E. Sheldon, *Pounders of Grain: A History of Women, Work, and Politics in Mozambique* (Portsmouth, NH: Heinemann, 2002), 48. And finally, on Matekenya and his family, see Owen J.M. Kalinga, *Historical Dictionary of Malawi* 4th ed. (Lanham, Maryland: Scarecrow, 2012), 286–7, and David and Charles Livingstone, *Narrative of an Expedition to the Zambesi*, 24–6, 449–50. On Quelimane and a description of Mozambique Island in the nineteenth century, see Frederick Lamport Barnard, *A Three Years' Cruise in the Mozambique Channel for the Suppression of the Slave Trade* (London: Richard Bentley, 1848), 51, 71–2, 110–11.

2   For French Charlie's shop and provision procurement business, see Sulivan, *Dhow Chasing*, 207–12. Details for William Dillon come from a portrait and family letters and Dillon's abbreviated diary described in descendant Julia Turner's *Dr. William Edward Dillon: Navy Surgeon in Livingstone's Africa* (British Columbia: Friesen Press, 2014). As always, details of navigation, weather, and activities on board *Daphne*, including the sad case of Tom Hurrex, come from *Daphne*'s log, National Archives ADM 53/9582. The resistance of wind and current are also documented in Sulivan to Leopold Heath, 11 Oct. 1869 in Slave Trade Records of the East Indian Station, National Archives ADM 127/40. Historical moon phases are available from nasa.gov. On Jumah Jin discovering the root of the terror in the town, see a letter of Sulivan quoted in 'Reports from Naval Officers', *Anti-Slavery Reporter*, 1 July 1871, 171. Other details, including Africans seeking refuge on board, come from Sulivan, *Dhow Chasing*, 219–45; and also Sulivan to the governor of Mozambique, 31 Aug. 1869, in House of Commons Parliamentary Papers, 8 Feb.-15 Aug. 1876, vol. 28, *Fugitive Slaves*, 178; and Sulivan to Heath, 11 Oct. 1869, in the same source at p. 178.

3   For the British in the Persian Gulf generally, including the slave trade there, the Great Game, Banian supremacy in various markets, customs farming in Muscat, and the pearl industry, James Onley, 'Indian Communities in the Persian Gulf, c. 1500–1947', in Lawrence G. Potter, *The Persian Gulf in Modern Times* (New York: Palgrave Macmillan, 2014), 231–66, particularly 254–6. For the pearl diving industry and slavery, Jerzy Zdanowski, *Slavery and Manumission: British Policy in the Red Sea and the Persian Gulf in the First Half of the 20th Century* (Reading, Berkshire: Ithaca, 2013), 75–6. For Pelly generally see Frederic Goldsmid, 'Obituary, General Sir Lewis Pelly', *Proceedings of the Royal Geographical Society and Monthly Record of Geography*, New Monthly Series, 14 (1892),416–21. Details come from a letter from Lewis Pelly to Colomb of 24 Apr. 1869, British Library India Office Records Mss Eur F126/42, ff 28–9, in which Pelly uses the word 'row' and mentions his suspicion of Russian or French prodding in Tehran. For the details of the Persian Gulf chief's complaint to Persian Gulf political resident Lewis Pelly, see correspondence between Pelly, Heath and Colomb between April and July 1869 in House of Commons Parliamentary Papers, 1870 [C.141] Class B, *East coast of Africa. Correspondence respecting the slave trade and other matters*, 86–90.

4   For Colomb and the *Dryad*'s time at Ceylon (now Sri Lanka), including his delight at seeing anything green, see Colomb, *Slave-catching*, 284–95. Other details come from *Dryad*'s log, National Archives ADM 53/9913. *Forte*'s log mentions rockets fired from shore, National Archives ADM 53/ 9931. The text of Heath's orders to Colomb is at House of Commons Parliamentary Papers, 8 Feb.-15 Aug. 1876, vol. 28, *Fugitive Slaves*, 177, and, as copied by Heath himself, 10 Oct. 1869, Slave Trade Records of the East Indian Station, National Archives ADM 127/40.

5   For Heath finding that Colomb had fully answered Pelly's objections, see House of Commons Parliamentary Papers, 1870 [C.141] Class B, *East coast of Africa. Correspondence respecting the slave trade and other matters*, 89–90. Kirk's complaints about the interpreters in Heath's squadron and Heath's response are preserved in Leopold Heath to Secretary of the Admiralty, 31 July 1869, Slave Trade Records of the East Indian Station, National Archives ADM 127/40. The enclosures containing Kirk's complaints appear much later in this large volume. For Madagascar consul Pakenham's frustration with Heath's squadron, see the same source, communications between Pakenham, Heath, and others, on pp. 18–30. For Heath's intention to speak to the escaped captives taken to Seychelles aboard the *Nymphe*, and Heath's pointing out to Pakenham the unabated trade to Madagascar, see the same source, Heath to the Admiralty, 22 Sept. 1869 (referring to his activities in July), on p. 92. And see, for Heath's further words for Pakenham, House of Commons Parliamentary Papers, 8 Feb.-15 Aug. 1876, vol. 28, *Fugitive Slaves*, 180. Details of the departure and weather come from *Forte*'s log, National Archives ADM 53/9931.

13. 'Swell his sail with thine own powerful breath'

1   Moses D.E. Nwulia nicely paints the picture of the French officer arriving at the court of the sultan from Réunion in *Britain and Slavery*, 31; other details come from his ch. 2, pt. 3. For more on the *engagés* system generally, and the number carried to French islands in the 1850s, see Paul E. Lovejoy, *Transformations in Slavery: A History of Slavery in Africa* (Cambridge: Cambridge University Press, 2000), 181. For an early eyewitness to the French 'free emigrant labour' scheme, see Lyons McLeod, *Travels in Eastern Africa*, vol. 1 (London: Hurst and Blackett, 1860), 120–5 and elsewhere. For Livingstone, see David and Charles Livingstone, *Narrative of an Expedition to the Zambesi*, 623.

2   On the frequency of dhows flying French colours and being un-searchable, see George Sulivan to Leopold Heath, 11 Oct. 1869, in Slave Trade Records of the East Indian Station, National Archives ADM 127/40. Details of this period of hunting off Mafamade Island come from *Daphne*'s log, National Archives ADM 53/9582. They also come from a report on this period sent by Sulivan to Heath, 11 Oct. 1869, as cited above, which includes his thought that the dhow passed him in darkness. Geographical details about Mafamade and the surrounding area come from James Horsburgh, *The India Directory, or, Directions for Sailing to and From the East Indies*, vol. 1 (London: W.H. Allen, 1852), 258–9, and, with additional details about the appearance of the island, Alexander George Findlay, *A Directory for the Navigation of the Indian Ocean*, 3rd ed. (London: Richard Holmes Laurie, 1876), 358. Other details of the hunt off Mafamade, including Sulivan's familiarity with the island and his memory of dysentery sweeping the *Castor* come from Sulivan, *Dhow Chasing*, 214–15. With regard to enemy fire and the armaments of slavers, see HMS *Star*'s experience in taking fire and finding significant weaponry on board a slaver in Walter de Kantzow's letter of May or June reported in *Anti-Slavery Reporter*, 1 Oct. 1869, 271. De Kantzow is not named, but his identity is easily detected based on the locale of the capture and the total of captives taken off the dhow, 236, later published in official reports. For the disappearance of crewmembers from Lyra near the River Antonio, Parliamentary Papers vol. LXXV (Feb.-Aug. 1866) 37, *Slave Trade*, 85–6.

3   Details for *Daphne*'s hurry to Mayotta come from *Daphne*'s log, National Archives ADM 53/9582. Insight into Jumah Jin (bin Moosa, not to be confused with the Jumah bin Moosa who served on *Dryad*) come from British Library IOR L/PS/9/48 Secret Letters Received from areas outside India, 'Evidence of Juma bin Moosa', a statement given in regard to the HMS *Star* affair, burning the dhow of Vizier's sister, 3 May 1869, 1–2. Also for Jumah Jin, see Sulivan, *Dhow Chasing*, 247–50. For Sulivan's belief that he was not intercepting slavers in the Mozambique Channel because they were hiding behind the French flag, and for his broaching it with the governor of Mayotta, see George Sulivan to Leopold Heath, 11 Oct. 1869 in Slave Trade Records of the East Indian Station, National Archives ADM 127/40.

4   For the experience of *Nymphe* stalking off the coast of north-west Madagascar and navigating to Majunga, see *Nymphe*'s log, National Archives ADM 53/9548. The appearance of the approach to the fort comes from Colomb, *Slave-catching*, 327–28. On Meara's talk with authorities at Majunga, including his belief that the Malagasy did secretly carry on the trade and force silence on their people, and also his encounter with Africans at Boyanna Bay, Madagascar, see Edward Meara to Leopold Heath 29 Oct. 1869, in Slave Trade Records of the East Indian Station, National Archives ADM 127/40.

5   Details of Heath's thinking at the moment of writing to Pakenham from Seychelles, having received the sworn depositions from Ferejd and Malbrook, come from Heath to Pakenham, 14 Aug. 1869, in House of Commons Parliamentary Papers, 8 Feb.-15 Aug. 1876, vol. 28, *Fugitive Slaves*, 180. In the same source, pp. 180–1, are the depositions themselves of Ferejd and Malbrook. Other details come from *Forte*'s log, National Archives ADM 53/9931.

14. 'Stand upon the foaming shore'

1   Gwyn Campbell, 'Madagascar and the Slave Trade, 1810–1895', 213 and elsewhere. For the Indians dominating the financing of the slave trade to Majunga, see his 'Madagascar and Mozambiques in the Slave Trade of the Western Indian Ocean', in William Gervase Clarence-Smith, ed., *The Economics of the Indian Ocean Slave Trade in the Nineteenth Century* (Abingdon: Routledge, 1989), 172, 185 and elsewhere.

2   For Colomb's period in the town of Majunga, see Colomb, *Slave-catching*, 318–46. This includes his thought that Meara had exposed the Majunga authorities since they did not bother reporting the illegally imported Mozambican captives until after he found them out. This is also suggested at pp. 307–8. For some additional details about the chase that occurred while Colomb hosted Governor Ramasy, see Colomb's report on this cruise to Commodore Heath, 1 Oct. 1869, Slave Trade Records of the East Indian Station, National Archives ADM 127/40. Additional information about *Dryad*, including the material of its decks, come from *Conway's All the World's Fighting Ships, 1860–1905* (New York: Mayflower, 1979), 55–6; Colomb's love of the Malagasy language is documented at p. 306. Data for Midshipman Gerard Brooke come from *Dryad's* Establishment Book, National Archives ADM 115/290, and his service record, National Archives ADM 196/38/175. More details from the period at Majunga come from mid-September 1869 entries in *Dryad's* log, National Archives ADM 53/9913.

15. 'Traitors ensteep'd to clog the guiltless keel'

1   For the slave trade bureaucracy and Wylde, see Keith Hamilton, 'Zealots and Helots: The Slave Trade Department of the Nineteenth-Century Foreign Office', in *Slavery, Diplomacy and Empire: Britain and the Suppression of the Slave Trade, 1807–1975* (Eastbourne: Sussex, 2009), 31–4. I cannot quite agree with my colleague Dr Hamilton in the credit that he gives Wylde for stimulating action on the east coast. I believe that he and Dr Huzzey, in his excellent *Freedom Burning*, draw far too direct a line between Wylde and ultimate results in the form of the Frere mission. For more on Wylde, see his memo of 31 Mar. 1869 in National Archives FO 84/1310 in which he promotes the idea of a single port of debarkation from the mainland for captives bound for the Zanzibar slave market. He proposes a slow abolition of the trade over a course of years with the sultan of Zanzibar being compensated for the loss in taxes on slave imports. Meanwhile, he was both against a larger naval presence on the coast and confident that enforcing existing treaties at the points of sale would work. Wylde based much of his confidence that the east coast trade would eventually be eliminated on the fact that the west coast trade had been ultimately stopped. But that was over the course of decades and was to some important degree because of historical changes at the points of sale on the other side of the Atlantic. The evidence suggests Wylde was slow to come around to the idea of the total prohibition of the trade at sea, following Heath and the squadron's officers who came to that conclusion far earlier then he did. See Howell, *The Royal Navy and the Slave Trade*, 88. Ch. 3 of Huzzey's *Freedom Burning* is also an excellent source for the growth and operations of the abolitionist bureaucracy in London and includes Palmerston blaming the Admiralty for sending only its slowest tubs to do suppression work. For Wylde's extreme statements about the squadron acting practically like vigilantes, and his belief that Heath's ships would make them 'come to grief', see his letter to H.C. Rothery, 28 July 1869, inviting Rothery to join the inter-departmental committee to write new orders for the suppression of the east coast slave trade, National Archives HCA 36/5. The Foreign Office received Bombay's concerns and those of Russell at Aden around late May 1869, Admiralty to Clarendon, 24 May 1869, in National Archives FO 84/1310. Those reports seem to have convinced Wylde that the Navy was out of control; see his memo of 27 May 1869 in National Archives FO 84/1310, 263–5.

2 Details for Heath's visit to Zanzibar and subsequent trip to Aden come from *Forte*'s log, National Archives ADM 53/9931. Dr John Kirk related this conversation about leaving suspect slavers in charge of governors along the coast in a letter to the government of Bombay: Kirk to C. Gonne, 24 Aug. 1869, British Library IOR L/PS/9/48, Secret Letters Received from areas outside India, 1–3. The same letter reveals that this is when Kirk revealed to Heath that he had ruled against Edward Meara and the *Nymphe*'s officers in the Keonga dhow case. And more information about Heath's confrontation with Kirk and Heath's ongoing conflict with the Foreign Office, Arthur Otway in particular, comes from Heath to Secretary of the Admiralty, 22 Sept. 1869, which is copied in full in Slave Trade Records of the East Indian Station, National Archives ADM 127/40, n.p, and as an extract in House of Commons Parliamentary Papers, 1870 [C.141] Class B, *East coast of Africa. Correspondence respecting the slave trade and other matters*, 92–4. This source includes the evidence that the dhow in question carried enslaved Africans, equipment, and an expired pass. On Kirk's concern with the reputation of Britain in those waters, see a letter of the same month to the Foreign Office on the subject of the Keonga incident: Kirk to Earl of Clarendon, 8 Aug. 1869, in the same issue of Parliamentary Papers, p. 53. On Kirk ordering the restoration of the slaves that came off the suspect dhow, see Edward Meara to Secretary of the Admiralty, 27 July 1870, in Foreign Office, *British and Foreign State Papers, 1870–1871* (London: William Ridgeway, 1877), 360–1. For the new rumours of Livingstone being seen, see John Kirk to C. Gonne, Sec. to Government, Bombay, 31 Aug. 1869, British Library IOR L/PS/9/48, Secret Letters Received from areas outside India.

16. 'Vouch with me, heaven'

1 For the division of the finders' fee paid to Portuguese officials by *engagés* dealers, see McLeod, *Travels in Eastern Africa*, 306. For other details in this section, see Nwulia, *Britain and Slavery*, 32–3. A description of Epidendron Island comes from Alexander George Findlay, *A Directory for the Navigation of*

the Indian Ocean, 3rd ed. (London: Richard Holmes Laurie, 1876), 357. Details of target practice at Epidendron Island and the chase of the Portuguese schooner come from *Daphne*'s log, National Archives ADM 53/9582. George Sulivan to Leopold Heath, 11 Oct. 1869, in Slave Trade Records of the East Indian Station, National Archives ADM 127/40. For Sulivan's belief that the Arab slavers absorbed the blame for the Portuguese slave trading, see *Dhow Chasing*, 230. Further details about the capture of the schooner, the children on board, and Sulivan's thinking and suspicions come from both *Dhow Chasing*, 231–2 and George Sulivan to Leopold Heath, 11 Oct. 1869, in Slave Trade Records of the East Indian Station, National Archives ADM 127/40; Sulivan's awareness of the increased scrutiny placed on the squadron comes from a kind of warning circulated among the squadron by Leopold Heath, namely Kirk's complaint about poor interpreters leading to allegedly false seizures, signed by all captains on the station, 6 May 1869, in Slave Trade Records of the East Indian Station, National Archives ADM 127/40. In the same source there is a circular sent by Heath and signed by all of the squadron's captains except Sulivan, repeating the Admiralty's admonition to take captures into a port with a Vice-Admiralty judge in it whenever possible; Heath to squadron, 5 Jun. 1869. Far more direct would have been recent conversations with Captain De Kantzow, though there is no documentary evidence for these.

2   For George Sulivan's return to Mozambique Island to condemn the Portuguese Schooner bearing enslaved children, see *Daphne*'s log, National Archives ADM 53/9582. George Sulivan to Leopold Heath, 11 Oct. 1869, in Slave Trade Records of the East Indian Station, National Archives ADM 127/40, for a number of details including the governor of Mozambique saying that the 'free' children 'belonged' to the Indian merchant and especially for his thinking about taking the schooner to the Cape of Good Hope, and Sulivan, *Dhow Chasing*, 231–2. For physical details of the town, see William Devereux, *A Cruise in the Gorgon* (London: Bell and Daldy, 1869), 62.

3   On the failure of Churchill's initiative to divest Kutchees of their slaves and Kirk's requirement to publish news otherwise in August 1869, see John Kirk to Sec. Government, Bombay, 16 Aug. 1869, House of Commons Parliamentary Papers, 1870 [C.141] Class B, *East coast of Africa. Correspondence respecting the slave trade and other matters*, 54. Word that the British community at Zanzibar understood that the Omani slavers who battled the *Nymphe*'s crew walked free comes from H.A. Fraser, William Tozer and James Christie, *The East African Slave Trade, and the Measures Proposed for its Extinction: As Viewed by Residents* *in Zanzibar* (London: Harrison, 1871), 53. Dr Christie writes that the identities of the slavers in question were common knowledge in the town.

4 Details of the crossing to Mauritius come from *Dryad*'s log, National Archives ADM 53/9913. Examples showing Colomb's strong sense of his own coolness, dispassionateness, lack of sentimentality are many in his memoir, but see for good examples, *Slave-catching*, 265, 270, 279–82. See these pages and 271, 274, 277, too, for the experience of having the Africans on board the *Dryad*. In the same source on p. 280 Colomb states that he did not need to draw on sentimentality to take the right action in fighting the slave trade. For Colomb's acknowledgement of and rejection of sentimental views of Royal Navy sailors, see P.H. Colomb, 'The Evolution of the Blue Jacket'. For another example of 'mother-henning', this one from the *Nymphe* before Meara took command, see *Letters of Bishop Tozer and His Sister*, 169. For the arrival at Mauritius and Colomb's sense that it was 'European' and thus to his prejudiced mind 'civilised', see *Slave-catching*, 346–50.

5 For British outrage at French and Portuguese hypocrisy, see Nwulia, *Britain and Slavery*, 33–4. Details come from Deryck Scarr, *Slaving and Slavery in the Indian Ocean* (Basingstoke: Palgrave Macmillan, 1998), 68–74 and elsewhere, and his *History of Seychelles since 1770* (London: Hurst, 1999), ch. 3. See also Richard B. Allen, 'Maroonage and its Legacy in Mauritius and in the Colonial Plantation World', *Outre-mers* 89 (2002), 131–52; and his *Slaves, Freedmen and Indentured Laborers in Colonial Mauritius* (Cambridge: Cambridge University Press, 1999), 136–51 and elsewhere; and for details including the fact that indentured servants to Mauritius were members of a slave caste, see his 'Slaves, Convicts, Abolitionism and the Global Origins of the Post-Emancipation Indentured Labor System', *Slavery & Abolition* 35 (2014), 328–48. See also Clare Anderson, 'Convicts and Coolies: Rethinking Indentured Labour in the Nineteenth Century', *Slavery & Abolition* 30 (2009), 93–109. For details including the rate of indentured labourers' successful court cases on Mauritius in the 1860s, see Alessandro Stanziani, 'Debt Labour and Bondage: English Servants Versus Indentured Servants in Mauritius, from the Late Eighteenth Century to Early Twentieth Century', in Gwyn Campbell and Alessandro Stanziani, eds., *Bonded Labour and Debt in the Indian Ocean World* (Abingdon: Routledge, 2015), 75–86. For other details including the protests against 'apprenticeship', see Moses D.E. Nwulia, 'The "Apprenticeship" System in Mauritius: Its Character and Its Impact on Race Relations in the Immediate Post-Emancipation Period, 1839–1879', *African Studies Review* 21 (April 1978), 89–101. On the welcome reception of the deposited refugees on Seychelles, see Mahé merchants' petition of 24 November 1869 to Leopold Heath in National Archives, East India Slave Trade Records, 1869, ADM 127/40. On the welcome reception African refugees received in Mauritius, House of Commons Parliamentary Papers, 1871 [C.340] Class B, *East Coast of Africa. Correspondence respecting the slave trade and other matters*, 8. **6** For Colomb's observation of the accommodations for the Africans on Mauritius and his gloomy perceptions of their fate, see *Slave-catching*, 346–50.

17. 'False as water'

1 For details about the day Edward Meara paid Hamed bin Sahel see National Archives ADM 53/9548 HMS *Nymphe* Log. Heath's letter bearing news of promotions, received Sept. 1869, comes from Admiralty to Leopold Heath, 23 June 1869, in Slave Trade Records of the East Indian Station, National Archives ADM 127/40. For Kirk's belief that this was important for convincing the Arabs of British justice, Kirk to the Earl of Clarendon, 8 Aug. 1869, in House of Commons Parliamentary Papers, 1870 [C.141] Class B, *East coast of Africa. Correspondence respecting the slave trade and other matters*, 53. Meara knew of the reminder to tow condemned ships into port if at all possible because he signed Heath's circular on the matter: Slave Trade Records of the East Indian Station, National Archives ADM 127/40, Heath to squadron, 5 June 1869. More details of the meeting at which Meara paid the dhow owner at the British Residency come from John Kirk to Secretary of State, Foreign Affairs, 18 Sept. 1869, British Library IOR L/PS/9/48. Details of the layout of the British Residency at Zanzibar and the surrounding area come from Richard Hayes Crofton, *The Old Consulate at Zanzibar* (Oxford: Oxford University Press, 1935), inset map. That Kirk took Meara aside to blame Bombay for ordering restitution to the slaveholder taken at Keonga comes from Edward Meara to Secretary of the Admiralty, 27 July 1870, in Foreign Office, *British and Foreign State Papers, 1870–1871* (London: William Ridgeway, 1877), 361.

2 Kirk to C. Gonne Sec. to Govt Bombay, Political Department, 21 Sept 1869 and 4 Oct. 1869, both at British Library, India Office Records, L/PS/9/48.

3 For the period of Sulivan arriving at Zanzibar just after Meara's paying of the allegedly aggrieved dhow owner, see *Daphne*'s log, National Archives ADM 53/9582. For his visit to Jumah Jin's widow and his visit to the Zanzibar slave market, see Sulivan, *Dhow Chasing*, 247–54. Most details come from Sulivan's book, but some details of Zanzibar streets outside the slave market come from slaver-hunter William Cope Devereux, assistant paymaster on HMS *Gorgon* in 1861. See his *A Cruise in the Gorgon* (London: Bell and Daldy, 1869), 100–3; generally, Devereux had a very low opinion of the honesty of the men on his ship with regard to their slave-trade policing. Other details come from Leopold Heath's aide-de-camp Percy Scott, who was there in the same years as Sulivan: *Fifty Years in the Royal Navy*, 29.

4   The period of *Nymphe*'s hunting off the Horn of Africa, including target practice and daily work, is described in *Nymphe*'s log, National Archives ADM 53/9547. Crew details come from the *Nymphe*'s Establishment Book, National Archives ADM 115/691. The Sept. 1869 message from Kirk to Meara is recorded in Edward Meara's report to Commodore Heath, 26 Oct. 1869, in Slave Trade Records of the East Indian Station, National Archives ADM 127/40. For Meara's thinking relative to Kirk's decision that the refugees from slavery should be returned to the victor in his Vice-Admiralty court, see Edward Meara to Secretary of the Admiralty, 27 July 1870, in Foreign Office, *British and Foreign State Papers, 1870–1871* (London: William Ridgeway, 1877), 360–1. There is no evidence to indicate the moment he decided to ignore D. Kirk's order.

5   The description of Tamatave comes from Devereux, *A Cruise in the Gorgon*, 291. Other details of the stop at Tamatave come from *Dryad*'s log, National Archives ADM 53/9913, and Colomb, *Slave-catching*, 350–1. Some details of the proceedings at the consul's house come from a series of letters between T.C. Pakenham and Commander Colomb and Pakenham and the Earl of Clarendon [Foreign Office], Aug.-Nov. 1869, in House of Commons Parliamentary Papers, 1871 [C.340] Class B, *East coast of Africa. Correspondence respecting the slave trade and other matters*, 4–8. For Colomb's aims in returning to Majunga to try to trap the officials there, including the hope to help Heath defend Meara by giving a counter charge, see Colomb's report on this part of his cruise to the commodore, including his racist theory that the Malagasy race-deficiencies were in part to blame, 31 Dec. 1869, Slave Trade Records of the East Indian Station, National Archives ADM 127/40. For Colomb's obvious delight in the surprise he would spring on Governor Ramasy at Majunga, as well as all of the other details of this incident, see Colomb, *Slave-catching*, 350–6.

18. 'The desperate tempest'

1   For the ants – I suspect he was writing about termites – eating the ornithological collection, see *Dhow Chasing*, 214–15. Information about Sulivan and *Daphne*'s arrival at Bombay in October 1869 come from *Daphne*'s log, National Archives ADM 53/9582. Also from his extensive report, Sulivan to Leopold Heath, 11 Oct. 1869 in Slave Trade Records of the East Indian Station, National Archives ADM 127/40. This report reveals that he had read in that period the criticism of the squadron moving between officials. One clue is that in his *Dhow Chasing* (p. 259) Sulivan makes particular reference to a condemnatory April 1869 letter from the Bombay Government to the Zanzibar Resident. The details of Sulivan's angry reaction to Bombay's interference come from this important document. The details about Royal Navy officers being condemned to Bombay suppers, including the sights on Bombay roads, come from Colomb, *Slave-catching*, 89–91. But unfortunately Sulivan does not provide the date of the supper in question. It might have been late 1868, but given the comment of the official and Sulivan's presence in Bombay then, late 1869 seems a better guess. The quote of the official comes from *Dhow Chasing*, 3. The direct quote from Sulivan's report to Heath comes from the 11 October 1869 report referenced above. Abdul Sheriff reports the short supply of ivory in 1868 in *Slave, Spices, and Ivory*, 135.

2   For the weather for 1 Nov. 1869, *London Daily News*, Tuesday 2 Nov. 1869, 7. For Clarendon's cigarette habit, Edward Hertslet, *Recollections of the Old Foreign Office* (London: John Murray, 1901), 121. H.C. Vivian is pictured on a carte-de-visite from this period at the National Portrait Gallery, item NPG x13266. One of Dickens' first jobs was court reporting from the Doctors Commons, which is both a place name and the name of the society of lawyers who practised its special law. The Dickens quote is from *David Copperfield*, ch. 23. On the friendship of William Wylde and Henry Rothery, see Howell, *Royal Navy and the Slave Trade*, 15. There is not much information on Fairfax beyond the Navy List and his service record, National Archives ADM 196/36/1115. An image of Arthur Otway is in *Vanity Fair*, 8 Feb. 1879. On Wylde and Rothery taking the lead on the committee, see Howell, *Royal Navy and the Slave Trade*, 61. Details from this section, including the meeting location, report drafts, manuscript notes on the proceedings, letters, and others, come from the file of papers generated by the committee: National Archives HCA 36/5. In this file, for Vivian warning about the interruption of hunting, see Vivian to Rothery, 16 Nov. 1869, 1. There is an 1860s portrait of Lord Clarendon at the National Portrait Gallery on a carte-de-visite, item NPG x29291, and a painting of Gladstone's entire cabinet by Lowes Cato Dickinson, 1869–1874, item NPG 5116. Information on Clarendon's philosophy comes from an excellent *Dictionary of National Biography*

(2004) article by David Steele and from Huzzey, *Freedom Burning*, 59–60, 63 and elsewhere. The report of the Slave Trade committee that included H.C. Rothery is located in National Archives HCA 36/5, Papers and correspondence of the East African Slave Trade Committee. The section quoted here is on p. 5. For the thinking of the East African Slave Trade committee, its allegations, even thoughts revealed in the margins, see this same collection of papers. The 'purchased at too high a price' quote comes from an annotation that Lord Clarendon made in the margins of a memo. This is cited in Richard Huzzey, *Freedom Burning*, 80. In the same source see p. 78 for Clarendon's damping down the zeal of diplomats.

3 The letter from Lord Clarendon's office citing the squadron for incorrectly rescuing fugitives from slavery is dated 6 Jan. 1870, in Slave Trade Records of the East Indian Station, National Archives ADM 127/40. For the Somerset trial, Steven M. Wise, *Though the Heavens May Fall: The Landmark Trial that Led to the End of Human Slavery* (Boston: De Capo Press, 2005). Caroline Shaw offers an excellent overview of this issue and tells the story of this matter coming to a head in the mid-1870s in *Britannia's Embrace: Modern Humanitarianism and the Imperial Origins of Refugee Relief* (Oxford: Oxford University Press, 2015), ch. 7. For the Foreign Office's official pique toward Sulivan, see the Admiralty letter conveying the news in Secretary of the Admiralty to Leopold Heath, 7 June 1870, in Slave Trade Records of the East Indian Station, National Archives ADM 127/40.

4 For Dr O'Connor's small stature and good company, see National Maritime Museum, William Henry Maxwell Journals, MAX/1, Section 1868. Details about the tale of Sabourri and the death of John Shilston come from Colomb, *Slave-catching*, 434–40. See also *Dryad*'s log, National Archives ADM 53/9914, *Dryad*'s Establishment Book, National Archives ADM 115/290, and Dr Daniel O'Connor's service record, National Archives ADM 196/9. It seems most likely that Sabourri was a student of Bishop Tozer, among Tozer's small group of students at Zanzibar, but I cannot find proof of this. Colomb's family background comes from the *Dictionary of National Biography*, 1901 Supplement, vol. 2 (New York: Macmillan, 1901), 49–50. Little is known of Dr O'Connor's background, but he is always mentioned as Daniel O'Connor, Esq.

5 The appearance of the Colaba lighthouse is provided by a watercolour pasted in the log of Frank Fauwell, National Maritime Museum, LOG N/D/13. Other details of the appearances of the ships already in harbour come from *Nymphe*'s log, National Archives ADM 53/9548. Commodore Heath describes his captains as zealous and energetic in his 22 Jan. 1870 report on the year 1869 in Slave

Trade Records of the East Indian Station, National Archives ADM 127/40. Leopold Heath's anger at the report of the committee is evident in multiple sources, but these particular thoughts come from his official response to the revised instructions, Confidential letter, Heath to Sec. of the Admiralty, 25 Mar. 1870, in National Archives HCA 36/5, Papers and correspondence of the East African Slave Trade Committee. For Heath's feeling that capturing ships with only a handful of captives on board was now practically outlawed, see Heath to Secretary of the Admiralty, 12 Jan. 1870, in Slave Trade Records of the East Indian Station, National Archives ADM 127/40. For Heath's feeling that the new rules would negatively affect the activity of the captains on the squadron, even embodied a threat, see Heath's annual report on the slave trade in the 22 Jan. 1870 document cited above, no page number, but his point no. 14. For Sulivan's angry response to India and London, see Sulivan to Leopold Heath, 11 Oct. 1869, in Slave Trade Records of the East Indian Station, National Archives ADM 127/40. The formulation offered here reflects his prose in *Dhow Chasing*, 3. Colomb, Sulivan and Heath wrote that the officers on the station shared the view that the new instructions badly hamstrung their efforts, practically limiting them to capturing fully laden slavers, though experience showed that perhaps most of the trade was carried on in much smaller numbers: Colomb, *Slave-catching*, 453; Sulivan, *Dhow Chasing*, 2; Heath, Confidential letter, Heath to Sec. of the Admiralty, 25 Mar. 1870, in National Archives HCA 36/5, Papers and correspondence of the East African Slave Trade Committee. Word of the Royal Humane Society awards came from the Admiralty to Leopold Heath, 21 Sept. 1869, in Slave Trade Records of the East Indian Station, National Archives ADM 127/40. On Heath writing that the new instructions 'will diminish the number of captures very largely', see his confidential letter referred to above.

19. 'After every tempest come such calms'

1   On the departures of Colomb, Heath and Meara and the numbers of East Africans taken from slave ships, see *The Times*, 9 Apr. 1870, 12; 24 Jan. 1870, 5; 20 May 1870, 12. On the rough totals of those lifted from slave ships, Howell, *Royal Navy and the Slave Trade*, 73, and House of Commons Parliamentary Papers, *Slave trade (tonnage bounties, &c.). Return of vessels captured for being engaged in and equipped for the slave trade* (411), 1870. For totals from 1870 and the fact that freed Africans were restored to slaveholders, House of Commons Parliamentary Papers, *Trade; Slave Trade*, LXXI (Feb.-Aug. 1875) 933–9. Dr

NOTES

Lindsay Doulton researched the suppression of the East African slave trade from the point of view of the navy, imagined Africans, and imagined Arabs within British popular culture in her DPhil thesis, 'The Royal Navy's anti-slavery campaign in the western Indian Ocean, c. 1860–1890: race, empire and identity', University of Hull, 2010, and I found ch. 8 especially helpful; my findings might adjust her chronology a bit earlier since much, though certainly not all, of her newspaper material is from the 1880s. For a good overview on the culture of newspaper reading in this period, Mark Hampton, *Visions of the Press in Britain, 1850–1950* (Champagne-Urbana: University of Illinois Press, 2004), ch. 1. For the rise of visual culture in newspapers of this period, see Henry Miller, *Politics Personified: Portraiture, Caricature and Visual Culture in Britain* (Oxford: Oxford University Press, 2015), ch. 7. For the 'barbarous and backwards races' see First Lord of the Admiralty George Goschen to Gladstone, 19 Sept. 1871, British Library, Gladstone Papers, Add MS 44161, 177–82. For a few examples of the newspapers reporting battles and tragedies, see *Illustrated London News*, 27 Feb. 1869, 216; *Morning Post* (London), 22 Nov. 1869, 5; *Daily News*, 25 Nov. 1869, 5, *Mission Life*, 1 Jan. 1870, 64; The *Anti-Slavery Reporter* published tales of rescues and reported their agitation aimed at the Foreign Office in *Anti-Slavery Reporter*, 1 Oct. 1869, 256, 271. There are many more examples and many items are reprinted in newspapers across the United Kingdom. Searching the British Library's Newspaper Archive produces at least sixty stories on the squadron or closely related material; this does not include *The Times*, but that newspaper showed less interest in the squadron, at least until 1871. The publishing of the Parliamentary Papers, or 'blue books' containing Heath's correspondence with London and his officers' with him, helped motivate action: *Hampshire Telegraph*, 1 July 1871, 8, and a collection of press clippings in *Anti-Slavery Reporter*, 1 July 1871, 143. For the *Anti-Slavery Reporter* turning Heath's reports into copy and for its outrage when George Sulivan was criticised by officials for having rescued runaways, see the same issue, p. 171. A commenter in 1873 wrote that Heath's reports stirred interest; see this item, too, for the press arousing interest in Britain, generally: *Ocean Highways: The Geographical Review*, Oct. 1873, 290. For the 'rebuke to Captain Sulivan', see *Anti-Slavery Reporter*, 1 July 1871, 169.

2   *Reading Mercury*, 25 Sept. 1869, 4. *Christian Observer*, Oct. 1869, 785. *Morning Post (London)*, 22 Oct. 1869, 3. *Penny Illustrated Newspaper*, 4 Dec. 1869, 2 (illustration on page 1). *Western Times*, 24 May 1870, 2. *Pall Mall Gazette*, 12 May 1871, 5. *Anti-Slavery Reporter: Under the Sanction of the British and Foreign Anti-Slavery Society*, Letter to the editor by James Haughton, Dublin, 21 July

1871, 206. *Anti-Slavery Reporter: Under the Sanction of the British and Foreign Anti-Slavery Society*, 1 July 1871, 171. *Mission Life*, 1 Jan. 1870. The Anti-Slavery Society wrote to MPs in advance of MP Charles Gilpin's plans to advance a Bill for the repeal of existing treaties with the sultan of Zanzibar. Gilpin was a Quaker, abolitionist, activist for prison reform, the expansion of the franchise, and more. See evidence of the letter-writing campaign at *Freeman's Journal*, 28 June 1871, 3. For the importance of the rediscovery of Livingstone to the new focus on the East African slave trade, hand-in-hand with news of the Royal Navy's adventures, see Richard Huzzey, *Freedom Burning*, 152.

3   Richard Huzzey puts this better than I do: 'To assess the politics of Britain's diplomatic and naval campaigns for suppression means analysing a curious mixture of imperial bombast, calculated realpolitik, economic pressure and anti-slavery sincerity. It would be impossible to impose a clear typology on the varied opinions of ordinary Britons.' When it comes to how the 1871 Select Committee came into being, no easy causal calculus is possible either. 'The Politics of Slave-Trade Suppression', in Huzzey and Burroughs, *The Suppression of the Atlantic Slave Trade*, 44. See also his *Freedom Burning*, 89. For officials' objections to stringent anti-slave trade efforts on grounds of expense and so on, see William Mulligan, 'British anti-slave trade and anti-slavery policy in East Africa, Arabia, and Turkey in the late nineteenth century', in Brendan Simms and D.J.B. Trim, eds., *Humanitarian Intervention: A History* (Cambridge: Cambridge University Press, 2011), 263–6. For the Treasury's advice to Gladstone's government, *Slave Trade on the East Coast of Africa* (November 1871), British Library, Add. MSS 44,617, vol. DXXXII (June-Dec. 1871), 132. For the Gladstone cabinet bowing to pressure, see R.J. Gavin, 'The Bartle Frere Mission to Zanzibar', 136–41. Richard Huzzey analyses Gladstone's view on slavery and the slave trade in 'Gladstone and the Suppression of the Slave Trade', in R. Quinault, R. Swift and R. Clayton Windscheffel, eds., *William Gladstone: New Studies and Perspectives* (Aldershot: Ashgate, 2012), 253–66, especially 265–6. I also draw from Roland Quinault, 'Gladstone and Slavery', *Historical Journal* 52 (June 2009): 363–83.

4   Heath's service record shows that he was still serving on the committee considering torpedo defence during this time; National Archives ADM 196/1. The charge for his train fare from Portsmouth is shown in the appendix of the House of Commons Parliamentary Papers, 1871 (420) *Report from the Select Committee on Slave Trade (East Coast of Africa)*. The sole other hearing taking place had to do with the disposition of new land reclaimed from the Thames with the completion of the new main drainage of London and Thames embankments,

Pall Mall Gazette, 29 July 1871, 1. Weather conditions come from *The Times,* 21 July 1871, 11 (reporting the previous day's weather). For Rigby's individual efforts against the trade at Zanzibar, see Christopher Palmer [Lillian] Rigby, *General Rigby, Zanzibar, and the Slave Trade* (London: Allen and Unwin, 1935), 9, 141–2, and elsewhere. Gilpin is pictured in *Vanity Fair,* 18 Jan. 1873, and his portrait is in the National Portrait Gallery, item NPG Ax8579. Sir John Hay is pictured in *Vanity Fair,* 23 Oct. 1875. George Shaw-Lefevre is pictured in the *Dictionary of National Biography.* Russell Gurney's portrait by George Frederic Watts is at the Tate Britain, item N01654. A portrait of Arthur Kinnaird is on a carte-de-visite in National Portrait Gallery, item number NPG Ax8643. The minutes of evidence reveal that Heath was in the hearing room during Rigby's interview, but could not hear all that was said. House of Commons Parliamentary Papers, 1871 (420) *Report from the Select Committee on Slave Trade (East Coast of Africa);* together with the proceedings of the committee, minutes of evidence, appendix and index, 52. Rigby's passionate evidence is on pp. 42–52. A description of Gurney's soft-spoken, gentlemanly air and dark, keen eyes is related in his *Dictionary of National Biography* entry. Heath's interview is transcribed in Parliamentary Papers, 1871 (420) *Report from the Select Committee on Slave Trade (East Coast of Africa),* 52–6.

5   Details from the select committee hearing come from House of Commons Parliamentary Papers, 1871 (420) *Report from the Select Committee on Slave Trade (East Coast of Africa),* 249–58. Data about the eventual successful attack on Lagos comes from House of Commons, Accounts and Papers, *Consuls; Slave Trade* (47, part 1) vol. 103 (Nov. 1852-Aug. 1853), 309–18. For Heath and Rothery exchanging insults through their letters and reports Raymond Howell, who relates this exchange in his *Royal Navy and the Slave Trade,* 62–3. Henry Rothery's testimony comes from pp. 60–3 of the report cited above.

6   Philip Colomb's interview before the committee is at House of Commons Parliamentary Papers, 1871 (420) *Report from the Select Committee on Slave Trade (East Coast of Africa),* 81–5.

20. 'May the winds blow till they have waken'd death!'

1   Edward Meara and the widow Ellen Renshaw were married at Piccadilly on 12 May 1870. *Pall Mall Gazette* 14 May 1870, 5. Per his service record he arrived in England on 14 April; National Archives ADM 196/13. On the birth of Ida Meara at Clarence House, *Cheltenham Looker-On,* Saturday 22 July 1871, 10. The

Mearas lived in Clarence House, Promenade (on Imperial Square), Cheltenham. The house still stands. Details of the house staff come from the 1871 census. For Edward and Ellen Meara travelling to Bath, *Cheltenham Looker-On*, 8 Apr. 1871, 218. For a trip to the seaside, *Cheltenham Looker-On*, 6 Aug. 1870, 506. For patronising charities, *Cheltenham Looker-On*, 24 Sept. 1870, 611. For attending balls, *Cheltenham Looker-On*, 9 Dec. 1871, 716. On the order to refund £933 for a prize judged not be a slaver, *Pall Mall Gazette*, 1 July 1871, 9. For the text of Meara's letter to the Admiralty written in Clarence House, see Edward Meara to Secretary of the Admiralty, 27 July 1870 in Foreign Office, *British and Foreign State Papers, 1870–1871* (London: William Ridgeway, 1877), 360–1. Edward Meara retired as part of an initiative to 'buy out' executive officers on the Navy List who had little prospect of promotion given the crowding on the list but were drawing half-pay, which was expensive to the state. Meara was promoted to Captain and retired to draw his pension from 1873. See *Morning Post*, 5 Mar. 1875, 7 which suggests that Meara took an active interest in this new program.

2   The 1871 Census nicely places George Sulivan in the modest house 12 St Peter's Road, Mylor parish, Flushing, along with the other inhabitants and servants in the house. Google street view provides the view, along with Hugh P. Olivey, *Notes on the Parish of Mylor, Cornwall* (Taunton: Barnicott and Pearce, 1907), 3. The layout of the house and garden are briefly described in Henry Norton Sulivan, *Life and Letters of the Late Admiral Sir Bartholomew James Sulivan*, 6. Details about Henrietta and others in the family come from there: pp. vii-viii, 394, 416 and elsewhere. Details about Henrietta's advice on observing the Sabbath come from her serial letter to George Sulivan, Sulivan papers held by the Hodson family, 28 Nov. 1849. The Bartholomew James book cited above makes his strict Sabbath observance clear too; p. xxxi. Data on Thomas Ball Sulivan comes from the *Dictionary of National Biography* 55, (London: Smith, Elder, and Co., 1898), 157. The detail about the Sulivan name being a ticket to respect and kindness in Cornwall comes from Henrietta Sulivan to George Sulivan, 10 Aug. (no year given), in the Sulivan papers held by the Hodson family. Details about George Sulivan's great naval family come from Bartholomew James, *Journal of Rear-Admiral Bartholomew James*, ix. For the Foreign Office's official pique toward Sulivan, see the Admiralty letter conveying the news in Secretary of the Admiralty to Leopold Heath, 7 June 1870, in Slave Trade Records of the East Indian Station, National Archives ADM 127/40.

3   For Colomb's speech and answers to questions on this occasion at the Untied Service Club, see *Journal of the Royal United Services Institution* 16 (1873), 455.

For a newspaper interpretation of the meaning of the 1871 Select Committee's report, see *Morning Post*, 12 Aug. 1871, 6. There are many examples of the issue being actively kept in the public eye before Henry Bartle Frere's mission of 1873. For some, see Henry Bartle Frere and George Sulivan's friend Horace Waller's campaigning among Evangelicals and Quakers in *Anti-Slavery Reporter* 18 (Mar. 1872), 9–10, 46–60. Lieutenant William Henn was called 'effervescent' by Stanley, 'energetic' by Sulivan. Sulivan, *Dhow Chasing*, 251. Even after the Select Committee of 1871 called for decisive change, the wheels of parliament and government moved slowly while a certain consensus was formed, public pressure rose, and Gladstone's government landed on specific course of action led by specific personnel. See, for an example of parliament continuing to talk about the right time and type of action, *Hansard Parliamentary Debates*, House of Lords, 23 July 1872 (vol. 212), cc 1608–20, in which some members push for action sooner, others later.

4   Heath was promoted admiral in late 1871. For one of several examples of Heath presiding at a shareholders' meeting, see *Western Times*, 13 Feb. 1872, 8. For Heath at a royal levee, *London Standard*, 15 Mar. 1872, 3. I am grateful to Mr. J.J. Heath-Caldwell for the invaluable service of transcribing the diary of Leopold Heath's son, Arthur Raymond Heath. This provides an invaluable glimpse of Leopold Heath as father. It details his frequent trips to London, daily activities, his patience with his children, even the talk about selfishness as the fundamental human motivation that seemed, given the context in the diary, to be motivated by Arthur's exposure to the ideas of Herbert Spencer. I am grateful for his transcription of Mary Emma Heath's diary, as well, which provides hints of her fondness for Leopold and reveals that Arthur was called 'Artie' in the house. The diaries are available online at http://www.jjhc.info. From Arthur's diary, I draw from entries including, but not limited to, 13 Jan., 29 Jan., 2 Feb., 11 Feb., 14 Feb., 26 Feb., and 5 Mar. 1873. For the news reporting the Bartle Frere mission's progress see, just for one example, *Hampshire Telegraph*, 1 Feb. 1873, 10. See also R.J. Gavin, 'The Bartle Frere Expedition to Zanzibar', 122–48. And for the discouraging reports in the newspapers at this particular moment, see *Liverpool Mercury*, 18 Feb. 1873, 6. For Leopold Heath's ongoing public work against the East African slave trade, see *Morning Post*, 13 May 1874, 6. The Frere mission to Zanzibar was a topic of the Queen's New Year speech in 1872. Other details for this section, including the fact that he was approached to join parliament and the Board of Admiralty, plus his motivations for retiring, come from Heath's own hand transcribed in his nephew George Heath's *Records of the Heath Family* (published privately), 1913. Rumours of the possibility of running for parliament to serve at the Admiralty come from *Hampshire Telegraph*, 1 May 1872, 2. For Heath becoming a board member for the Devon and Cornwall railway company, see *Exeter and Plymouth Gazette*, 10 Feb. 1872, 2. Arthur Heath's diary hints that his father was motivated by the unwillingness to be away and his new City interests.

5   The members of the squadron that had written publicly included Lieutenant Challice, with his article, 'In Pursuit of Slavers', *Dark Blue*, 4 (1872): 303–7 and a letter to the editor of *The Times*, 14 Nov. 1872, 5. Challice also contributed the pamphlet, *Remarks on the Scheme for the More Effectual Suppression of the Slave Trade* (London: J. Wingfield, 1869). Lieutenant William Henn had contributed drawings including one of the Zanzibar slave market to the *Illustrated London News*, 8 June 1872, 1. Sulivan's own photographs of refugees from slavery on board *Daphne* were published in *The Graphic*, 8 Mar. 1873, 168. It is certain that Sulivan followed some of this activity from clippings found in his personal papers preserved by the Hodson family, e.g. *The Times*, 2 Nov. 1872, 4. This letter was written by an officer recently on the station, probably from *Daphne*, *Nymphe*, or *Dryad* given the author's awareness of the Mozambique Channel trade. The letter also condemns the Indian government's complicity or at least lack of concern over the trade. Sulivan had also made a clipping of a report on a meeting at Mansion House, London, attended by some very influential politicians and activists. This was probably the 4 Nov. 1872 meeting, though that detail is not included in the clipping. The information that Sulivan wrote his book in order, at least in part, to instruct Sir Henry Bartle Frere and his mission comes from Sulivan to the Secretary of the Admiralty, no date, but around 1872, in the Sulivan papers preserved by the Hodson family. The mission to Zanzibar consisted of Sir Henry Bartle Frere, Reverend G.P. Badger, Mr Clement Hill of the Foreign Office, Captain Charles Jago, R.N. (later Captain Fairfax), Charles Ewan Smith, Frere's secretary, Charles Grey, and Frere's son B.C.A. Frere. See John Martineau, *The Life and Correspondence of Sir Bartle Frere*, vol. 2 (London: John Murray, 1895), 70–106. This account, based almost entirely on Frere's letters, describes his negotiations at Zanzibar, the intrigues of the French there, a trip to Majunga where Meara had had his intense stand-off, and reveals Frere's awareness of Portuguese complicity in the trade from Mozambique. This rare book is digitised and available to read online.

6   Hawarden Castle in Flintshire became Gladstone's through his wife. The Foreign Secretary to whom Gladstone wrote was Granville Leveson-Gower,

Lord Granville, Lord Clarendon having suddenly died in his office in June 1870. For Granville and the 'Anti Slave Trade people', see Granville to Gladstone, 16 Sept. 1872, in Agatha Ramm, ed., *The Political Correspondence of Mr. Gladstone and Lord Granville, 1868–1876*, II (London: Royal Historical Society, 1952), 347. Granville's word for Kinnaird was 'officious', in Granville to Gladstone, 19 Nov. 1872, *Correspondence of Mr. Gladstone and Lord Granville*, 364. For the Queen's speech mentioning the East African slave trade, see *Quarterly Review* 133, Oct. 1872, 522. For the cabinet bowing to pressure, see R.J. Gavin, 'The Bartle Frere Mission to Zanzibar', *Historical Journal* 5 (1962), 136–41. See also Huzzey, 'Gladstone and the Suppression of the Slave Trade', 253–66, and Quinault, 'Gladstone and Slavery', 363–83. Gladstone's term 'negrophilists' comes from this article as does his view that Africans were a 'lower race' and of 'lower capacity', pp. 377–9, as does Quinault's conclusion that Gladstone viewed abolitionists with 'distaste', also p. 377. For Sir Henry appeasing the abolitionists, see Granville to Gladstone, 19 Nov. 1872, cited above. For Gladstone's concerns about the use of force and his interest in whether a means for enslaved Africans to be borne from the coast to Zanzibar could be preserved, see Gladstone to Granville, 7 Nov. 1872, in *The Political Correspondence of Mr. Gladstone and Lord Granville*, 359.

7   Doulton nicely covers the way Colomb's and Sulivan's books were reviewed by a wide variety of periodicals in 'Royal Navy's Anti-Slavery Campaign', 274–7: *The Athenaeum*, 3 May 1873, 560; also 17 May 1873, 624–5; *British Quarterly Review*, 58, July 1873, 224; *The Examiner*, 7 June 1873, 595; *Illustrated Review*, 8 May 1873, 489, and Apr. 1873, 437–8; *London Journal*, 25 Jan. 1873, 56. For the abolitionist press: *Anti-Slavery Reporter*, 1 July 1873, 154; *Christian Missionary Intelligencer*, June 1873, 177–88, 186, 181; *English Churchman*, 3 July 1873, quoted in the *Christian Missionary Intelligencer*, Aug. 1873, 253. For details about the course of the Frere mission and subsequent blockade, see Howell, *Royal Navy and the Slave Trade*, 89–95; see also Gavin, 'The Bartle Frere Mission', throughout. The newspaper coverage of the signing of the treaty was particularly celebratory and proud: *Western Daily Press*, 18 June 1873, 4; *Glasgow Herald*, 18 June 1873, 6; *Dundee Courier*, 18 June 1873, 2.

21. 'Here is my journey's end'

1   On the officers advising Frere to secure a guard ship at Zanzibar, see George Malcolm to Henry Bartle Frere, 24 Mar. 1873, National Archives 127/41, and

Frere to Lord Granville, 4 Apr. 1873, FO 84/1391, 175–80. An image of *London* as headquarters at Zanzibar appears in *Illustrated London News*, 17 Dec. 1881, 268. George Sulivan also owned a photograph now in the Sulivan papers preserved by the Hodson family. Henrietta Sulivan died 22 June 1873. Details of *London*'s arrival come from *Morning Post*, 7 Jan. 1875, 5. See also Howell, *Royal Navy and the Slave Trade*, 114–15. Details of *London*'s arrival in Zanzibar, *Daphne*'s appearance later, and other details are drawn from HMS *London*'s log, National Archives ADM/10589. I borrow the final sentiment from Raymond Howell, who puts it nicely: 'Sulivan never allowed the admiralty to forget the *London* on its isolated station.' The ongoing work of *Daphne* after Sulivan's return to England is documented in the Scottish National Archives, Journal of Commander J.M. Hope, GD 364/2/115. This is an excellent source but proved beyond the scope of this book.

2   The final scene is drawn from Sulivan, *Dhow Chasing*, 32–3. And the 'still, small voice' that Sulivan recalled is from 1 Kings 19: 11–12.

3   In the five years after its arrival, the boats of the *London* removed around one thousand abductees from slave ships, whether on the open sea or up rivers. Reports on the slaver interception are documented in the 'returns' listed in National Archives, Slave Trade Advisor Report Books, HCA 35/82–6. Howell's *Royal Navy and the Slave Trade* is excellent on the period after the signing of the Frere treaty with Barghash, ch. 5 and elsewhere. And see Christopher Lloyd's *The Navy and the Slave Trade: The Suppression of the African Slave Trade in the Nineteenth Century* (London: Cass, 1968), 269 and elsewhere. The key recent scholarly monographs on the Indian Ocean slave trade come from scholars William Gervase Clarence-Smith, *The Economics of the Indian Ocean Slave Trade in the Nineteenth Century* (London: Frank Cass, 1989), Gwyn Campbell, *The Structure of Slavery in Indian Ocean Africa and Asia* (London: Routledge 2003), and Deryck Scarr, *Slaving and Slavery in the Indian Ocean* (London: Palgrave 2002).

INDEX